Steps of Faith around the World

STEPS OF FAITH
Around the World

Encounters with God at Work in the Cities

Edwin R. Orton

BIRMINGHAM CITY MISSION

Copyright © 2012 Edwin R. Orton

Published by Birmingham City Mission
75 Watery Lane Middleway, Birmingham B9 4HN, UK

Production by Deo Publishing
PO Box 6284, Blandford Forum, Dorset DT11 1AQ, UK

A Deo title

Cover design by Bernard Madden
Printed by Henry Ling Ltd, at the Dorset Press, Dorchester,
DT1 1HD, UK

British Library Cataloguing-in-Publication data
A catalogue record for this book is available from the British
Library

ISBN 978-0-9518307-2-7

Dedicated to

Dorothy Laura Orton

*my amazing wife and fellow-worker for more than sixty-two years
without whom this book could not have been written*

and to our four wonderful children

David, Esther, Ian and Martyn

who often suffered from having an absent Dad

Contents

Foreword

As I read this manuscript I could only think, what an amazing man, and realize it is because he has AN ALMIGHTY AND AMAZING, AWSOME GOD!

As you read this you will go in your mind from nation to nation where Edwin has ministered. You will see though his eyes and get something of his heart.

He has been and still is a marathon runner in God's great race and leaves behind a great legacy.

I know his prayer is, like mine, that some will catch a vision to pray for these nations and some of the people and ministries mentioned. I believe others will be led by the Holy Spirit to head out to work in some of these needy places, especially Pakistan.

I am always amazed at how far people go and the big expense just for a holiday, and I try not to be judgmental, but at the same time some people are saying that short-term missions is too expensive and the money spent could be used elsewhere. What a contradiction. I am glad people invested so that Edwin could make these trips. Only eternity will tell the story.

Edwin and his wife Dorothy have been a huge help and blessing to Operation Mobilisation, not only in India which is mentioned here, but also in the UK and around the world.

All kinds of workers are still needed and I pray that you will take time to read this book and consider getting more involved in God's great global work.

I have known Edwin for over 40 years. Here are the words that come to mind when I think of him. I pray they will be a reality in my life and yours:

VISION – GRACE – OBEDIENCE – LOVE
PRAYER – HARD WORK – FAITH
PERSEVERANCE – DISCIPLINE – PATIENCE
THANKFULNESS

The list could go on.
Thank you Edwin.

GEORGE VERWER

Acknowledgments

Many names are mentioned in this book and without those people it would not exist. Likewise there are others who have made valuable contributions to the stories but whose names do not appear; there are simply too many to mention by name. However, I do want to express my gratitude to everyone who has been involved, especially those who have prayed this book into being.

Numerous members of Birmingham City Mission are to be thanked for their help and encouragement as well as continuing in their important work during my many absences while travelling abroad. Special thanks should be given to my hard-pressed secretary, Pat Lambon, who typed up my voice-recorded diaries, alongside her many other duties.

Operation Mobilisation figures large in these events and I want to acknowledge the practical help given me by so many in making arrangements for travel, accommodation and itinerary on a multitude of occasions. Their prayerful fellowship has been a vital part of this journey.

Thanks must be given to Kingshurst Evangelical Church members for their untiring and generous support over the years, especially Chris Hakesley who continually urged me on, and his daughter Dawn who read much of the text and made helpful suggestions. Likewise I want to thank my friend Trevor Davies who spent many hours reading my scripts and sharing ideas for the structure of the book.

Finally I want to thank my family for their longsuffering during my frequent absences overseas, and for the unstinting support of each of my four children, and particularly David, who has had the onerous task of getting this book into print. Thanks too to my granddaughters Susannah and Abigail, who worked hard on my diaries. My deepest thanks must be given to my wife Dorothy, who accompanied me abroad on many occasions but always gave me the support without which I could not have exercised the ministry described in this book.

Steps of Faith around the World are of course faltering steps, following where the Lord has led. For mistakes I have made I ask for forgiveness, for the abundance of His blessings I give Him all the glory.

Introduction

"**D**o you have to board another plane after you arrive in Dubai?" I asked the young woman sitting next to me. She had arrived late just before the aircraft took off and now we were well on our way, and apart from a smiled hello we had not spoken. I could see that she was a sophisticated, intelligent lady by the way she was dressed and by her constant, competent use of her handheld computer, and I did not want to intrude. However, she was travelling alone and my question was intended to be helpful.

"Yes, I'm flying on to Karachi", she replied. As soon as I said that I knew the city, had visited it and many other places in Pakistan, a pleasant conversation began. She was interested to know that I had visited Islamabad, Rawalpindi, Peshawar and Lahore, where she had never been. It transpired that she was returning home for the first time in three years after studying engineering in Birmingham. This surprised me and we talked a little about her chosen subject. Pakistan produces some very good mechanical engineers but I did not expect this dark-eyed, attractive, well-dressed young lady to be one of them.

I suppose it was because of my age (three days later I had my eighty-second birthday) that she felt it safe to talk to this English fellow-passenger. I too was travelling beyond the destination of this flight and would be going on to Kolkata in India. It was her turn to be surprised so I gave my reasons for the journey, that I was visiting teams of young people who were bringing relief to the poorest of the poor in the great cities of the sub-continent.

We fell silent for a while, each busy with our own thoughts. In my case I was praying, and praying for her. Actually I had already done so as it is my custom to pray that I might sit beside someone I could talk to about the Lord. My friend and companion, Mark Lacey, was on my right next to the aisle and my new friend was on my left beside the window. At thirty-five thousand feet above sea level there is little to see outside the windows. The video screen on the back of the seat in front of me was showing films of many kinds but none of them appealed to me.

On checking in at Birmingham airport I had had difficulty with my hand baggage. Some airlines allow a laptop in addition to a cabin bag but Emirates asked that one bag be put in the hold. I was therefore separated from things which I needed on the journey, including books. Fortunately I had slipped a small red Gideon New Testament into my coat pocket and was able to read that on the plane.

Again I spoke to my new acquaintance and asked if she knew the book I was reading. When she said no I told her that this was part of the Bible and asked if she had seen a copy before. She thought that her father had possessed one once but she herself had never read it. I then proceeded to tell her a little of the contents of the New Testament, that it told the story of Jesus, his birth which Christians celebrate at Christmas, his life and character, his teaching and miracles, his death and resurrection. This I related briefly, being sensitive of the fact that she was most likely a Muslim with very different views.

The flight continued and I paused to reflect that among the three hundred or so passengers on board I was privileged to sit beside this young lady and talk to her about Jesus. Meals were served and soon the atmosphere changed as we began to near our destination. I quietly said to her that when I made a new friend on a journey I usually gave a small gift but this time I was separated from my goods. The only thing I could give to her was this New Testament, which was not in mint condition. Would she mind receiving it from me? To my delight she received it gladly, saying she would look forward to reading it. Here was a young Pakistani university graduate who had spent three years in my city, Birmingham, England, and had not heard of the primary text that had shaped our history and caused the Christian message to be taken around the world.

This recent encounter occurred just over 70 years after the seeds of being a missionary were sown in my mind. In the 1930s my family, although not church people, thought it right to send us to Sunday school, where I heard that one of the members had gone as a missionary to China and that this was, somehow, a good thing. I was 10 years old. By the end of the Second World War I had become a Boy Scout troop leader. I was at a Scout camp in Worcestershire when the atomic bomb was dropped on Nagasaki. The news of VJ Day was all the talk of the town when I cycled back to Birmingham.

At the Sunday school where I was now a teacher the young instructors would walk together after classes. During one of these walks, Jean Tyler, a young woman I knew from school days, talked to me of a book she was reading about a missionary to China. She offered me the book to read and I was hooked. "This is what I want to be", I thought, and went to my church leader to tell him as much. "Give it six months", was his response, "and then come back." The account of my journeys that follows should convince the reader that the call was not just a youthful fancy!

I understood that a missionary was someone sent by God and with something to share of his or her own experiences of God. But I did not know Him. During this time I had discovered a leaflet with a Bible verse where Jesus tells his hearers to "seek first the kingdom of heaven" with the attached promise that, "all these things (material needs)" would be added. Was this a promise? Was it for me? I managed to get hold of a small-print Authorised Version of the Bible and ended up reading it in secret, by torchlight in my room, because my mother was worried that it would not be good for me.

Although gripped by the words I was determined to know if there was a reality behind them and asked God earnestly to show himself to me. I had been working as a plumber's apprentice and, before the Health and Safety Executive was heard of, was working with a ladder on the roof of a two-storey house. The ladder slipped and the next thing I knew was I had fallen to the ground in soft sand, having just missed a fence. I dusted myself down in front of a quickly assembled crowd of bewildered residents. The noise had attracted them in expectation of seeing some serious injury. Though shaken, I simply stood and pondered the significance of this escape.

On Sunday evenings I would often walk along the Coventry Road from Hay Mills and pass "The Swan" hotel at Yardley. One evening in September 1945 there was a group of Christians preaching in the open air and giving out leaflets. I did not want to be associated with them but took a tract and walked on beside the cemetery. As I walked it was as if a hand was placed on my shoulder and the words "Go back" filled my mind. That incident became a turning point in my life for it led to my hearing the good news of Jesus and the beginning of a lifetime following him one step at a time.

Seldom do I read introductions to books. I like to get on with the story and avoid the politics. Nevertheless, there are points which deserve explanation and that may be helpful to the readers. The title of this book, *Steps of Faith around the World*, like the title of my recent book, *Steps into the City*, was chosen for its simplicity. The thought is that all journeys, long or short, are only a series of steps. Even the conquerors of Mount Everest did so (and still do so) one step at a time.

Most of the "steps" recorded in this book were dictated into my mini-recorder very soon after they occurred. This ensured accuracy in the details but it sometimes assumes too much background knowledge on the part of the reader. Some re-writing was required, but much of the script is published in its original diary form. It must be remembered that the daily diaries were dictated at night often after a long, tiring day in the heat and pressure of a tropical country. In some cases the notes were typed exactly as spoken, not in the best literary English. Occasionally the story is told from outlines jotted down at the time. Text from the diaries is distinguished in the typesetting by indentation on the page. My hope is that it is readable and meaningful.

It is important to realize that these "steps" were not carefully planned by the author. They seemed to follow naturally one after another, but they were not by my design. All I did was follow one step at a time. However, the journeys described are not recorded in strict chronological order but are grouped geographically. Also in some cases names have been changed for security reasons. The following pages sketch some attempts which in my own feeble way I have made to encourage others to spread the good news of Jesus Christ wherever they may go.

PART I: STEPS INTO EUROPE

1

First Steps into Europe

From the beginning of my Christian life I felt the call to overseas missionary work. After training at the Missionary School of Medicine in London in 1952, my wife Dorothy and I did our best to prepare for a move towards India. This was soon after the partition of India and the formation of Pakistan – developments associated with much bloodshed and political instability. Our applications for missionary work were therefore declined. The farthest we got was to Essex, to the east of London, where we were able to visit the Indian crews on board P & O liners at Tilbury docks.

It was not until 1973 that we first crossed the English Channel. That was a trip by car to Strasbourg in order to bring back our son David and all his gear at the end of his year at university in France, a requirement towards his degree in Biblical Studies and French.

The following year we made two journeys across the English Channel: one to Berlin, where we visited the parents of Annette Kretschmer, whom David was hoping in due course to marry; and the other, first, to Belgium to attend a conference of Operation Mobilisation.

Across the Channel to Belgium

The OM conference in Zaventem was an unforgettable experience for the thousands of young people from many different nations and cultures who attended. There were

numerous meetings large and small where the buzz of interpreters formed the background to each event. Bright singing
of modern Christian songs preceded each address, and there
was plenty of laughter and much prayer. Prayer times were
held in twos, threes or small groups. Each prayer time was
introduced with news from abroad with statistical and
geographical information. These presentations were made by
bright, enthusiastic young leaders, among who shone Peter
Conlan, whom we had known from summer camp days in
Malvern. It appeared that the chief organizer was a young
American called Jonathan McCrostie, who later planned the
routes the teams would take as they left for their assignments
throughout Europe. The main speaker was George Verwer,
the founder of Operation Mobilisation, who inspired everyone
with his zeal and wholehearted commitment to the Lord and
the cause of world evangelisation.

The conference continued for a week and was an exercise
in community life on a scale which we had not experienced
before. There was no preferential treatment, all were expected
to help with the chores, eat the same simple meals and live and
sleep with few comforts, but with joyful comradeship. The
conclusion was like a military operation as teams were
organized and equipped ready for deployment.

Several hundred vans and cars laden with young people,
their personal luggage and boxes of books and Christian literature made a wonderful spectacle as they moved out from the
conference, destined for several countries throughout Europe.
Our Ford Escort estate car transported Dorothy and me
together with our youngest son Martyn and a young woman
OMer who could speak Italian. We were bound for Italy.

Through the Alps to Italy

The journey took two days. We camped first in a heavy
thunderstorm in the south-east of France and then, having
driven through tunnels in the Swiss Alps, we pitched our tent
just off the motorway south of Pisa. We spent a short while

looking at the Leaning Tower of Pisa, and next morning we proceeded to our first team venue near Viterbo. As there was no room for us in the house where they were staying we put up our tent in a nearby park. It was there that we all met for a time of worship, and as it was Sunday we had communion. During the afternoon we visited an extinct volcanic lake and bathed in the cool water. The spiritual conversations together with a good deal of fun and laughter were to be the norm for this tour. The young people we were visiting were highly motivated and enthusiastic. They were freely giving their holiday time to reach out with the good news of Jesus to many Italian people who had never heard the gospel. Living by faith and trying to communicate in a foreign language was a new experience for them, as was living together with people from different cultures and denominations.

Dorothy had to return to her work in Birmingham, taking Martyn home with her. But first we spent a day sightseeing in Rome where we explored the Forum and the Coliseum, viewing with awe the place where so many Christian martyrs paid the ultimate price. Then she left by train on what became a very difficult journey home in a crowded compartment lacking any kind of refreshments, including water. However, they arrived home safely while I continued my itinerary alone by car.

We had unsuccessfully tried to find our next destination at Adelphi. This is a glorious spot where we sat sipping iced tea, beholding a breathtakingly magnificent panorama of beautiful Italian countryside. That night we spent in the car before taking Dorothy and Martyn to the railway station. As I returned to look again for my next venue, I met along the road Les Wade, an OM leader who had been with us at the conference in Belgium. He was returning from the very place that I was looking for and therefore was able to give me clear directions. As he left he said, "I think they have room for you." Later I discovered that this remark was to be taken literally, as the church was so small that when the team put down their sleeping bags at night there was just room for one more. The room was triangular and we all slept on the floor with our feet towards the narrowest point.

It became my practice to lead a Bible study with the teams early in the morning and then go out with them on evangelism, which was mainly in the form of selling Christian books and giving out tracts in Italian. It was hard work, especially in the August heat, but generally the young people from different countries all practising the local language were well received. We were grateful when kindly locals offered us huge delicious peaches freshly picked from their gardens. In the evenings we met for times of worship or sharing our testimonies with our new friends.

One team I visited in Latino was sleeping under the vines belonging to a friendly farmer. His family invited us for a meal on a beautiful patio in the warm summer evening. The team leader confided in me that they had a problem in that they were being overfed with pasta. Whenever they emptied their plates they were refilled. When they could eat no more the main course arrived! The foreign visitors had not understood the Italian custom that to clear the plate was to ask for more. Nor did they realise that the pasta was the first course of the meal!

My next appointment was with a team working in a poorer housing area of the city of Rome. It took a long time to find the team's address, as I could not ask bystanders, having no knowledge of Italian. When I did find the small church where the team was billeted it lay below the embankment upon which the road was built, so leaving the car I walked down the hill to confirm that I was in the right place. On seeing me the team gave me a warm welcome. As we stood chatting for a few minutes an Italian lady arrived carrying a book. Immediately I recognised it as my Bible, and it dawned on me that someone had been in my car. I raced back up the hill and found that a thief had opened the hatchback and removed all my belongings. The only clothes I had left were those that I was wearing. Even my toiletries were missing.

Fortunately my documents and money were safely hidden. The young OM people were marvellous. In no time they had spent what little money they had to provide me with essential items, including a towel. Although we had not met before I was treated as a member of their family. Later on when I was visiting a team near the sea the boys were bathing and I watched in the hot sunshine. One of the team, Jonathan Souray, asked why I didn't join them. On hearing that my bathing trunks had been stolen he produced a spare pair which he said had belonged to his father! Soon I was splashing with them. A year or so later Jonathan came for a gap year of training with the Birmingham City Mission but I still kept the trunks!

Several other teams were visited in the area and among one of them was a mechanic. He was there to serve all the teams in the district; the word 'Mobilisation' carried with it all the ingredients of repairing and servicing vehicles. After meeting him I moved to a team that was camping under canvas at an official site. Their Volkswagen van had broken down so I was despatched to collect the mechanic, who promptly came and fixed the problem. The sun was so hot that it was decided to move the team to another site in a cooler place. I was given brief instructions about the new venue before I left to return the mechanic to his base.

There were many miles between these teams and as it was beginning to get late I was anxious to find my team, where I had left the few belongings which I now had. The route took me around the Roman Outer Ring and I was looking for the trunk road number which I had been given. Finally I saw it and left the ring road, eagerly looking forward to finding the new camp and having a meal, for I was now quite hungry. The road seemed endless, I was travelling towards a mountainous region and it was getting dark and there was still no sign of the camp. Suddenly there was a loud hissing noise from my Ford engine. All the warning lights came on and the car came to a standstill.

Now I am no mechanic so all I could do was open the bonnet and peer in. It was a moment of truth when all I was sharing of God's faithfulness and the way He answers prayer would be put to the test. True, I had taken the precaution of paying for a foreign extension to my subscription to the UK Automobile Association breakdown service, but how do you access that in the middle of nowhere? I could see the lights of a village in the distance. It appeared that I had broken down at a road junction where a lane left the main road. I began to walk towards the lights and eventually found a bar. By some means I told the woman barkeeper that I needed a telephone and that my car had broken down. Then came the next problem, for although I could make a call to the number in my AA book there was nobody there who could speak English and I couldn't understand Italian. There is little sense in making gesticulations to someone over the phone. Eventually I gave up and walked back about half a mile. I returned at the double when I realised that I had left my wallet beside the phone. It was still there.

When I returned to the car it was getting dark and I still had no idea how I would get mobile again. As I stood there, disconsolate, I was suddenly hailed from across the road by a man speaking in English, "Can I help you?"

What a relief that was, and soon I was explaining my predicament to this angel who had appeared from nowhere. In fact this Italian gentleman had learned English while he was a prisoner of war in Britain and now he lived in a fine house just opposite where my car had broken down. He had noticed the UK number-plate on my Ford and saw my comings and goings and now offered assistance.

First I was invited into his house and shown the bathroom. After all my adventures that hot day I obviously needed a wash. Afterwards I was escorted to the dining room where a beautiful Italian meal awaited me. The man's wife was called Lydia, and she was all her namesake must have been to Paul in the first European church at Philippi so long ago.

It took some time before the phone call was made to the local breakdown service regarding the stranded car, but this time my new friend did all the talking in Italian. He was able to explain the situation and tell them exactly where the vehicle was. All we had to do was to wait.

From our vantage-point on a bank overlooking the road I was looking at my car when suddenly a police car arrived. The policemen were looking at this foreign car and I began to worry because I had no papers or passport with me, and little money.

While the officers were inspecting the vehicle I noticed the flashing lights of the breakdown truck. It was time for me to go down and face the music.

My Italian friend kindly accompanied me and interpreted for me. The patrolmen did their best at putting the engine right but finally gave up saying that they would have to tow the car to a garage for repair the next day and they would take me to a hotel for the night. At this I became horribly aware of my lack of funds in addition to my isolation from my documents and OM friends.

Just then a figure was seen passing on the other side of the road and the policeman who had begun to talk to me in English hailed him. When he came the officer introduced him as a friend who was also the best mechanic he knew. Having heard of my dilemma the man tinkered about with the engine for less than two minutes and then told me to sit in the car and start the engine. It started first time and purred into action. He then declined payment, for which I was very grateful, but I gave him a gift of the little money I had with me.

Finally, I sought help in locating the camp site where my OM team had moved to. To my great relief the breakdown patrolman said he knew exactly where it was and if I just followed him he would lead me to it.

Before leaving I was able to make a gift to Lydia and her husband of two Christian books in Italian, *Peace with God* by Billy Graham and *Tortured for Christ* by Richard Wurmbrand. Unfortunately I had no means of contacting that couple again but prayed that their kindness to me would be repaid by them coming to the Lord.

Soon I completed the itinerary which had been given me in Belgium but had a couple of weeks remaining to work with the OM teams – still without my baggage which had been stolen earlier. My remaining razor was poor and eventually it fell apart and became unusable. I had arrived at a small church at Ostia near which a tent mission was being held. It was late and I was tired and was soon joined by Ray Lynse, an American OM Leader whom I had met in Birmingham in 1972. Ray had once been a wealthy man in the oil industry of Alaska and California but now lived a life of poverty and total commitment to the work of Operation Mobilisation. All his belongings were kept in a small bag, yet when he heard of my predicament, he immediately produced a spare razor for me. He could speak Italian and was an enthusiastic open-air preacher and on another occasion we worked together among hundreds of students gathered on steps of Perugia University. Having passed on his razor he said that like me he was exhausted and needed to sleep. As there was nowhere else allocated for us he put down his bedroll in the centre aisle of the church, whereupon I did the same, and despite the comings and goings of excited participants of the nearby tent mission we were both soon asleep.

So far the teams I had ministered to were boys. I was asked to visit a girls' team. They had spent a few weeks in Turkey, where they had been arrested for distributing Christian literature. Some had been beaten, so they were forced to leave the country. Being unwilling to return home they decided to join fellow OMers in their work in Italy. There was no knowing exactly where they would be staying as at that time they had no fixed address. I was given a telephone number with the suggestion that I visit a farmhouse near Perugia. I should expect to receive a call. At last it came and I was given the name of a village near Assisi and told to be on the main road at one o'clock in the afternoon. I was to look out for and follow a white VW Beetle car. By the time I arrived I was nearly out of petrol but there was no time to do anything about that, and when I saw the car it immediately moved off and I just had to follow. We travelled several miles and climbed a steep hill, and the car stopped outside a farmhouse at the top of the hill. It transpired that the homeless team had enquired at an estate agent's in the village and he had kindly offered the use of half the house, which had been renovated ready for sale. It was quite unfurnished but the girls had gratefully accepted and had now made themselves at home.

There were twelve girls in their late teens and early twenties and each came from a different country and spoke a language of their own. Fortunately for me they could all speak English. There were two rooms, one was mainly used as a bedroom and the other as a lounge and dining room. We had a lovely time of Christian fellowship and they gave me food. Their main request from me was that they should have a communion service as throughout their time in Turkey and now in Italy they had had no one to officiate. I gladly agreed but said that we would need bread and wine. Bread they had, and also a white tablecloth which they put on the floor as there was no table. One of the girls went to the house next door, which was inhabited by a local farming family. She returned with a bottle of wine in a basket.

It was now dark and only candles gave light to a beautiful scene which I will never forget, those twelve lovely girls seated on the floor around the improvised communion cloth. I was reading to them the wonderful words of Jesus when he asked his disciples to remember him by sharing bread and wine when there was a knock on the door. Then entered the whole family from next door! Of course there was some embarrass-ment and confusion but it soon emerged that the girl who had asked them for wine in her poor Italian had given the impression that it was for a party and that they were invited! It was all taken in good part and I had a lovely opportunity of telling them through one of the girls who spoke perfect Italian what the communion was all about and how God loved them so much that He had given his Son for them too. The gospel message was well received and eventually our visitors kindly left us alone.

We finished our service by candlelight, but suddenly the whole room was filled with light! The girls had been in the dark throughout their time in the house not knowing that there were electric lights in the room. Only the fuses were missing and our neighbours had understood this and replaced them without being asked. We just praised God for all the wonderful way He had led and provided.

Time and space prevent me from relating the other adventures which we encountered in Italy on this occasion but this was a taste of what was to come. It will have to suffice to record my sense of privilege if not awe to have followed in the steps of St. Paul by sharing the good news of Jesus Christ in the city of Rome and visiting the great Coliseum where so many Christian martyrs laid down their lives. We are but shadows of those who have gone before.

That summer in the magnificent land of Italy is indelibly etched in my memory. The beauty of the mountains, trees and flowers; the warm sunny evenings; the friendly country folk and the unforgettable sounds of Italy will always remain with me. So also will be the joyful spirit of the teams of young people who made up Operation Mobilisation at that time.

2

Beyond the Berlin Wall

On 3rd September 1939 I well remember as a ten-year-old sitting with our family around the 'wireless' listening to Prime Minister Neville Chamberlain announcing that we were at war with Germany. During the six succeeding years we were to discover personally the grim reality of childhood in wartime: nightly bombing through the Blitz; sleeping in air-raid shelters; rations and food shortages; an interrupted and shortened education; evacuation to temporary families far from home; and a host of other hardships. My brothers, Ron and Dennis, were conscripted into the army; Ron in particular saw terrible bloodshed and barely escaped with his life. Our neighbour's son spent years in a dreadful Japanese prison camp.

For us the Second World War ended with the cessation of hostilities in 1945, though it took many years for the country to recover. The construction of the new Coventry Cathedral, which opened in 1962 on the same site as the cathedral destroyed by German bombs, reflected a spirit of reconciliation as we began putting the war behind us.

The situation in Germany was more complicated. Apart from the enormous loss of life and the devastation of property, the British, American, French and Russian victors had divided up both the country and the city of Berlin. Soon there were just two political regimes facing each other, the Communist East (East Germany [DDR] and East Berlin, its capital) and the Capitalist West. Being one hundred miles inside the DDR, West Berlin was a thorn in the side of the Communist bloc.

To stop a steady drift of population to the West, the government of the DDR isolated West Berlin. In 1948–49, all access routes by road, rail and water were closed in what was known as the Blockade. For almost a year the Western Allies had to fly in all supplies for the population in a monumental Airlift. Then in 1961 the DDR built the Berlin Wall, dividing families and friends and creating huge distress to thousands of people. For decades, travel between West Berlin and West Germany was possible only on a small number of closely guarded rail and road transit routes.

At the British city mission leaders' meeting in 1976, held at the London City Mission holiday centre in Felixstowe, an invitation to a conference in Berlin was received from a group of European leaders. It seemed unlikely that anyone would attend from the UK, but as my son David and his wife were living in West Berlin at the time, I agreed to attend. On hearing that I planned to drive there, Rev. Duncan Whyte, head of LCM, asked if he could accompany me.

The 1977 conference coincided with the 100th Anniversary of Berliner Stadtmission (Berlin City Mission), which arranged some wonderful public meetings in the Kongresshalle. At the formal meetings David interpreted for me, but that was a major effort as in German tradition the thirteen speeches were long and without any informal breaks. On other occasions the city mission provided a variety of music and a special youth event took place in the basement on the Thursday evening, a superb example of effective communication of the gospel to modern young people.

The event in Berlin was also attended by representatives of European city missions from Helsinki (Finland), Oslo (Norway), Zurich (Switzerland), Stockholm (Sweden), Amsterdam (Holland) and a number of cities in Germany. It was the second conference of the organisation which became known as the European Association of Urban Missions (EAUM), the first having been held in Geneva in 1974. It became clear that this coming together of missions from various countries was in part a reply to the division of Germany, which had not only geographically divided Berlin but also the Berlin City Mission. An international conference was respected by the Communist government of the DDR and became a means of communication and encouragement to Christian believers in an atheistic state. On other occasions I was privileged to attend similar gatherings in Helsinki (Finland), Gothenburg (Sweden), Prague (Czech Republic), and Zurich (Switzerland).

The Berlin Wall was not only a political statement; it was a reality which we experienced in person in 1977. The city mission's celebrations took place on both sides of the Wall, which meant we had to make our way through the strict bureaucracy and border guards. In order to travel without interference from West to East Berlin, the strategy was to split into groups of about a dozen, crossing the Wall at different official checkpoints. Then we were paired off by language. Each pair had a map, marked with a different route from the others, leading from the checkpoint to the DDR mission headquarters. By this means we were viewed as tourists and were able to arrive at our destination unchallenged. A united church service was held in the centre of East Berlin at the Marienkirche (later the gathering point for protest meetings in 1989, which eventually led to the fall of the Wall).

At that time the Berlin City Mission (East) was led by Dr. Paul Toaspern, a brave, godly man who suffered much for his stand for Christ. He and his wife and daughters were living in West Germany when people were fleeing there in their thousands from the Communist East. When the Berlin Wall was being built they prayerfully decided to go against the flow, from West to East, so they could help the believers left there. Paul was a university Professor in two disciplines as well as being a writer, poet and musician. Before the Wall came down he was forbidden to travel to the West, even to attend his mother's funeral. But he was allowed to travel east to such countries as Bulgaria, Romania and the Ukraine. The contacts he made were invaluable for fellowship of missionaries and many were invited to the World Conference, which was held in Birmingham in 1991. After the Wall came down in 1989 I invited him on to the board of the City Mission World Association. I was delighted that he later also came with us to visit the Bombay City Mission in India.

It was in April 1989 that an EAUM conference was held in Dresden, DDR. Alan Cutler of Birmingham City Mission accompanied me. We flew to West Berlin and traveled to the East by train and were met in the DDR by Manfred and Renate Koloska. Manfred was pastor of a Berlin City Mission church, where I preached on several occasions. From Berlin Alan and I were taken to the city of Dresden, in the southeast of Germany, which is well-known as a city destroyed by Allied air-raids towards the end of the Second World War. By the time of our visit the city had been almost entirely rebuilt as had it had been before the war.

The local authorities made us very welcome. On the day of our arrival we were put in the charge of a woman civil servant who showed us around, gave us all pocket money in DDR currency and even bought us ice-cream! In the evening we were given an official welcome by the Burgomaster and then given complimentary tickets for a performance in the newly rebuilt opera house.

The conference itself was held in a small convent where we were adequately housed and fed. Reports were given by a wide range of representatives from city missions in Munich, West Berlin, Berlin-DDR, Bielefeld, Plauen, Mecklenburg, Leipzig, Karl-Marx-Stadt, Zwickau, Český-Tešín, Vienna, Linz, Zurich, London, Birmingham, Oslo, Stockholm and Turku. Despite language differences there was a strong spirit of Christian love and understanding, especially for those missions under the restrictions of atheistic governments. We made many new friends and hoped we brought encouragement to those who were unable to travel outside their own country or hear news of the wider Christian community.

We returned to East Berlin and were given hospitality by the Koloskas. On May Day while Communist political rallies were being held we walked in the eastern shadow of the Berlin Wall and I remarked that I didn't think that the Wall would last much longer. He replied that if it did not come down in his lifetime he hoped it would during the lifetime of his children. In November of that very year I received this message from him: "My dear Prophet! The Wall is down!"

It was along the traffic corridor from West Germany to West Berlin that Dorothy and I had travelled to meet David's future in-laws in 1974, and later I drove Duncan Whyte and my daughter Esther and husband Jeffery to the 1977 conference. We have since made a number of journeys by road and by air to that great city, more easily so since the Wall has come down. In March 1997 I was honoured to be Guest Speaker at the 120th Anniversary of Berliner Stadtmission in Berlin. As I stood before such a large congregation, preaching on Hebrews 12.1-2, I was humbled to be part of God's wonderful work among the nations. Surely the Lord has been with us.

The Man Who Fought on Both Sides in the War

The life of the man to whom this title relates tells the tale of much of European history in the twentieth century. At the European conferences I frequently met a stockily built, elderly man who was always warm towards me. Although he was gifted in a number of languages, English was not his strongest, and yet we struck up a friendship which eventually led to his telling me his story.

Bishop Wilhelm was from Silesia in the south of Poland and he invited me to visit his home when I travelled to Prague. From Prague to Silesia is quite a train journey but I felt it was important to make the trip. Once we had met up (despite some confusion over the station of my arrival), I was interested to see that he lived in the bishop's house next to the church and the building belonging to the mission he once led.

He arranged for me to stay in the mission headquarters, a beautiful modern building. As I couldn't speak the Czech language it was difficult to communicate but the joy of their singing and worship times made it clear that I was among the Lord's people. At that city there is a bridge which separates the

Czech Republic from Poland. Wilhelm took me across to meet many of his friends and see the glorious scenery of the forest. One Sunday I was privileged to preach in a modern Polish church, the pastor interpreting for me. It was crowded with young people who made me very welcome.

The account of his life went some way to explain his situation. Silesia had long had an identity crisis, and at the outset of the Second World War Wilhelm was a young man in the Polish part of Silesia. When the German army invaded he was conscripted to join the *Wehrmacht* and sent away to train. Despatched to the front in the Italian campaign, he was captured by the Allies, becoming a P.O.W. The British asked him why he, a Pole, was fighting for the Germans, given that many Poles were fighting with the British in the Allied forces. He explained his situation and was offered the chance to change sides and rejoin the war on the other side; this he did.

After the war, Communism had taken over his homeland and most of his compatriots. Rather than go back to a devastated Silesia he accepted the offer of emigration to Canada, but Wilhelm wished to return home. An intelligent man, he became a student in the engineering department of the university. Eventually when the university discovered that he was not a Communist party member and was, in fact, a Christian, he lost his position. Friends suggested he study theology through the Lutheran church and he did this with great success, in due course becoming a bishop and leader of their Český-Těšín City Mission, caring for people with both spiritual and physical needs.

When the Berlin Wall fell he was again stripped of a position, but this time in the church! This was because of his life story and the fact that he had worked for both sides. He was tainted by the suspicion of collaboration with the Communist government, a charge that was very painful to him. He was allowed to keep the house but his work in the Mission was unrecognised despite the fact that the work had been set up on good foundations and grew in strength.

A while later he came to Birmingham, as his young grandson was learning English, and we had the opportunity to share together. A key moment was when he revealed his sense of betrayal and his feelings of bitterness towards an individual who had done him great harm. He was able to forgive the man and found the peace that had eluded him for too long. A month or two later I heard that he had died and received a letter from his family thanking me for this significant encounter.

The story of Bishop Wilhelm Stonowski would warrant a book by itself.

3

Through the Pyrenees to Spain

A significant contact with wide-ranging repercussions was made during a deputation visit I made to the Railway Mission in Worcester, a work which was later to develop into the fine Wood Green Evangelical Church. The person in question was John Sanders, who went to Madrid to serve the Lord by teaching English at the Centro Cultural Evangelico. From there he wrote to ask me to visit Madrid and do a feasibility study for setting up a city mission. I accepted.

The journey from Birmingham to Madrid was full of adventure and excitement as I decided to combine a trip visiting and encouraging OM summer teams in France with this project in Spain. I was advised to bring accommodation with me, in the form of a camper-van. The cost threatened to be prohibitive, until Jean Roberts, a member of Kingshurst Evangelical Church, and her husband Neville kindly offered us the loan of their caravan. Neville even gave me a briefing on how to attach and tow the caravan. Evidently I had not paid close enough attention, for at the M1 Toddington service station, as I pulled away from the petrol pumps I noticed my caravan overtaking me! Thankfully it came to rest before the trip came to a premature end. We drove on through London and on to Dover. Our first experience of taking a caravan on to a cross-Channel ferry was safe enough, though the readjustment of mirrors for driving on the right was irksome. This was long before the days of the GPS/"satnav" and my first mistake in France was to turn left at Calais and head towards Dunkirk. I knew I had to turn right for Paris and soon found myself on a very minor road in the countryside. Ironically, another caravan-tower who had spotted me thought it a good idea to ask for my advice on how best to pull the things. I didn't let on that this was my first towing experience!

The roads widened and we reached the Parisian suburbs and visited the church at Romainville co-founded by John Pennell, one of the original Covenanters at Kingshurst who had gone to join OM France and had married Elise and settled there. He is still in that country doing a great work having recently come through a very difficult illness; his three children are serving God in three different parts of France.

From Paris we travelled to Bourg, where our son Martyn was leading OM teams. They were staying in a village outside the town and we had difficulty in finding the address. Eventually we were hopelessly lost and pulled up at the side of the road. Neither of us could speak French so it was difficult for us to ask directions. The only people we could see were a young couple walking on the other side so I crossed over and asked if they could speak English. To my surprise they answered in perfect English and, furthermore, the address we were looking for was very near and they were going there and could take us! Once again we found that the Lord was with us.

Our next destination was a visit to a team near Grenoble. It was their day off, so we took time to do some sight-seeing. We had not realised that we would be in such a beautiful location in the French Alps. We parked the caravan in a car-park and drove up to les Deux-Alpes, where we were overcome by the beauty and grandeur of panoramic views of the mountains. There we sensed the presence of God and were delighted to find in a prominent place with such a splendid background a large wooden cross. We had passed the ski-lifts and beautiful chalets, but here was a reminder of the purpose of our missionary journey. I still treasure the photograph I took of that cross on such a fine, sunny day.

The journey south was both interesting (for one thing we saw the famous unfinished bridge at Avignon) and eventful. Our route was blocked at one point by the "Tour de France" cyclists. We had to take a detour, leading away from our destination. On taking a left turn I was horrified to be faced with a steep incline – a huge obstacle for my small car towing the caravan. However, we made it by changing down to first gear!

When we arrived at the top of the hill we were in a narrow lane passing through farming country. As we were travelling we became aware of a car behind us sounding its horn. I could see an impatient young man in a sports car. I thought it best to stop. I explained that I could not pull over and that tooting the horn would not really help. He said that he was looking for a way round as well and suggested he lead the way as soon as possible. We eventually found a place where we could pass us and he led the way. Unfortunately his sense of direction was no better than mine and we ended up in a farmyard. Embarrassed, he drove off without a word! Nor did we say anything to the French country folk whose Sunday afternoon had been disturbed by an English car towing a strange caravan, scattering their chickens and frightening their dogs. We beat a hasty retreat.

Surprisingly, we did make it to the Mediterranean, where we camped by the seaside, then on to Barcelona with a stop at a campsite on the road to Valencia. Finally we drove across the sierra to the capital city, Madrid. There we had to negotiate the narrow streets, ill-suited for caravan towing. We reached the centre and parked outside the Baptist Church. The minister of this church was a very impressive, tall man. Jose Borras had left the Roman Catholic priesthood and after much soul-searching and prayer and decided to join the Baptist movement - which was considered a cult in Spain. I preached to a very welcoming congregation in this church next day and set out the challenge of city mission. John and Olga Sanders kindly gave us hospitality in their home and during our stay introduced me to church leaders interested in the setting-up of a Madrid City Mission.

We also took the opportunity to do see some of the sights, visiting the "Valley of the Fallen" with its enormous cross surrounded at its base by huge statues of beasts representing the four evangelists, and an impressive basilica to remember the victims of the Spanish civil war. What was especially poignant was that the building of this monument had cost hundreds of lives. Republican prisoners had been offered remission from prison if they worked on the project; the conditions of this forced labour were appalling, and there was a terrible toll on lives.

I had to get back to Birmingham to conduct a wedding and needed to set out for the return journey. This coincided with a change in the weather, which hit the headlines as torrential rain and hurricane-force winds caused roads to be closed and travel to be disrupted over a wide area. We set off anyway and, at the border of France and Spain, we looked around at what resembled a disaster zone; there was no alternative but to keep driving. We made the wedding date as planned.

Later Visits

My subsequent visits to Spain were made by air. First I was invited to speak in a number of local churches in May 1984 on the subject of city missions and the possibility of forming one in Madrid. My teaching was warmly received and it became clear that there were some who would take up the challenge.

John Sanders also arranged for me to fly to Barcelona, where he met me at the airport. I was to talk to students in the nearby Bible School at Castel de Fels. It was, as always, a delight to speak to and answer questions from young people eager to find the will of God and serve Him.

On another occasion I accompanied Madrid City Mission workers to a central open air meeting in the famous Plaza Mayor and then walked with them to their nearby base, which provides food and clothing for homeless people, where I was given a tour. I was amazed at the standard of orderliness, efficiency and compassion, such as I had rarely seen elsewhere. Among the voluntary workers was a bright young Christian woman who later applied for further training with Birmingham City Mission. She spent a year with us; we were impressed by her dedication to the Lord and her desire to win others for Christ. However, that was not the end of her story, for she fell in love with David Clover, a fellow-student. Later they married and worked for a time with Madrid City Mission. On another visit to Spain I spent time with them and they showed me around the city and took me to view the famous Goya and Picasso collections in the Prado museum, one of the finest art collections in the world. Among other things we also visited the impressive El Escorial monastery.

In Madrid I was pleased to be shown the Plaza de Toros, so different from its namesake, the Bull Ring in Birmingham – which of course never saw a bullfight. This was a sporting occasion, drawing many spectators. Besides the splendid sculpture of the matadors I noticed nearby a statue of the British scientist, Sir Alexander Fleming, whose discovery of penicillin led to the saving of many matadors' and toreadors' lives.

A few years later I was invited to speak at the annual meeting of Madrid City Mission. It was well attended and clearly the new mission had won a place in the life of the city. A number of meetings were arranged for me, one ending at about 10 p.m., when I was asked if I would speak at a house meeting. Thinking that my programme was already full I asked, "When?" and they replied, "Now!" I went, and found a hastily gathered crowd in an upstairs apartment. Their spiritual hunger was heart-warming, and it was with difficulty that I tore myself away.

On the way back to our accommodation it was suggested that we stopped for a meal. We drove up to a large department store. I was amazed that in the small hours of the morning the place was crowded and there was a long queue for the restaurant. "We can't wait any longer here," said my host, "let's go home and cook a meal!"

This was (and is) typical of life in Madrid. The city was quiet in the afternoons while people had their siesta. But in the evening it all came to life, families with children playing out at all hours while adults promenaded the avenues. The warm summer evenings were noisy social occasions when people met and enjoyed one another's company.

Spanish Protestant Christians were enjoying a freedom which they had not had for generations but they were experiencing difficulties with so-called missionaries from outside the country. I attended one church which was built with foreign money and run on foreign lines. National Christians tended to resent the intrusion and lack of knowledge of the culture and history of Spanish believers. The result was that the church was empty save for missionaries' families and other foreigners. For centuries local believers had suffered for their faith but had remained faithful to the Lord. Now they were being treated as if they had not existed and that Spain was a heathen land bereft of the gospel. With this in mind it was vital that any new work such as a city mission should be truly indigenous, self-governing, self-supporting and self-propagating. Although I have had little to do with their establishment, I have been pleased to see that city missions in Madrid, Barcelona and other cities in Spain are developing along those lines.

During this latter visit to Spain my host treated me to a day's outing to the beautiful historic city of Toledo. This was the capital of Spain at the time of Queen Isabella – who notoriously ordered the expulsion of the Jews but also commissioned Christopher Columbus's exploratory voyage on which he discovered America. We had little time but were able to see how the Jewish jewelry industry was still being practised. The highlight of my brief encounter with this place where Muslim invaders of Europe from Africa were finally repelled I was taken on a short tour of Alcazar, the impressive fortress palace which stands on the highest point in Toledo.

The formidable structure has been built and rebuilt over the centuries but more recently since the Spanish Civil War. Inside the palace I listened to a recording made during the siege, in which the leader is told by phone that the besiegers are holding his son, and that they will kill him if he does not surrender. The leader asks to speak to his son and then simply says, "Goodbye, son." How humbling it is to see what sacrifices some people are willing to make for others. O that we might be willing to make such sacrifices for Christ's kingdom!

PART II: STEPS INTO ASIA

4

Proving God in India

The vast sub-continent of India, with its wide plains, broad rivers, forests, mountains and deserts was first introduced to me by my father, Robert (Bob) Orton. During World War I he served as a soldier in the British Army and was posted to the East. With thousands of others he landed at Bombay, passing through the Gateway of India and on to the great Victoria Station. The steam railways and roads which the British built took them to cities like Lucknow, Kanpur and Lahore. Then came the long marches to Peshawar, Rawalpindi and Quetta. In the heat and dust under the hot sun and burdened with gear and weapons they experienced a thirst they had not known in England. Their ration of liquor was gratefully consumed, and could become a craving that persisted long after their return home. It was after my father had been drinking, for usually he was a quiet man, that he would fascinate us with his stories of India's millions and the British Raj. Words like Kashmir, Khyber Pass, elephants, jungle and snake charmers roused my curiosity and desire for adventure.

At junior school my teacher Miss Penny inspired us with stories of British heroes; Nelson, Wolfe, Livingstone and Clive of India. She also read us stories from Rudyard Kipling: Rikki Tikki Tavi the Mongoose, Mowgli and others from the *Jungle Book*. Soon I found Kipling's book *Kim* in the public library and entered into Indian culture as he saw it. Finally Miss Penny introduced us to a young soldier, a former pupil of hers, who was on leave from India. My love for India, though my knowledge of it was only sketchy, had begun.

Many years went by before I had any hope of visiting the land of my dreams. As I have recorded in the story of my conversion to Christ, the first Christian book I read was *The Triumph of John and Betty Stam*. They were missionaries of the China Inland Mission and it was CIM that published that powerful book. It was natural that in contemplating missionary work my thoughts would turn to China. Soon I was reading the life of Hudson Taylor, the *Growth of a Soul*, written by Mrs. Howard Taylor. Whenever I heard of CIM meetings being held in Birmingham, London, or later in Malvern, I was sure to attend. China did not, however, have the same draw upon me as India.

In the decade following the end of World War II in 1945 momentous changes took place across the globe. The United Nations was inaugurated, the State of Israel was born, Winston Churchill declared that an Iron Curtain had fallen across Europe, and India gained its independence from Britain. Each new development brought its own pain and bloodshed. Multitudes were massacred as Muslims and Hindus regrouped to form East and West Pakistan and Palestinians and other Arab nations rejected the new Israeli nation. Communism engulfed the great Chinese empire and Christian missionaries were expelled.

No new missionaries would be sent to China in the foreseeable future, and things were becoming more difficult in India too. By the time I had finished training at the Glasgow Bible Training Institute and the Missionary School of Medicine it seemed impossible for me to go to the East. God had other things for me to do and we have seen how he led into church planting in Essex and Birmingham and the founding of city missions there and elsewhere at home and abroad. In fact I was forty-four years old before I even crossed the English Channel to Europe, far less to the Middle East.

The winter of 1978 was particularly cold in England. At the soup kitchen in Bromsgrove Street, Birmingham, we were busy, as homeless men crowded into the warm room, appreciating the hot food given to them. It was January and a thin covering of snow lay everywhere when the news was brought to us. There had been a fire in the crypt at St. Chad's Roman Catholic Cathedral. For many homeless people in Birmingham this was their only night shelter. As two men died in the fire the crypt was closed and the temporary residents were turned away. What were they to do? Where could they go? These were the questions put to me by Birmingham City Mission staff members.

There had been no real option; it was agreed that the mission centre would remain open, make-shift bedding would be found and the men would sleep on our premises. Our staff were magnificent, volunteering to stay on duty all night when necessary, some even sleeping on the floor with the men.

Of course I had to take my turn and at the end of the long evening I found space to sleep on the floor of my office, a little room on the second floor. It was after one of these shifts that I went home and climbed into bed at 8 a.m. Three hours later I rose and was just getting dressed when I was struck with the incredible pain of sciatica. For ten weeks I was confined to my room and unable to do my usual work.

George Verwer, International Co-ordinator of Operation Mobilisation, was due to preach in our home church at Kingshurst. It was a very special meeting and I was deeply disappointed not to attend. However someone kindly arranged a telephone link from the pulpit to my bed. During the conversation I had with George I was amazed when he asked if, when I recovered, I would be willing to go on his behalf to visit teams in India.

Some weeks later I contacted Peter Conlan, one of George's aides, in case I had misunderstood, and it was confirmed that I should go. In August 1978 I arrived at last in India.

My flight to India in August 1978 was my first flight anywhere, and it was one to remember. Wesley Erpen, then on BCM staff and later to become its Director, offered to drive

me to Heathrow Airport. That was fine until we were nearing
our destination but then there was a complete snarl-up of
traffic. The time was ticking by and I became anxious about
being late. Finally, I decided to go the last few hundred yards
on foot, only to be stopped by a policeman. Apparently there
had been a warning that a bomb had been planted in the
terminal, and no one was allowed in. When I remonstrated
that I would miss my flight he said that airlines would delay
planes leaving. He was wrong. When eventually I reached the
check-in desk I was told the plane had left.

The next few hours were spent looking for an alternative
flight. My flight had been via the Middle East, on Kuwait
Airlines. Their next flight to Delhi was a week later. This
meant that I had to go to a travel agent in central London and
arrange to travel with a different airline, in this case Trans-
World Airlines, on a plane which had come from USA and
bound for Delhi. Wesley and I slept at the house of OM
friends and next morning I left for India.

Stepping out of the aircraft in Delhi, I thought I was in the
slip-stream of the jet engine because of the hot air which met
me. It was of course my first experience of a true Indian
summer and although it was 3.30 in the morning there the
temperature was very high. On the air-conditioned Boeing
747 I had needed a warm pullover, but this I quickly removed.

Imagine my situation, in which each step was new to me:
the queue for passport control and immigration, surrounded
by hundreds of Indians returning home, collecting my luggage
(at that time there were no baggage trolleys at Delhi airport!)
dealing with customs, fighting off numerous offers to carry my
bags, and eventually finding the exit.

Exits at airports are one way only, there is no turning
back. On reaching the outside gate I realised that I had no
Indian money, as rupees could not be bought at a bureau de
change outside India. The arrival hall itself was poorly lit, but
outside beyond the exit lights it was dark and unwelcoming.
At any moment I expected someone to emerge who would

recognise me and transport me to my accommodation. No one appeared, and I just felt stranded.

From London I had sent a message to OM India, then based in Bombay, telling of my changed flight, different airline and expected time of arrival. Clearly the message had not arrived in Delhi. Worse still, I had no name, address or telephone number of any friend or contact in that city, nor did I know how to negotiate this foreign culture without money or guide. Although surrounded by beggars with hands outstretched I felt utterly alone. Besides that, the whole episode since leaving home had taken two days and two nights of stress and I now had a king-sized headache!

Suddenly I was startled by a brisk movement behind the low fence against which I stood. I turned sharply and there I beheld a sparrow, a house sparrow such as is common in my native country. The surprise had made me jump, but as I watched the small bird all my tension began to ebb away. I remembered the words of Jesus, "Are not two sparrows sold for a penny? Yet not one of them will fall to the ground apart from the will of your Father.... So don't be afraid; you are worth more than many sparrows" (Matthew 10:29-31).

For an hour or so I just stood and relaxed. The Lord was with me and He had just spoken to me through a sparrow. Gradually it became light and as dawn broke I became aware that a number of Muslims around me were at prayer facing towards Mecca. I scanned the motley crowd, typical of those who hang around airports and railway stations, especially in the East. Many were still sleeping on the ground, having nowhere else to go.

Soon the departure building became visible through the early morning mist and I decided to move in that direction. It was a busy and more organised place and I quickly found somewhere to exchange money. Then I rummaged through my belongings and found the telephone number of the Bombay office of OM. Thankfully India is a country where English is widely spoken. Soon I was told how to make a phone call to Bombay. How pleasant it is to hear a friendly

Christian voice in such circumstances. I was supplied with the number for Enoch Antony, the brother who had been here to meet me from my original flight. His instructions for using a Bombay 'Ambassador' taxi were clear and finally I had the joy of seeing this fine man standing in the street near his home, waving his arms in welcome.

Arriving in a culture and environment so different from our own can be both exciting and frightening. It is so easy to make mistakes which can have a lasting effect upon both us and our hosts. How glad I was to find sympathetic and loving understanding in my first Indian home! Throughout this tour I began learning quickly how to cope with Indian toilets and bathrooms, sleep on Indian beds and eat Indian food. Enoch Anthony's wife seemed so aware of my lack of experience of the sub-continent that she took great trouble to make my entrance to Indian culture as easy as possible. Their two children helped. Perhaps it is because I have four children of my own, or because all my life I have worked with children in Sunday School, clubs and camps, or because I served as a school teacher, that I have found it easy to relate to boys and girls all around the world. Here in Delhi I was surprised to find that the children whom we met, no older than ten years, were being taught Shakespeare. Their books and writing materials were somewhat primitive by English standards but their thirst for knowledge was great. Not only were we able to discuss some of Shakespeare's plays but they were delighted to learn that I lived within twenty miles of his birthplace, Stratford upon Avon, and could tell them much about his childhood environment.

A short time later I was off to my next destination, Bangalore. P.M. John, the OM leader for South India, was my host and it was he who met me at the airport and in whose house I stayed. The house was also the team base and there were people coming and going frequently. On one occasion I arrived there in the night and was found a three-tier bunk bed, I being in the middle and one man at floor level and another above me. However, when I arose in the morning I discovered that the men had both left and another two had taken their places!

At Bangalore I had my first experience of auto-rickshaws. These small three wheeled vehicles propelled by noisy two-stroke engines were a cheap means of transport. My friends always told me to keep out of sight while they haggled over the price. If the drivers saw Westerners like me they would ask twice as much for them. During my visit in 1978 the roads contained many bullock carts, horse-drawn carriages and wandering animals of all sorts, but few cars. The British 'Ambassador' taxi was actually made in India, as any foreign car was so heavily taxed as to make it prohibitive for them to be imported.

At first I could not get used to the noise of India. Such windows that they had were kept open because of the heat. Every sound from the street was heard. The harsh call of the crows could be heard from morning to night. Street sellers of every kind called out their wares. Cheerful boys shouted as they played cricket in any feasible spot. Beggars, some being young children, whined their plaintive pleas, while toothless barefooted old people shook their collecting cans. It is a land of superstition and – to a Westerner – strange sights; one is confronted almost every day by some new exotic spectacle.

Bangalore was – and still is – a beautiful city, but now the streets are thronged with traffic of every kind, large foreign cars, an assortment of taxis and small Japanese vehicles and thousands of auto-rickshaws belching out their exhaust fumes almost in competition with the heavy Tata trucks. The pollution forms a deadly smog. Added to that of course is the natural dust which arises following months of hot, dry weather. The monsoon rain is very welcome. Even so, Bangalore is resplendent with wonderful flowering trees, even in winter, and of course the palms and numerous other tropical trees are alive with parrots and other exotic birds and butterflies.

Many of the fine palatial buildings were built by the British as they chose Bangalore as their seat of government in the south. The area is on a plateau, making it much cooler than other cities in the southern sub-continent. Bangalore is now the Silicon Valley of India, with its large commercial centres for the computer and information industry. The Indian government long since replaced the British, but there are still Victorian parks and museums. The shops on the M.G. Road are reminiscent of London's West End, and now there are towering hotels to dominate the skyline. But London does not have the magnificent lively bazaars of Bangalore.

As in most large cities in India, Bangalore has its poor and its slums. On my first visit I borrowed a bicycle and P.M. John showed me where the poor lived. Though the conditions are not as bad as in some cities I was much moved by the poverty and suffering which I observed. It is gratifying to know that today, more than thirty years later, OM India Good Shepherd Ministries have a number of social, medical and spiritual activities in those very areas. Many years later, in 2009, I was invited to speak to a large evening ceremony in a Bangalore slum in which more than forty ladies were graduating after a training course in tailoring. Their joy in the midst of such poverty lit up the darkness. Members of a sponsoring church in Singapore were there to present awards and share their faith with a smile.

Trip to Mysore

The Bangalore-Mysore road proved to be a delightful introduction to rural South India. Accompanied by a young OM Indian lad we went on a crowded public bus, stopping only for a comfort break; there were no public toilets! We passed through lush green paddy fields, and sugar cane, flanked by rows of huge palm trees. Occasionally there were heaps of water melon and coconuts for sale from vendors who obviously lived with their produce. Along the road we passed many ox-carts, the oxen plodding leisurely along with their sleeping drivers. Many oxen had their long horns beautifully

decorated with ornaments and bright colours. I was told that
they knew the way home and did not need guiding – though
being without lights they were a hazard to other road users at
night.

Mysore had been the home of Maharajas and it still had an
air of opulence and grandeur. On entry we passed a regal
domed monument heralding the way to the Maharaja's Palace.
But that day all was quiet and the palace was closed.

We found the place where the OM team was supposed to
be billeted but no-one was there. My guide was embarrassed
by this as he knew I was hungry. However he found me a
rather grand hotel and I went and had a meal in the hotel
restaurant. I was the only person there and felt extremely
conspicuous while wondering where the rest of the team was.
My guide made inquiries and found that the team had moved
into the mission station of the missionary Hilda Baker, a few
miles to the south, towards the Kerala border. We travelled to
her compound and I was given a corner bed with a mosquito
net and was introduced to the OM team. Chelladurai was the
leader, and I was to form a life-long friendship with this lovely
young man of God.

I was invited to be part of the team, to teach and to travel
with them on foot into the villages. There were no roads, only
narrow footpaths. On one occasion someone shouted, "Snake,
Snake!" I had just stepped over it and – I was told – it was
venomous!

We went to a village where there were many carts with
barrels – the local water supply. Children gathered around me
(the only white man) and I taught them Christian choruses.
Chelladurai was able to translate into Kandahar, the local
language. The team were visiting the people and passing out
tracts and selling gospel packets.

On Saturday we came across an area where they were
building the Pagoda Dam, without mechanical equipment and
largely supplied by women carrying materials on their heads.
The workers who were resting spoke Telegu, and to my

amazement Chelladurai again was able to translate my preaching perfectly.

At evening to my surprise around the back of the dam we came upon the famous Brindhavan Gardens with all kinds of exotic trees and flowers. There was a bench at the end, offering a view down upon them, and as I sat down suddenly all the lights came on and the floodlit fountains started up in beautiful colours and in all sorts of magnificent shapes. This was a spectacular tourist attraction, thousands of visitors coming by coach, car and every conceivable mode of transport. It was a fitting ending to a wonderful week.

Hilda Baker

Hilda came from my own home city, Birmingham, and had studied to be a nurse at Dudley Road Hospital, where my wife also trained. She went out as a missionary from the Methodist church but, after Partition, when Pakistan was separated from India, things changed. Millions lost their lives as the two sides fought as they tried to relocate their communities. Later most of the British missionaries were expelled and different denominations came together to form the Church of South India (CSI). Unfortunately squabbles and corruption soon developed. Hilda therefore bought her own property so that she could work without fear of exploitation or corruption.

Hilda took me around her district to a village to visit a very sick woman, dying of tuberculosis. Her house was no more than a bivouac of sticks, like the other dwellings in the village. She had no proper floor covering, no bed sheets and no furniture. She simply lay on the earthen floor in such poverty. Hilda had brought various items for her, and I was asked to lay hands and pray for her.

As we travelled in her old car she threw out Christian leaflets to those we passed by. "This may be the only good news of Jesus they ever hear," she declared. Once when questioned by a young man in his twenties why she, a foreigner, remained in India, she replied, "I am not a foreigner; I have been here for more than thirty years, and therefore I am more Indian than you!"

In her mission compound Hilda worked with the children while their mothers were at work all day in the cotton fields, providing food and shelter from the hot sun. In the grounds Hilda also showed me a huge well, around 12-15ft in diameter. "This is where Hindu extremists threw the body of an earlier English missionary after they killed him," she informed me.

A few years later Hilda retired to a mission house in Mysore. By this time she was very old and Dorothy and I visited her and urged her to return to England. "No", she said, "India is my home and the Indians are my people." I learned some time later that she had passed away.

Chelladurai

On our return to Mysore after finishing the work with Hilda Baker we were told we were scheduled to conduct an evangelistic campaign with a whole week of meetings. Posters had already been prepared giving my name as speaker! Then they announced that since several nurses had given their lives to the Lord we were to hold a baptismal service. We were right next to a Muslim quarter, separated from it only by a high wall. As soon as we started singing and praising God, large numbers of people from the Muslim side crowded around to see what was going on. "Brother," I said to Chelladurai, "This is too good an opportunity to miss. Let's stand on the wall – I will preach and you translate for me!"

We did just that, a tall, dark South Indian and a short, white Englishman, standing side by side next to a tank of water which served as a baptistery and preaching to a street full of Moslems and Hindus who had gathered to watch. Later, as years went by and occasionally our paths would cross we would often greet each other with, "Remember the wall!"

Chelladurai was born into a strong Hindu family and brought up by his father who was a practising shaman. After his father's death he was put into a Catholic hostel and became a devout Roman Catholic, but he still lacked peace in his heart. In 1973 he attended a youth meeting which led him to study the New Testament and finally give his life to Christ. Later, he joined OM and became a team leader in Bangalore.

During my time in South India he was my constant companion, guide and translator. We travelled together overnight to the southern city of Trichy, where we visited an OM girls' team. After a time of Bible study and prayer they showed us around. The building they were billeted in had once been the vicarage to a large Anglican church but had long since been vacated. They found the room in which they were living filled with rubbish, rats and snakes! To confirm this they opened the back door to show me all they had removed!

The girls, all Indian except one white Canadian who acted as cook while we were there, had visited all the homes in the town and wanted to show me the city. From the vantage point of the Rock Fort, up the steps to the Hall of a Thousand Pillars, the shrine of Shiva and the temple of Ganesh we had a magnificent view of the Cauvery River and the plains beyond. On the way up I was asked to pay at a kiosk for taking my camera with me. Within this temple, where I had seen hundreds of people worshipping Hindu idols, I noticed a large wall calendar hanging in the official's booth, and I asked him what the numbers on the calendar stood for. As he didn't know I explained that the date 1978 was the number of years since the coming of Christ. I went on to share the gospel with him.

On another occasion Chelladurai escorted me to the Gold City of Kolar to visit another OM girls' team who were engaged in church planting. As in other cases we travelled overnight in keeping with Indian culture, arriving in the morning and leaving in the evening. They asked for a communion service, at which I was pleased to officiate, and I noticed that their leader did not look well. When she was out of the room I enquired and the girls told me she was ill and had spent the previous night in hospital but could only afford the price of one night.

After she returned I suggested that I should lay hands on her and pray for her healing. On leaving Kolar I was grateful to the Lord that she was much better, and she accompanied me to the bus. Years later I was in the home of an OM leader in Hyderabad and thought that his wife looked familiar. She was in fact Esther, the woman we prayed for in Kolar.

Kolar was the city where Chelladurai and his lovely wife Stella made their home. Their daughters, Grace and Glory, have completed this wonderful family, who serve the Lord faithfully.

5

On Top of the World in Nepal

As cold water to a thirsty soul so is good news from a distant land. So says the wise Solomon in Proverbs 25:25, and it is very true. Those who have left home comforts to embrace a foreign culture for Christ's sake know only too well how out of touch and isolated they can feel. When someone from the home country, even though a stranger, speaks our native tongue with our own colloquial accent we are cheered as if a shaft of sunlight has broken through the monotony of a cloudy day. This is even more so when the words spoken are as a message from God. Surely such words revive our souls and renew our flagging spirits.

Such was the purpose of my visit to Nepal in September 1978. This land on the roof of the world had long been a forbidden Shangri-La in my imagination. A white blank space between India and China kept its secrets, for no white man, no missionaries, no Christians were allowed in. At Bible College we prayed and soaked up any information of that mysterious land. Now, however, things had changed. In the early 1950s the door was opened and news began to trickle out of opportunities and challenges to explore this incredibly beautiful Hindu kingdom and share the gospel with its peoples.

Several friends of mine had already made amazing progress from that occasion when Hillary and Tensing had stood on the peak of Mount Everest until my more humble brief visit. Ron Byatt, a teacher from Romford, Essex, had gone as a missionary and returned with glowing accounts of development in education in Nepal. Others whom we had known as nurses in England waxed lyrical about the new Shining Hospital at Pokhara. Now it was my turn, not to trudge the long mountain pathways, crossing swaying narrow bridges over gorges above turbulent waters, but to fly as a passenger in a small plane up the valleys and into the Tribhuvan airport.

I was met by a tall, lean, fair young American from California named Alan Meyer. We had first met in Birmingham in 1972 when as newly-weds he and his wife Julie were part of the vanguard setting up the OM Conference. There I had observed their untiring commitment to serve the Lord in any practical way He ordained. Alan was an ingenious mechanical engineer who used all his skills to keep the OM teams on the plains of India mobile and as comfortable as conditions would allow. By the time we were reunited they had acquired two beautiful children, and I think a third was on its way.

At that time the Cold War was still on and Kathmandu was much like Berlin and other cities being courted by East and West alike. The shrewd Nepalese made the best of it so that finance and investment were welcomed from both sides. New roads, bridges and buildings bore witness to this. But manufactured goods were scarce and spare parts hard to obtain.

Operation Mobilisation had begun its work in India in 1964. At first donated trucks were driven overland from Belgium through Yugoslavia, Turkey, Iran and Pakistan. On arrival in India the vehicles were allowed six-month visas, after which they had to leave the country. Those six months were well used, as teams of young people travelled carrying large quantities of Christian literature, Bibles and gospel packets. In the heat and dust of the Indian plains the workers toiled in spreading the good news of Jesus Christ to many millions who had never before heard His name. It was exciting but often dangerous as opposition grew to what some deemed to be a foreign western religion.

After six months the trucks were driven to the Nepali border from where a mechanic received it for maintenance at the OM base in Kathmandu, the base being a garage belonging to a local hotel whose owner was sympathetic to the cause. The border crossing was a two-way transaction as each vehicle was exchanged for another, freshly repaired and serviced, and for which there was a new six-month visa. Generally this system worked well, but the drivers and mechanics in this remote land earned my deepest respect.

A tour of the base revealed how adept at economising and improvisation the mechanics were. Nothing was wasted: no screw, no spring, no part of motor body nor engine; all was conserved for possible later use. When trucks were no longer fit to travel the long rough Indian roads they were made serviceable for local journeys in Kathmandu and sold to local buyers who would turn up cash in hand, eager for a bargain.

My task was to see that the workers were in good shape. Mainly they were very fit physically, though there were those who had been sent to Nepal to recuperate after the exertion of OM missionary endeavour, which was a kind of protracted pilgrimage. The chief need was to give encouragement and spiritual counselling allied to sound Bible teaching. Mission workers experience all the doubts and fears, hopes and aspirations that people at home do, only more so. Often the only people to whom they can turn are the very people they have problems with. It is therefore of great value for someone from outside, even outside the organisation, to be there to listen and bring comfort. Throughout my short stay I made it my business to spend time alone with each worker on the base.

There was another 'Alan' at the base but he was always busy elsewhere until the day before my departure. Then I met him. He was a cheerful, capable Londoner with a cockney accent. We took time out together and he gladly accompanied me to my first experience of dining in a Tibetan restaurant, when we ate their delicious 'dumplings'. There were many Tibetan refugees in Nepal and one day I was able to visit a camp, meet their people and even buy some of their hand-made goods. Many of these are marketed in the West by Tearcraft.

After our meal Alan took me for a drive up the Kathmandu Valley to a small isolated mountain, which we ascended. The views were magnificent overlooking the bright green terraced hillsides surrounded by the snow-capped Himalayas. At the top of the hill stood an ancient monastery, containing both a Hindu and Buddhist temple. Climbing out of our old Ford Transit van we were surrounded by excited children. Nearby, many large monkeys and baboons eyed us inquisitively. We hoped that they would keep their distance.

As we were about to enter the oriental monastery we looked down the mountain road and were astonished to behold a cavalcade of limousines such as I had never before seen in the East, moving rapidly towards us. Alan and I stood aside as the fleet of motors drew up. They were obviously officials, as each black car bore the double triangular flag of Nepal and the red starred flag of Communist China. It was evident that here was a government touring party being escorted by Nepali officials. We were aware that negotiations were taking place to open the borders of these two countries to tourism but that the move was regarded with suspicion. For us at that time an encounter with natives of mainland China was an exciting opportunity to share the gospel with those who have never heard. My heart quickened as a group of about forty well-dressed Chinese left the vehicles and began to follow a smart Nepali army officer and his retinue. We joined the procession which led into the monastery library, an obviously antiquarian treasure. The Nepali guide spoke in his own language and an interpreter translated into Mandarin.

Being engrossed with the spectacle I was surprised to receive a nudge from Alan, who quietly produced from his shoulder bag a handful of Christian literature in Chinese. "You go that way and I'll go this", he whispered and immediately began to move around the outside circle of tourists, distributing his leaflets with a friendly smile. I could do no other than what he did, I going clockwise while he went anti-clockwise. By the time we met completing the circle the literature had disappeared. He quickly drew me outside and towards the van. "Now run!" he cried, and we were soon diving into the vehicle and driving down the hill. Not only had we broken Nepali law, which at that time frowned upon free distribution of religious tracts, but we had also passed them on to subjects of another nation which strictly forbad the propagation of the Christian faith!

Second Visit to Nepal

This time, in 1982, I was going to visit David Moulden and his wife Sarah. David was from my church in Kingshurst, Birmingham and had responded to my challenge and appeal for mechanics to serve with OM in India. David was a trained mechanic, was well qualified and also a devout Christian. It was a big sacrifice for this young newly married couple to leave home comforts to serve in the sub-continent. The rigours of travelling on Indian buses carrying tools to repair broken-down trucks in remote Indian villages needed someone tough and determined. David was that man.

They had asked for some spare parts for a heavy diesel engine which were unobtainable in Nepal. OM leader, Gary Dean, met me at Heathrow Airport with the new items still in boxes. Of course I had little idea of what they were and my first hurdle was to get them through security and on to the plane. First Gary had to make them a gift to me so that I could answer the questions truthfully when asked if they were mine. Next I had to pack them myself, which meant rearranging my luggage before checking in. Even in those days security was tight, so I prayed hard that I might not be challenged. All was well and I made it all the way to Delhi.

Mike Wheate met me at Delhi airport, a more pleasant arrival than on my first visit. The OM base in Delhi was a kind of transit centre, and there were several folk from round the world who were travel-worn and in need of counselling and refreshment. To help with this, Mike persuaded me to stay there for a few days. I pointed out that I had a flight booked for Kathmandu and that David Moulden was expecting to meet me. Mike said that he would take care of that, change the flight and telegraph David about the new arrangements.

Eventually I arrived at Tribhuvan airport, together with a group of Australian tourists. We had to form two queues at the customs checkpoint and I was dismayed to find that we were all required to open our baggage for inspection. When it came to my turn I was questioned about the motor engine parts which the official unpacked from their boxes. The problem was that he could speak little English and I could speak no Nepali. In answer to his "What's this?" I resorted to making noises like an engine, to no avail. He repeated his English vocabulary several times until he remembered his other words, "Wait here". Then he disappeared.

The queue opposite was moving slowly but ours was at a standstill. The Australians behind me began to express their frustration in colourful language. As I stood there I noticed a door open to a large store-room which was full of confiscated goods. I began to suspect that my engine components brought all this way from UK would end up there, and would not play the vital part of rescuing OM trucks. Furthermore I was not in the habit of paying bribes.

Quietly I decided to re-pack the boxes with the unidentified pieces of engineering. Then I called across to the officer manning the other queue and asked him to put his mark on the baggage so that I could leave. To my amazement he stepped across and did it, at which I grabbed my belongings and fled!

Once outside the airport building I looked for David or someone else sent to meet me. I looked in vain. As usual I was surrounded by beggars and doubtful characters that were keen to deprive me of my goods. After half an hour or so, and I was already late from the various delays, I realised my predicament. I had no address or telephone number of anyone who could help me. Where could I go and where would I spend the night?

It is strange how in times of emergency the mind is quickened and insignificant items are suddenly remembered. As usual at times like these I prayed for God's help and guidance. Vaguely I remembered the way to the garage which had served as the OM mechanics' base. A small Nepali taxi had driven up so I decided to go on board and trust the Lord to guide. The driver spoke no English but he understood my one instruction when I cried, "Kathmandu!" We sped along the winding road towards the city. Suddenly we were passing over a fine bridge above a ravine. My memory was jolted reminding me of a left fork ahead. This I called out and indicated and the driver obeyed. Then I remembered that there was a carpet store on the corner of the road leading to the base. To my relief, there it was, carpets stacked up. Again I shouted, this time waving my right arm. We drove on, and after a few hundred yards came upon the garage, where we stopped. Fortunately I did not remove my luggage or let the taxi go. The place was deserted except for a couple of angry-looking dogs.

There again I experienced a strange quickening of my memory. At a meal in the OM base in Delhi we sat at several tables. There had been a conversation at a table near me, not at the one where I ate, and I had overheard them talking about the new house which the team had acquired in Kathmandu. I had not consciously listened or even attempted to memorise the description. Now it came forcibly to me. The house was a mile or so from the garage, surrounded by a garden, had a flat roof, red bricked around the ground floor and white around the upper.

Boarding the small Nepali taxi again, I urged the driver to go on up the narrow winding lane. We had little idea where we were heading. I was praying hard while keeping my eyes peeled. I don't know how long we travelled but we took many turnings and travelled several miles. Then I saw a building which exactly matched the description which I had inadvertently overheard in Delhi. By this time my Nepali driver understood me when I called him to stop. Leaning out I called to a Nepali man working in the garden, "David Moulden?" He did not respond. Then I called "OM!" He looked up with a broad smile and outstretched hand. I had reached my destination.

Of course the problems on my arrival were caused by a failure in communications, there being no telephone service available at that time and the telegrams explaining my delay had just not arrived. David had kindly been to meet planes for three days but since no message had reached him he had then given up.

I cannot claim that my two visits to Nepal made a significant difference to the life of the nation or even to the progress of Christian mission there. But of this I am confident, whenever we obey the Lord and do His work, he always has a purpose and nothing is wasted. We must trust Him for results. For me it was a time of wonder and encouragement. Hopefully my experiences which have been shared with others have proved a blessing over the years.

The Story of Pastor Joseph

Take, for instance, Pastor Joseph, who was brought to visit me in Kathmandu. This lovely, typically stocky Nepali gentleman quietly told me his story. As a child he had been brought up on a peaceful country small-holding containing their thatched house where they lived upstairs and kept chickens and small animals below. There was land to grow rice and fruit and keep a couple of cows. Joseph's parents and his older brother were very happy, if uneducated and un-travelled. All was well in their beautiful surroundings among banks of rhododendrons in the shadow of snow-capped mountains. Then calamity came. First his mother became sick and died, and soon after so did his father. Presently the landowner arrived to collect his rent, and as the boys could not pay they were evicted from their home.

The two young lads aged eight and ten were destitute, nor was there any to help as all the neighbours lived at subsistence level. Advice was given them to leave the country and seek their fortune in a distant Indian city. The journey was long and arduous and they were often hungry and thirsty, simply living on what they could find or was given to them. Eventually they arrived in Darjeeling, a city the like of which they had not experienced before. Never had they seen such crowds or heard such noise. At first it seemed exciting but they soon learned that a city is a lonely, uncaring place. They were still hungry but found that now they were competing with many other orphan children on the streets as well as beggars of every kind. One day as they were pushing through the crowded bazaar the boys became separated, never to see each other again.

It was while Joseph (the name which he adopted later) was stealing fruit out of sheer hunger that he was caught by an irate Hindu farmer. The man shook him and told him he should return to his parents. Tearfully Joseph told him his tale of sorrow and fortunately the farmer took pity on him and invited him to be his own buffalo boy. Though it meant long hours and sleeping on the floor of the farmhouse Joseph cheerfully accepted; after all, it meant food.

Sadly the farmer's wife was not so enthusiastic and often Joseph felt rejected after a beating. However there were compensations, for in the farmer he had a father figure whom he could ask questions. One was regarding a picture hanging on the whitewashed wall of their sparsely furnished room. Who was the man in the picture? The farmer had been reluctant to say, except that no, he was not his father, brother or friend in the village. Eventually he said that his name was Jesus, and that he was a person Christians followed.

Joseph had never heard the name Jesus or the term Christian before. Somehow he became fascinated by the man in the picture. The farmer told him all he knew about Jesus, but that was little. He gleaned that Jesus was good and kind, had taught wonderful things, healed the sick and cared for the poor. Joseph longed to meet him, but then he learned that he had been killed, but what was that about him coming back to life?

One evening Joseph had a particularly bad time with the farmer and his wife and he went to bed sore and tearful from a beating. He determined that he would run away, so next morning he took his basket as usual to collect food for the buffaloes, but as soon as he was out of sight of the farmhouse he dumped it and fled. All he wanted to do was escape from his misery and, if possible, find Jesus.

As I listened to the Nepali pastor telling his story I was touched by the fact that many, many other children could tell the same story. How many have no one to love and care for them, and how many have never heard the name of Jesus?

Joseph had no idea where he was going. He just got as far away as possible and then began asking passers-by if they knew where Jesus lived. No one had even heard of him. "Not in our village," they would say, "try the next." After days of disappointment and hunger and nights sleeping out under the stars, Joseph remembered the farmer telling him that Jesus was the one Christians followed. Now he began to ask also where the Christians lived. Soon he was told of a village further along the road where he would find a Christian. The boy ran on to find the place and asked for the house in which a Christian lived. There was a door which he knocked and a man appeared. "Does Jesus live here?" asked the lad excitedly.

Joseph told me that the man was a Roman Catholic missionary, who took him in, gave him food and shelter and let him join an orphanage, where he received a good education and where he learned English. He also learned about the Gurkha regiment in the British Army where many young men from Nepal served. The years went by, he studied hard and became a soldier, but he forgot about Jesus. It was only after he failed military exams to become a Gurkha officer and decided to leave the army that he began to have serious thoughts about Christ again.

Our meeting was coming to an end so I was not able to learn the story of the intervening years. But what was he doing now, and why had he been brought to me? He told me of his conversion experience and growth in Christ, how he had returned to Nepal and become a pastor of a small group of believers and how they had been persecuted. He had just been released from prison having served three years for baptising new believers. He recounted how he had been away from home preaching when police had raided his house looking for him. When he had returned home he was advised to run and hide, but instead he had gone to the police station and asked why they wanted him. He told me how they had listened intently as he shared with them his testimony to Christ. Later they arrested him and beat him, knocking him to the ground. As he described to me his sufferings, I said how sorry I was to hear it. "Don't be sorry for me," he replied with a warm smile, "Suffering for Jesus was the greatest experience of my life."

That interview with Pastor Joseph was in itself worth my effort and expense to visit the magnificent land of Nepal. However, there were many more memorable events and contacts made during that visit but I only have time and space to mention them briefly.

One Sunday in Nepal

The King of Nepal was no mere constitutional monarch. He was involved in government down to the smallest detail. David and Sarah had taken me up a mountain from where we could see Mount Everest. On the ridge was a Buddhist shrine with bell and prayer flags. From there was a spectacular view. Looking to the northwest we could see another mountain, from which I was told one could look into China. The following Sunday it was suggested that we might go up there. The OM Transit van could also go quite a long way up, so we could ride. This was important as I was still suffering from sciatica and climbing was limited.

We drove from the house to the far end of the valley, where there was a gate straddling the road leading up the mountain. To our surprise the gate was closed and guarded by policemen. They told us that we needed a pass in order to enter. When we enquired where a pass could be obtained we were told we had to get one from the King! The van was left at the foot of the mountain and I bravely volunteered to do the climb, which was not too steep, but long. We were already high up and they told me the peak was 10,000 feet above sea level. That is low by Himalayan standards.

The grandeur of the panoramic views from the summit was breathtaking. Even here there were many Tibetan prayer flags. How we longed that these dear people should come to trust the Living God and not be bound by futile attempts to earn salvation.

As you would imagine the whole trip had taken much longer than expected and we had to hurry down not only to beat nightfall but also because I was due to preach in a Nepali church. Driving back to the house to get a change of clothes we passed someone on a bicycle on his way to the service. We were able to pass on the message that we would be coming but that we would be late.

The Nepali believers met in a hired room. When we arrived the place was in darkness, due to the proverbial power cut. However, candles revealed a good number of local people seated on the floor. Their upturned faces beamed a welcome and as we were late we were soon sharing God's message through a Nepali translator. Who would forget the joy of teaching God's word to such an audience in the flickering candlelight on a warm evening in Kathmandu? They were mainly new believers who had received the gospel gladly, if amid danger and persecution. On my earlier visit I had preached in a Nepali church in a different building. They told me that the churches in Nepal had grown since the beginnings in the 1950s to about three thousand members in 1978. On the second occasion in 1982 they informed me that the numbers stood at about twelve thousand. The body of Christ in Nepal has continued to grow and we can only marvel at the power and grace of God in calling out a people for His Name.

My words can never do justice in describing the beauty and romance of the land of Nepal, even the small areas that I saw. On the other hand it is impossible to portray the sense of darkness and bondage to idolatry which I witnessed in that place. Once I watched as worshippers arrived in coach loads to queue before a huge stone image lying on its back. The area was fenced, so entry was made through a gate at which they paid a priest and collected puja to put on the idol's head.

Another day we visited an enormous Hindu temple straddling a river during a festival. Many buses full of pilgrims had travelled from India to worship there. On one side lay an open sacred field where naked holy men covered with ashes taught groups of disciples seated around smoking fires. A bridge spanned the river to the main temple area, but a notice in English proclaimed, "Hindus only."

From our vantage-point we viewed the crowds of pilgrims thronging up the steps and alleyways placing offerings to the numerous deities, overlooked by a series of large stone platforms. On these were built stone cubicles where elderly people were left to end their days. There the families built funeral pyres and burned the bodies before throwing the ashes upon the river below. I noticed that when the pilgrims opposite concluded their oblations they bathed themselves to wash away their sins in that same river.

Even in the capital city we observed numerous shrines where worshippers did their ritual washing and paid their respects to what, to our eyes, were hideous images. There were also Tibetan Buddhist temples where splendid prayer banners fluttered forlornly in the wind.

But we were encouraged to see signs of Christian grace, such as the small orphanage run by a former Salvation Army woman married to a Nepali businessman. The place was poor and far from the standard we would expect in the West, but it provided security and shelter to dozens of destitute waifs from the street.

Then we visited a factory set up for Tibetan refugees where various textiles were produced. These people had lost everything as they fled from the invading Chinese Com-

munists but were working hard to provide for their subsistence.

We also visited a small leprosarium where poor destitute
sufferers of the disease and its consequences found shelter and
earned a meagre living by making leather goods. Some were
blind, others had only stubs for fingers and yet they punched
holes in the leather and inserted and tied the thongs skilfully to
create beautiful purses and handbags. These goods were
marketed in the West by Tearcraft. It was a joy to be an
eyewitness of these endeavours and also meet those who
benefit from this partnership.

The missionary community was close and denominational
barriers non-existent; all worked for the common good. Many
of the medical and educational institutions, if not all, would
not exist except for the founding industry of Christian mission.
But there was a price to pay. One brief glimpse was afforded
me when I was asked to visit a young doctor who was himself
a patient in hospital. Few other visitors came to see him as he
was so far from home in England. He had been injured and
broken his femur in a motorcycle accident on a remote
mountain road. Having lain there some time he realised that
there would be no passers-by to help him, no telephone (it
was before mobile phones), no ambulance or emergency
service. Somehow, in agony, he made his way back on to the
vehicle and drove it back to his mission house, where he lived
alone. There he bandaged himself up and next day limped to
the road where the daily truck which passed for a bus would
come. This took him to an airstrip from which, after a long
wait, he was flown in a small plane to Kathmandu. Again he
had to help himself to a taxi and asked to be taken to the
hospital.

As he told me his story all the lights went out. Another
power-cut! These stories are surely but a glimpse of the tip of a
huge mountain of blessing in the land of Nepal.

"God moves in a mysterious way His wonders to
perform," says the hymn-writer. William Cowper goes on to
say, "God is His own interpreter, and He will make it plain".

Postscript

In March 2005 Dorothy and I were in Calcutta and stayed at a small hotel near the airport. Each morning we were awakened by a knock at the door by a servant bringing tea. He was a cheerful, friendly young man in a place noted for its staunch Hinduism and its poverty. He spoke little English but his appearance made me think that he was not from the locality. When I asked he told me he was from Nepal. I told him of my visits and gave my reasons for them, which helped me share my faith. I did not know how much he understood but he smiled broadly and went away. Soon he returned, bringing a book — a Nepali Bible. It became clear that he was a Christian and this contact was very precious to him. As he was learning English I found book, chapter and verse in his Bible and in mine and so communicated. I also gave him a booklet of scripture produced by the Scripture Gift Mission in English. By the time we left that hotel he had memorised most of it.

7

Pakistan Diary

The coming into being of Birmingham City Mission was partly due to the plea of Tom Bugby, a London City Missionary in Tilbury working among Asian seamen, many of them Pakistanis. Hearing in 1961 that I was moving to Birmingham he urged me to start a mission there to reach his men who had jumped ship and settled in the Midlands.

Early in the life of BCM (launched in 1966) we began training young people for Christian service at home or abroad. One who came on the course some years later was Rupert Abbott, who with his wife Janet had recently graduated from Leeds University. They had come to Birmingham to be social workers but were dissatisfied with their situation. Hearing of our student training course they felt led to apply. Rupert gradually gained confidence and became an excellent team member and later their leader. In his third year he asked if he could major on reaching Pakistanis in the city, of whom there were many.

My response was that if he was convinced that it was God's calling he would need to study their language (Urdu) and culture. He must look for accommodation in a district where they were living, such as Saltley, and that they should go on a visit to Pakistan. I also suggested that as I would be travelling to the sub-continent they could accompany me and they could stay in Pakistan for a month until I returned to the UK. They were told to go away and pray about the proposal.

A few days later they came back to me saying that they had prayed but felt the Lord telling them that they should stay in Pakistan for a year, not a month. I agreed and promised if they did that I would visit them; hence the experiences described in this chapter.

FROM MY DIARY

Arrival in Karachi (Saturday 23rd January, 1988)

My arrival in Karachi last night was rather bewildering at first. I had an easy passage through the exit immigration and health officials, and while other people were being searched and having their baggage sorted through Customs, I showed my British passport and was given an immediate OK into the country with no-one asking any questions whatsoever. However, I did take precautions and went to the bank within the airport area and purchased some rupees so that, should I need to pay for a taxi, I would have the money to do so.

As it was, there was no-one waiting for me when I emerged from the airport. I looked expecting to see David Moulden, Tim Farrell or Rupert Abbott, but no one appeared. There were a number of Pakistani people asking to help carry my gear or to help me find a taxi. They were not easily put off. One offered me cigarettes and obviously wished to get me under his wing so I would eventually pay out quite a bit more. However, I waved them all aside and continued to wait for my friends who were coming with a car. After about twenty-five minutes I was really beginning to think I'd been deserted. The plane had actually arrived fifty minutes early and I therefore explained to myself that was the reason no-one was there to meet me. In the event David had overslept and I noticed Rupert amongst the crowd, dressed as a Pakistani: it wasn't so easy to pick him out. By the time I had got to where he was standing he had disappeared again, but eventually I saw him and was able to attract his attention.

We then negotiated with a taxi driver, Rupert doing an excellent job in his Urdu, haggling over the required price. His Urdu seemed to be very good indeed and he communicates well. We next got into a very battered taxi which nearly got more battered as it tried to jockey between this one and that one, people getting in and out, pushing vehicles around so that we could eventually emerge from the taxi area.

It was quite a comfortable journey to David's home, an upper-storey apartment in a pleasant house with an adjoining, well-kept garden. The windows were covered in mesh to keep out the mosquitoes and other insects. Actually the mosquitoes still got in and there was a little electrical appliance which was kept alight to try to ward them off during the night. Out of the windows I could see a number of palm trees with coconuts growing and lots of other exotic plants. There was plenty of noise. This evening we were treated to several hours of rather loud music, and dancing. We went outside to see what it was all about, and I insisted it was all in my honour! In fact it was a wedding celebration and there were girls dancing to the music of double-sided drums and a kind of flute.

During the day I was visited by Rupert, Janet and the children and also Tim and Joy and their children (Tim and Joy Farrell were also ex-students at BCM and were now doing translation work with Wycliffe Bible translators). We had a lovely time of fellowship together and we were able to exchange news and really encourage one another in the Lord. It was lovely to see them all; they seemed to be quite happy and contented and in the will of God.

It was delightful to see how gratefully the gifts I had brought from England were received – not so much for what they were but for the thought and love behind them all. These friends are very much isolated in a Muslim community. We have been constantly reminded of Islam by the prayer calls throughout the day, and by the Muslim culture which surrounds us.

It seems that in a number of the churches the believers meet on Fridays because Sunday is the same as any other day here in Pakistan and the schools are open and people go to work and therefore it is not easy to arrange a normal Sabbath activity. However, there was to be a service in an Urdu-speaking church here in Karachi which David attended – and I was asked to be the preacher, through an interpreter of course.

The journey and the time difference were taking their toll on me, and I became quite disorientated. When I turned in, in the early hours of the morning, I was too tired to work it out, but I realised I had only had five hours sleep the night before. Even then the whole place was awake but I'd slept so soundly that David had left a note saying they had all gone out and to help myself to breakfast. I just about managed this and then lay on the bed again and went straight to sleep again. I felt a lot better, and by the next day I adjusted to the fact that there was a five-hour difference. In England we can feel put out by the one-hour change to our clocks for the summer months. My clock has changed by five hours in one night!

We have had some really good conversations, exchanging news of the Lord's work and also some spiritual conversations on the things of God. David and I concluded the evening with a time of prayer together and I felt it was beneficial to both of us.

Sunday 24th January

We were to spend the day on Karachi beach but first we needed to get some money. Rupert took me into the town, not too far. We walked to the bank and there I exchanged some travellers' cheques. This was quite a performance but fortunately Rupert had been there before. We went upstairs, sat down at a desk which was covered in all sorts of papers and files; there were many people around at other desks and we just sat and waited for someone to come and serve us. A man came and Rupert conversed freely with him in Urdu, explaining the situation. The man produced various papers and dealt with us quite smartly and cheerfully. He asked who I was and where I'd come from and had a little conversation with me. Eventually he wrote out two papers which I had to sign. He then asked for my passport, which he studied very carefully, for some reason looking carefully at the certificate of health that I'd received following my cholera injections. Armed with these papers we stood up, shook hands, exchanged greetings and then went down to the ground floor of the bank where first I presented the receipts to one man who looked at them carefully and then passed them to another man who was handling the cash. He counted out the rupees and then handed them back to another man who counted them all again and eventually we received the money.

Armed with our money we proceeded into the bazaar to do some shopping. We were looking for fruit and there was a little haggling over the price for bananas. We took a whole bunch, about a kilo, and some oranges. Then there were other fruits, rather like tangerines but as large as Jaffa oranges, and I think there must have been six of them. We paid less than 50p for the whole lot! Next we wanted to get some crisps so we bought them at a crisp shop. They were loose in glass containers so they had to be weighed and put into sealed polythene bags to take away. We next looked for a taxi and Rupert haggled over the price with one man. After quite a while he told him he wasn't free and was waiting for someone else anyway. We went to another one and argued over the price of that. He was asking far too much so we went to a third and, after quite a lengthy conversation, it was agreed that this man would take us to where Rupert was staying, pick up the family and take us to the beach. Later he would return to the beach to collect us. Finally a price was agreed. In fact when we got to the beach the driver decided to stay nearby. He was a very nice man and he stayed there all day then took us back. It seemed having got a price for a double journey he was content to accept that and enjoy the day.

We picked up Rupert's family who were staying at the house of a woman doctor. There was a couple there too who were visiting and touring the sub-continent. We took the taxi to the beach, which meant a drive right through the centre of Karachi: a large, very Indian city with crowds of people. There is no concept of lane discipline here. The cars were weaving in and out of carts drawn by camels or donkeys, sometimes two donkeys pulling a cart, between heavy trucks, all made up in glittering silver with lots of pictures, colours and reflectors. Each truck looks like a show-piece steam-engine or gypsy caravan and is much treasured by each driver. We passed a whole park of these, people working on them, taking wheels off, bonnets open, working on engines, and making them available for hire at any time. There were also lots of cycles, rickshaws (three-wheeler motorised), and an occasional donkey wondering around by itself. It was a very colourful, noisy place with hooters going constantly as we passed any vehicle. We got in between quite a number of trucks and they played very loud tunes on the horn. It looked dangerous at times, but we managed to come through unscathed.

As we crossed a bridge there was an appalling smell. All open sewers flow into this river and we were glad to get over it. We proceeded down the beach road and eventually found the houses, some of which were magnificent. We were shown one that belongs to a TEAM mission group, though other missionaries use it too. For us it was a landmark as we were to meet Tim and Joy there later in the afternoon. We were walking over the sand to the house when we realised we had brought no water with us. This seemed to be a serious deficiency – to spend the whole day in the heat and on the sand without water. We were very concerned about this. Water had been prepared for the trip but somehow had not been placed in the car. However, just at that point the door of the beach house opened and a little boy appeared. Rupert's boy, Thomas saw him and ran to him. It appeared that they were attending the same school and were mates and his family were staying in the house. We were welcomed onto the veranda, given the water, drinks and food we needed and had a lovely picnic together. Eventually we were joined by Tim and Joy and their children, also Joy's parents. The fruit which we had bought was very welcome.

It was a glorious day, as every day is here. There were no clouds and it was very warm in the sunshine (despite the fact it is still January). I didn't get sunburnt but I had to be careful and was glad of a little bit of shade under the veranda. The children played in the sea, and as there were very few other people around, they had the sea and the beach to themselves. The family staying in the house produced a dinghy for the children and took them out for a little cruise. There were also a couple of rubber tyres for them to use as lifebelts and to play with.

Then along came some Pakistani riders with their horses, offering to give rides. Eddie, the missionary from the hospital, had a ride on a horse. I was offered one but refused because I thought it might aggravate my back pain. Later, camels appeared; this time I was persuaded to take a ride on a camel. I was apprehensive, concerned that this might give me back problems for the rest of the tour. However, because they all wanted to take pictures of it for posterity, I agreed and they all enjoyed seeing me being lifted up on this camel. The guide was told to go very gently with me because of my back, but as soon as I was out of earshot, he started running and I had quite a run on the camel. To my amazement, when I returned, instead of my back feeling worse, I felt the discomfort had definitely eased. The bumpy ride seemed to have been beneficial to my back, for which I was grateful. It was a very funny and enjoyable time and we were all glad to be there. Eventually we arrived back at David Moulden's house. They were just about to leave for the service at which I was to preach, so it was a dash in, just a drink of water, change my shirt and put on a tie, get back in the car, and be whisked away across town to the service.

This was an Urdu service, entirely Pakistani Christian people, the women with their customary Pakistani dress and head-dresses, all the women squatting on the floor on one side of the building, and the men squatting on the floor on the other side. The church was quite full, I would think about a hundred people were there. They were singing from Urdu hymnbooks, and they had been going a little while – they thought we were not arriving, I think. I was a little surprised, because some of these Eastern church services go on for a long time and late starts are not therefore unusual. But this church was being led by two well-educated men and it seems that they were very disciplined with the time. There was no pressure put on me, however, but after they had sung and prayed, I was asked for the Scripture, which the leader read in Urdu from the Urdu Bible.

The reading I had chosen was the first chapter of Jonah. It was difficult having had little time to prepare and not quite sure where I was going or what I was expected to do, but I did decide eventually to key in with some views of Karachi. It occurred to me that although I had only been there only a matter of hours, I had seen Karachi from an angle that hardly any of them had seen, because I had flown in and I had seen Karachi from the air, and also I had arrived at night. So I talked about the beauty of the city as seen from the sky, and yet it could only be seen because of the myriad lights which were there – just small lights, but put together they showed this beautiful pattern. I then talked about Jesus, and that He had said that we were to shine as lights in the world, and that although we were in the midst of darkness, as there is such darkness in Pakistan – an overwhelming darkness – yet our light can be seen and Jesus said "Let your light shine before men that they might see your good works and glorify your Father in heaven."

It was a bit of a step from there to get back to Jonah but I talked about Jonah in the same sort of vein, that he was commanded to go to the city as we are commanded to go to the cities and the city of Karachi is a very needy one, and there he was commanded to go and preach the Word but he was disobedient. I encouraged the church members to be obedient to the Lord, to shine in the city and that by doing that they might be a witness, for they were in the midst of people. When the storm came in Jonah's case, each man called upon his own god and then they called upon Jonah to wake up and come and help them. But then he showed them that he belonged to the true, living God. If you read the end of that chapter you find that these men also feared the Lord and made sacrifices to Him. So I encouraged them to serve the Lord in the midst of their darkness and all the trials, that in the midst of that there will be those who will watch and they will come to know the Lord.

It was a lovely time. The interpreter was a former headmaster of a school and he had also been David Moulden's language teacher. He thought very highly of David, spoke about the way he preached and he also interpreted for him. This man knew Mr. and Mrs. Summers, who are WEC missionaries in Wolverhampton. David and Sarah's father came with me to the service. I believe the message was for us all.

Monday 25th January
Karachi Zoo

The morning began with Rupert calling for me and we first went to the home where they are staying. This is a beautiful house, belonging to a woman doctor whose husband is a civil engineer. From there we called a taxi and went to the zoo, taking the children with us.

Karachi Zoo is not exactly up to British standards. The care of the animals is not good, but there were many exotic birds. We saw quite a number of pelicans, vultures, eagles, peacocks, to name just a few. There was a beautiful white peacock which I'd not seen before. Among the animals was a fine leopard, a black panther, various kinds of deer, lions, and an elephant. Rupert had intended to get me to ride on an elephant and wanted a picture of that but was cheated of it because the elephants didn't give rides until the afternoon. We saw one poor elephant chained up. He couldn't move his feet at all and his water was several feet away from him. The intelligent animal decided to swing his trunk like a pendulum, in increasingly large arcs until eventually he reached the water and in a few seconds sucked up a great deal. I thought he couldn't have had much of a drink but he put the water in his mouth and when he'd had enough he emptied the rest out of his trunk – several gallons of it. We had a lovely walk. There were many trees in full blossom and green grass, rather like an English park. In fact, there in the middle of it all was a good old English Victorian bandstand.

At the end of our visit we took a taxi for a short distance and stopped when we saw a horse-drawn Victoria (a sort of landau carriage). There I sat with my back to the engine, that is the horse and horseman, and Rupert and Janet and the children sat opposite me. We had a leisurely trip on that and it took us to the mausoleum of Jinnah, founder of Pakistan, a national monument. I took some photographs of this and we went up and had a look round. We had to remove our shoes before entering and we bought a little information brochure on it. It was quite an imposing structure in an elevated position overlooking the city.

Afterwards we boarded a taxi back to the doctor's house and there we had lunch and I had quite a good conversation with the civil engineer. His father went there as a missionary, had little education, and was a self-taught plumber, but had an interesting story and worked there as a WEC missionary for some years. This man knew several people I knew, including Dennis Clark, but he has remained in Karachi and sees himself as a "tentmaker", working for his living and reaching out to other people in industry. He feels there is a great gap there, that we tend to reach the lower classes of people with our evangelism whereas we also ought to be working alongside those who are in high position, winning them for Christ too. They were very kind to us and we had a good meal. After playing with the children for a little while it was then time for Rupert and family to leave and they took a taxi to the railway station to commence their 26-hour journey home to Rawalpindi.

I returned to David Moulden's house and arrived in time to be told I was almost late for my next appointment but was first to be taken to meet Tom. Tom lives in an apartment at the back of this house. I went up to see him and also met his Iranian wife, a very beautiful girl. We talked together and enjoyed a cup of tea while he told me about the Iranian work. There was just time for a quick change before going with him by car to the meeting in a Southern Baptist church which was being made available for the Iranian work.

This was a very exciting meeting and there were about twenty young Iranian men. I was told that on a Sunday they have as many as 100 in the meeting. This meeting was really for the Christians, those who had turned to Christ. There is a high turnover of people, but the work is amongst refugees fleeing from Iran. They arrive in the country with no passport and with little money, in desperate straits. Tom and others go out on the streets looking for them, invite them round for fellowship and then the gospel is preached to them. They have had considerable success with people coming to Christ, who are then instructed and built up before they move on. There was a lovely testimony there. I was invited to give my testimony and talk a little about the work I was doing and then preach for half an hour or so, on 'The Secret of Contentment' in Philippians 4, urging upon them to be anxious for nothing, but to pray in all things. I talked initially about the formation of the church at Philippi, the small group in Lydia's home, the woman who was delivered from the evil spirit, then the conversion of the jailer. It seemed to be very appropriate and there were a number of people who spoke to me afterwards and appreciated that it was a message for them.

I was brought back by car, taking a short tour of some of the districts before we returned an Iranian family to where they were living, and that gave me another sight and smell of some of the poorer parts of Karachi.

Day with Tim Farrell
Tuesday 26th January

Tim Farrell and his wife Joy had both received training at Birmingham City Mission but were now working for Wycliffe Bible Translators in Karachi where they lived with their two children.

I was called for by Tim and Joy Farrell quite early this morning and taken to their home. This is an area not too far from the beach, although it's in a slum area populated by Baluchi people. The people live in small crowded conditions. The streets are narrow, lots of pot holes with people and children everywhere and women wearing burkas. It's quite common in Karachi to see people with black burkas. They cover their faces completely. Some have the old white burkas with the little net over the face. They can just see out and the garment comes all the way down to the feet. Men also have their own distinctive dress.

At Tim's home they had a small Japanese car and it was good to ride there. There is a small parking area inside their little compound. Inside, the home is quite roomy with a high ceiling, typical of the Indian home. Tim has a small office and he showed me the work he is doing. They have completed a small language book and have had it printed with beautiful coloured pictures done in the form of the alphabet or a simple children's primer using the Baluchi script. He is also working on another text, some which is from the Bible e.g. sections on Genesis, doing the flood story and other scripture portions. He has a Sharp computer which he values very much and this is helping him immensely. I was able to see the printouts and he demonstrated the method that they use.

While I was there two of his Baluchi friends arrived, young men, one clearly of African descent. This was an interesting point as I had noticed quite a number of people with African features and black curly hair which one would not expect to find in Pakistan. Apparently there are a lot of these people among the Baluchis. They seem to have descended from African slaves, evidence of the former slave trade in this area. These two young men were very bright, cheerful and friendly; they spoke some English, so I was able to converse with them. However, they regularly met up with Tim and acted as his teachers. He didn't have to pay them because they were only too happy to have something useful to do. The one looked a little like Muhammad Ali and we were joking about this as he was interested in boxing. Actually he was not quite so big as Muhammad Ali. The other chap was keen on cricket so we had some jokes about Pakistani umpires. Apparently he was on our side. These men came with us as we went out for a little tour in the car to collect a new battery as the one in his car kept failing and we were having to push start to get it going again.

We were given an impromptu tour of Karachi in search of an address and on arrival were escorted in customary Pakistani fashion into an office, where there was due ceremony with signing of books, friendly greetings, handshakes etc. We had called before to collect Tim's two girls. They both have blond hair and are very popular there and came away with key rings made by the firm. Having dropped off the two young men we returned home for a lunch of rice, salad and stew with Tim and Joy, and Joy's parents who are staying with them.

It had been planned that we would go on a circular rail trip around Karachi but decided to go down to Clifton Beach, yes *Clifton*! We joked about Clifton Bridge and in fact went over it. Actually we passed the embassies and various Ministries of Defence and saw quite a number of soldiers in that area too.

Having got down to the beach we first observed a man with a monkey who immediately began to perform for us. I'd never seen a monkey perform such antics. He stood to attention and saluted, danced, was given a stick and pretended to fight us, did all sorts of tricks, eventually feigning death. His head was covered in a scarf and whatever they told him to do he just flopped around and when it was taken from him he jumped in resurrection. I took a few pictures of it as I'd never seen an animal behave like this. I'm sure he could earn a fortune on TV. We had to make a little payment for him and then we went for a walk along the beach. There were the usual decorated camels and horsemen, not many people about. We walked right along and saw a couple of beached ship hulks.

This whole incident was most profitable spiritually. Had we been on the train I'm sure we could not have talked as we did. I was able to chat with Tim and Joy and they were able to share with me their thoughts concerning their situation and future. They were considering returning home in May. There is always the problem of a return visa but Tim is keen to get on a course which would in fact last a year and he would then return. It's the kind of course that would take him on to degree standard. A degree would be very helpful for much of his work, but also would improve his skills and knowledge for the work God has called him to do. They need prayer regarding this.

They shared with me concerning their home church. It is often forgotten that events at home, whether in families or churches, can have strong repercussions for the missionaries. They hear little snippets of information and mull them over and they can get very upset. There had been a division in the church to which Tim belonged and reports of it had reached them. This put them in great difficulty because, although they were sent out by the main church, the chief supporters were in the faction that had moved. We counselled them and I think they saw the need to be gentle and impartial in their approach to both sides of the dispute. They had been sent out by the whole church and they were all part of that church. But they have obviously been worried and distressed about this and it was good to be able to comfort them in this situation. So we spent a profitable afternoon together.

Finally, Tim and Joy brought me home about 6 p.m. to the Mouldens' flat. This gave me time to simply change, have a wash, and prepare to go out as I'd promised the Mouldens we would go out for a meal together. This was an opportunity to listen to some of their concerns and talk through various issues with them.

Rawalpindi

Wednesday 27th January

After lunch David took me to the airport. There were no problems, although it is sometimes difficult when you're the only English person in a crowd of passengers. The flight was brief. It had taken Rupert and Janet 26 hours to get from Karachi to Rawalpindi. The flight took me 1 hour 35 minutes. After collecting my baggage I was very relieved to see Rupert waiting for me. He has the use of a Lancer, a Mitsubishi model. It's in very good condition so we feel very well blessed. The drive didn't take long to the house of Dr. Stuart which had been loaned to them during their time here. I had never seen such a good house for missionary work as this one. There was a large hall with an open staircase. The rooms were very big with high ceilings and everything you could wish for. We had a lovely time. I was given a good English meal and played with the children a little while. Bryn and Thomas were both doing very well. Thomas had grown up a lot into a very sensible little boy. Bryn, too, seemed to be growing well. The children were put to bed and the rest of the evening was spent talking to Rupert and Janet over their experiences and sharing some of the news from Birmingham. It was a really refreshing time of renewing fellowship and I am sure this whole time in Pakistan with them will be of real benefit to them and to the work of the Lord here and in Birmingham.

Thursday 28th January

Today I woke to find the sky overcast and that it was raining and had been doing so throughout the night. It was also quite chilly, hardly what I expected to find in Pakistan. However, I had breakfast with Rupert and Janet about 8 o'clock then made a telephone call to Mike Wakeley of OM in Lahore. We were able to discuss briefly the plan of action for the next few days. It was arranged that I would travel with Rupert to Lahore on Sunday and have further discussions with Mike before proceeding with the next section of the tour.

As soon as we were ready we drove in Dr. Stuart's car into Rawalpindi and went to the Pakistan International Airways office to enquire about the possibility of a flight from

Rawalpindi down to Karachi on 14th February. We were able to make a provisional booking as money had not reached Rupert's bank and we had no time to exchange travellers' cheques, so we thought we'd leave the payment until later.

We then went to visit Agnes, a Canadian missionary living in Rawalpindi. Agnes used to work in Africa and when her work was finished she went home to Canada and after a while felt the Lord calling her to service in Pakistan. She is a midwife, regularly travelling out into the district some distance away to the north. Her home church has sent money to buy her a four-wheel-drive Suzuki and we were able to borrow that. Because of the wet weather we thought the road to where we were going would be impassable. As it happened the rain ceased but on the journey to the village we drove through an area where the road was being reconstructed. This was just an earth road anyway and very uneven; had we not had a four-wheel-drive vehicle we would have been in difficulties.

Pakistani Hospitality

We travelled to the village where ex-neighbours of Rupert live, a distance of over 40km from Rawalpindi. It was a most interesting journey, very much like India but with conditions somewhat better than I had experienced before. Eventually we were received by this neighbour from Birmingham. We were a little later than we had expected, but it turned out to be exactly the right time. This fine man had been in England for some years. He used to work at the IMI works in Witton and lived next door to Rupert in Chartist Road. We met a number of people who worked in Birmingham, Stourbridge, or Bradford; they spoke English with corresponding regional British accents and were very pleased to see us. We spent a short time with him in his home then accompanied him to do some shopping in the village. We were taken into a so-called Indian restaurant, although by "restaurant" standards it was rather basic, and we had a real Indian meal — portions of various meat dishes and buffalo milk, whey or yoghurt and vegetables and plenty of chapattis. I tried my hand — literally — at eating with my hand, always the right one, and it wasn't a bad meal. I had to be careful because I had been suffering from an upset stomach. We had a good long conversation about relationships between the resident population and those who work in England and make visits to Pakistan, cultural differences and various other things.

We walked around the village, meeting various other people. Wherever we went we were received warmly, invited to sit down in the small shops and introduced to various individuals, all of whom were pleased to see English people and many of whom could speak some English. One man who had once been in the army was very proud to talk to us because he had some knowledge of the British Army. It was a very colourful situation; the women with their dresses, children coming home from school, many of the girls with bright red shawls over their heads. We passed a few carts being drawn by camels, but there was much better transport with a lot of Japanese vehicles and we noticed a number of British vehicles. Apparently people buy minibuses in England and drive them all the way to Pakistan and sell them. They are glad to have the Pakistani currency, which cannot be taken out of the country; it can be invested in improved housing. These vehicles still have the GB or Union Flag sticker on the back, which you see as they drive around. There were the usual chickens running around, not so many dogs, goats, sheep and bullocks. Back at the man's home I took some photographs of his children. He had two buffalos in his yard. He had been very kind to Rupert and in fact he was the one who had met Rupert at the airport on his arrival in Pakistan and had taken him into his own home. He had even bought and fitted a western toilet especially for Rupert's sake. They were very kind to us and invited us to stay overnight, which is customary in Pakistani hospitality. However, as we needed to get back we declined. We negotiated the great trunk road, with its busy, apparently chaotic traffic. It was quite a dangerous road; occasionally one sees the wrecks of vehicles at the roadside.

We eventually arrived back safely without incident, glad to get back, exchange the car and come home to Janet. We had a nice tea together, played with the children, watched the English news on the colour TV which has been loaned to them. Actually it will be returned tomorrow, so that will be the end of that luxury. We saw some of the Pakistani items; apparently it is the regular thing immediately after the news to broadcast the whole Muslim prayer call, with pictures of Mecca, the mosques, and quotations from the Koran on the screen. Apparently quotations from the Koran appear frequently on national Pakistan TV, almost every few minutes. There is also commercial advertising on the single available channel, but the Islamic message is dominant.

Islamabad
Friday 29th January
Friday in Pakistan is the rest day. When President Bhutto was in power in 1975 he changed the rest day from Sunday to Friday. Most shops close on Friday, as do all government offices. Many churches, particularly the English ones, have kept in step with government policy. This morning we went to St. Thomas' Church in Islamabad, the capital of Pakistan, a large sprawling city of fairly new buildings. There is a huge modern mosque in the centre. The President's palace, the Congress House called the Secretariat, and the Parliament is centred here: a huge white complex which can be seen for many miles.

After the service Rupert took us for a drive into the hills to get a good view of the area. It was a marvellous sight; we could see the dam, the reservoir, and there were plenty of parks in this artificial new city with its straight roads, quite a fine place in my estimation. The road up the mountain was very steep and winding.

On returning to Islamabad we called at some shops and I met a young man who was working at the University but was particularly concerned with outreach to Afghans and Iranians. From him I learned that a number of Afghans had come to Christ. He mentioned a number of about two hundred, I think, now in the Delhi area. They were well satisfied with the progress they were making. He thought the work was rather slow but when seen from a distance this is surely a miracle. There was no Afghan church as such, but there were Afghan fellowships.

After lunch we went to visit the family of Rupert's teacher, the young man who had been a great help to him in learning the Urdu language in Rawalpindi. We went through the bazaar.

The family live in quarters belonging to the United Presbyterian Church of Pakistan. We visited the church itself, and I took a photograph from the front of the building. It is interesting to see an English building tucked behind such a Pakistani facade. The family we visited were real Pakistanis and yet with a Christian background. The boy's father was once the pastor there. He died about three years ago. The young man has two brothers and a sister, called Debbie. His mother is a very pleasant person. She didn't speak much English but seemed to be very responsive to spiritual fellowship.

The young teacher returned with us to Rupert's house. He wanted to have a personal private conversation with me. We talked for about an hour, mainly about England and general things of interest to both of us. I felt he had a very restricted view of the world, with very little idea of what Britain is like, and he didn't seem to know very much about his own country either. Yet he is studying for a B.A., and is still at college. One of his brothers is also at college with him studying statistics. His second brother is an anaesthetics technician in a local hospital.

Some of these people were to return to England tonight and it had been arranged that they should come to Rupert's on the way from their villages and have a meal here before going on to the airport. Rupert decided to lead them to the airport to ensure they would get there on time. We enjoyed a very warm conversation. There were six male members of the family and about the same number of women and they were all crowded into one four-wheel-drive vehicle. It is interesting to note that these men have Birmingham accents, at least the two who could speak English. One of them works in the central sorting office of the Royal Mail in Birmingham. Another one has two Indian restaurants on the Bristol Road in Selly Oak. He is quite an intelligent man with whom we had lengthy discussions. He is remaining here in Pakistan. The other one was over here briefly because of the death of their father. His body had been brought over to Pakistan for burial.

It is marvellous to see how Rupert is communicating with these people. A real loving relationship has been built up. They spoke so warmly to me too, two of the men embracing me before they left with a warm invitation for me to visit their village and be given hospitality. They asked me to come early so I could be shown around the farms. They have a number of animals and several houses and weren't sure how much land they owned. These people are quite well off. They have houses in England but have much more space in this country. They are of course all Muslims but they seem to be very open. I was pleased that before they left Rupert prayed with them.

Missionary Counselling
Saturday 30th January

This morning the weather was rather overcast and it was quite cold. Janet kindly took some washing from me and then after a mid-morning break we all went down to visit an OM couple, Craig and his wife from Canada, who have three small children. They were formerly working in India but were compelled, because of visa problems, to move to Pakistan. I am somewhat concerned for them as they seemed a little depressed and were unsure when asked the question: "What is your ministry?" They have been there about eighteen months and are mainly concerned with language study. His ideas on how to learn the language were not terribly satisfactory and I felt they weren't quite sure of their direction. We had a good conversation and prayed together, after which they both seemed to brighten up. We had lunch with them, and when eventually we left they were much more cheerful. The visit had certainly been worthwhile. It does seem to me that some of these OM couples that are in more permanent service need special pastoral care, encouragement and assistance in finding their role. Their house, which is of good quality, only about eighteen months old, surrounded mainly by school buildings, but its position does not serve well for them to be in touch with the local population. Perhaps that is one of their problems.

On returning home to Rupert's house we were able to see a little more of Rawalpindi and then Rupert took me into the bazaars so I could have a real look at Rawalpindi life and take photographs. I found it very exciting and stimulating. It is such a busy place with the usual tongas (small horse-drawn carriages), rickshaws, goats, bullock carts, everything you can think of. We called into a little café, or chai shop beneath the hotel where

Rupert and Janet first stayed when they arrived in Pakistan. They had been met by a Pakistani neighbour from Saltley (Birmingham) at the airport who took them to a hotel of a friend of his. It was a truly Pakistani hotel, hardly like a western one. It overlooked a very busy area of the inner city. It was very wet and muddy when they arrived and they were taken to a top room which was very small, dirty and sparsely furnished. They had been quite shocked at the situation at first, but told me that in the ten days they spent there they got to know the people and became quite adjusted to the place, although it was always noisy, on into the night. The chai shop where we stopped was also the place which provided them with food during their early days. A man in that restaurant had known Dr. Stuart and this linked up with the address which they had had in the first place. Dr. Stuart heard where they were staying and very soon invited them to come and live in her house. The Pakistani man who had befriended them was a Shiite who was a guide. He showed us a letter of thanks from a Cambridge University team which had climbed the second highest mountain in the world, K2, in November. He had served as a guide in that group. The man spoke very little English but was a very friendly person. It was lovely to see how these Pakistani men recognise Rupert and how he communicates with them. All this is as a result of the contacts he has made with neighbours in Saltley.

Having taken some photographs of the town, we returned to Valley Road, where we spent the rest of the evening together as a family. It was lovely to play some games with the children – hide and seek, and making paper aircraft. After the children had been put to bed we had some good spiritual conversations together and a time of prayer. I was able to make a telephone call to England and talk to Dorothy. It was nice to hear she was well and had made the trip up to [our daughter] Esther's safely. It was interesting to be reminded that the meeting at Kingshurst was to be addressed by Peter Maiden that very evening, so I was able to send greetings to him and the church.

Emmanuel Church, Rawalpindi

Sunday 31st January

The meeting today was at Emmanuel Church, Rawalpindi. After breakfast we were soon on the road as the service was due to commence at 9.30 a.m. We were there in good time but there were not many people there to begin with. Gradually they arrived. It was a meeting of the church originally planted by Ron and Rose Beckett, long-time friends of ours from Dudley. We were very warmly welcomed by the elders of the church, and especially by Samuel Gill, the son of the pastor, William Gill. The service was held in Urdu. There were no chairs, so we sat on the floor. I was glad to have a cushion to sit on and another for my back as I was able to lean against a pillar. There was an ordinary open worship service with plenty of chapati and local wine. I was then invited to preach and Samuel Gill interpreted for me. I gave them greetings, particularly from the Becketts as I had telephoned them shortly before leaving Birmingham. This was well received and I spoke on the text, Philippians 1:6: "He who began a good work in you will carry it through to completion until the day of Christ Jesus." The message was very well received, several people speaking to me afterwards concerning it, and it was evident it had been an encouragement to them.

After the service I was invited to sign the visitors' book and to meet the congregation, and then I took photographs outside the church of a group of young Christians. I was pleased to meet Brother Daniel, who is, I think, a colporteur and an evangelist. He has a very practical book van which opens at the sides so that all can see his Christian books. It is available outside the church and he uses it around the district quite a lot.

We then went to Samuel Gill's home, where we were given hospitality in the form of a cup of tea and biscuits; had quite a long chat with several people there and they were very pleased to see us and sent greetings to Ron and Rose Beckett and people who prayed for them. It was encouraging to hear how they had started the work there in a hired room and now they have this large church building. They have a daughter church at another location and their people go out on outreach.

Lahore

We returned to Rupert's home for lunch and afterwards took the long journey from Rawalpindi to Lahore. The road was reasonably good. We stopped on the way at a little chai shop and were immediately spoken to by two Pakistani men who were Christians and knew of the seminary where we are to work and preach tomorrow and later.

Arriving in Lahore we had some difficulty in finding the OM address, having to stop several times. It was dark and there were the usual crowded streets with rickshaws etc. We eventually found the base in a very busy area near the railway station. We were pleased to be met by OMers and to learn that Les Wade and family were nearby, and shortly afterwards they came in with Mike Wakeley. We had a good time of fellowship. Dot Wade had prepared the guest room for us, had made up my bed, had left a welcome note and a photograph. We felt really loved and cared for. We had a meal at the base, also a long conversation with Mike as he put us in the picture regarding the programme for the next few days and the kind of people I would be staying with. We were eventually glad to have a hot shower and then get into a good bed for the night. It was to be a short sleep – we were due to start early the next morning.

Gujranwala
Monday 1st February

We rose at 5.45 a.m. and prepared our own breakfast, got ourselves ready for the road by 7 a.m. We were called for by Melvin, a Sindh boy on OM. He speaks English, but not too well, and he was to act as our guide to Gujranwala. We now felt a little more Indian as we travelled through some very congested places. It was a bright sunny morning and very exciting. Eventually we turned in to the theological seminary. We had been briefed concerning this place by Mike Wakeley. It is an old American Presbyterian compound. The seminary was built as one unit but because of various political factions the whole compound is divided into three separate sections and they have nothing to do with each other! The section in which we were working has about twenty students. I was welcomed by the principal and other members of staff and invited into the chapel

to join in morning devotions with the students. I was invited to
speak and preached on the text Acts 27:23, "God whose I am
and whom I serve." Arthur James, vice-principal, interpreted for
me. I think the message was well received. At the end the
students trooped out and shook hands with me seriously one at
a time. We had a cup of tea with members of staff and then
there was the usual waiting about to decide exactly when we
were going. It was however very pleasant to sit in the garden
chatting. We were then joined by two other people and we left
Melvin to go back to Lahore and the rest of us went on to
Sialkot.

Sialkot

Sialkot is the place where John Hyde, 'Praying Hyde', was the
leader of a revival. I was told the way the Sialkot Convention
began: with thirty days of fasting and prayer. It was good to
arrive at Sialkot in the grounds of the bishop's house. There
were about twenty-five leaders: the bishop, and heads of
different organisations throughout the area. They were top
people. We sat down and I was asked to speak to the assembled
company briefly. There is clearly a problem with the principal
of the theological seminary in Gujranwala. Besides the fact that
the compound has been divided into three sections, a physical
wall having been erected to separate this seminary from the rest
of the area, there is evidently a spiritual problem.

After speaking to the leaders Rupert and I walked around for
a while, took some photographs and finally I was asked to speak
again. The message seemed to be well received. One brother
there was an elderly man, a well-known evangelist in Pakistan.
He has travelled widely, has been to Brazil, knows Dr. Drever
(former missionary), from Birmingham, and comes from the
district where Dr. Drever used to work. He is evidently a godly
man, well aware of OM, tells us he has been with the teams,
and has sometimes been physically attacked as he preached the
gospel with them. We had dinner in the open air, Indian style,
and later returned to Gujranwala, to the seminary.

In the evening I was invited to speak to the fellowship
meeting of the students. Rupert and I decided to hold a kind of
conversation and we had two interpreters to help us. This gave

me the opportunity to share what Rupert was doing in the country, why he had come etc., also for me to share a little of the history of BCM. I think it as a time well enjoyed and appreciated by everyone. We returned to our guest room tired but feeling it had been worthwhile.

Tuesday 2nd February

Today Rupert and I rose early, and were at breakfast for 7 a.m. We had some good fellowship together in the little room we shared last night. After breakfast we went for the first service, a devotional meeting in the chapel where I was invited to speak.

I gave an exposition of Isaiah 6, emphasising the need for a proper view of God before we commence serving Him. This was to be summed up in the expression, "Holy, holy, is the Lord of hosts." I then talked about getting right with God, having a fresh touch from Calvary and that we would be changed and given the commission to go into all the world and preach the gospel. The message was well received. We then had a break during which time I wrote several letters for Rupert to take away for posting.

We had a second meeting at 11 a.m. which was held in the open air. Chairs were provided. Rupert took some photographs. I gave an introduction to Paul's letter to the Philippians. I took the opportunity to talk about God's concern for the cities and the biblical base for city mission work. We continued with most of the first chapter of Philippians, and had lunch at about 12. Several students wanted to come for personal conversations.

At about 2 p.m., Rupert took me into the adjoining compound where he had had contact with a young couple, Michael Lacey and his wife, both from Preston, Lancashire. They arrived in Pakistan at about the same time as Rupert and Janet and had been up to the Murree language school, where Rupert had met them. On their arrival in Pakistan they found themselves in a very awkward situation. They were here under the auspices of the Church Missionary Society, having been invited to do certain practical work by a member of staff; but before their arrival this member had in fact left and they were soon told that their services were no longer required, or at least that the job they had come to do was no longer available. They had gone through a distressing time, having been pushed from one place to another without a settled home. However, I found them to be in very pleasant accommodation. It was a new house which had recently been built for them, Indian style, very clean, freshly painted, with good kitchen units and modern furniture, even a carpet on the floor. It was clear they were very pleased to have the visit from Rupert and me. We talked a lot about spiritual things, England, the future, their calling, how to go on with the Lord in difficult situations etc. They were a very pleasant couple and I understand they are on the BCM mailing list. We had a cup of tea and a time of prayer with them. Rupert travelled back to Janet in Rawalpindi, while I stayed on at the Theological Seminary.

At 4 p.m. there was another session, this time in the chapel. Arthur James interpreted again, as I expounded the end of Philippians 1 and the first few verses of chapter 2. Given the situation in this compound, with the present principal, who was once the principal of a larger complex and now not on speaking terms with people in the other areas of the compound, and with this kind of Berlin wall that had been erected between the two sections, it was a remarkable Word. I had been led to Philippians while praying about this visit back in England. I was emphasising this afternoon the need for unity, repentance, putting things right between brothers, emphasis on love, tenderness, compassion, and above all on humility. The message was very well received. Several students came and spoke warmly, thanking me and saying God had spoken to their heart and it was indeed a message they all needed at this time.

This time I was accompanied by students back to the guest house and clearly there were those who wished to talk to me on topics ranging from abortion to the difference between Paul's and James's teaching on the matter of faith and works. It was a good time but there was very little time to spend alone. We realised we had passed the time when we should have had a meal and it was almost time for the next meeting. However, they were very helpful as we went back to the dining area, which also functions as a sports room. This gave us the opportunity to play table tennis while waiting for the cook to prepare something. My meal consisted of some lightly fried bread (cook always insists on frying mine), with some jam, and two hard-boiled eggs. I also received a flask of tea, which was sweet and milky with a taste that doesn't really appeal to me! As I was about to eat the electricity went off again. This happens every night. It used to be at the same time but the time now seems to vary. Candles were brought and I finished my meal by candlelight.

The students arrived for the next meeting in the same recreation room. After some singing I taught them the chorus "God is good to me". A number of them cannot speak English, so this was also an English lesson. Arthur James came and joined us to translate. He looked very serious. I'm sure the Word he had been translating has got to him. I felt he was very moved after the afternoon meeting, but he then looked so angry and didn't have friendship or communication with me and tonight he refused to interpret, saying I should speak to them directly in English but to do so slowly and simply. Clearly I had to change the message, and I spoke to them from Isaiah 43:1-2, "Fear not, I have redeemed you. I have summoned you by name; you are mine. ... When you walk through the fire you will not be burned." This was the message on enduring persecution and that God would be with us. Because it was not being translated and because I had to make it as simple as possible with very few illustrations, we finished the meeting before time.

Wednesday 3rd February

The morning began with devotions, when I was asked to speak again. I continued in Philippians 2. Following that, the morning was free. At 12 o'clock I was sent for to go to the principal's home, where I was welcomed by his wife, daughter and, I think, another daughter and her husband. It's difficult to sort out their relationships as we were never formally introduced. There were two young boys and then a little girl of about three years. I was given hospitality with their meal and made very welcome. There was also another visitor, a candidate for the post of administrator for this college. He was a rather nervous man. I noticed that he smoked, and there was very little spiritual response. I would think that it would be a mistake if he were to be appointed. After the meal the principal, his son, the vice-principal, the visitor and I were packed into the Toyota car and went through the town of Gujranwala and out into the country, a distance, I reckon, of about 25 miles. Just as we neared the village to which we were going we passed the students who had gone ahead of us on cycles. There weren't enough cycles for everyone so someone was sitting side-saddle. I imagine they took it in turns as to who did the pedalling.

In the Punjab

We arrived at a country village where they speak Punjabi. It was very primitive, poor, with open drains, very low cottages, barefooted children. The road was virtually non-existent, just a rough cart track, and very bumpy. However, to my astonishment we arrived at the small gate of a school and there was a guard of honour. The path to the school gate and then on into the playground had been specially decorated in a kind of red carpet in my honour. It was done in three colours and when L looked carefully there were three different kinds of sand that had been laid out and the word WELCOME spelled out in English together with some other words in Urdu.

I was taken in and there at the head of this path was a table laid with plastic flowers on lovely tablecloth; quite clearly this was the place of honour. There were three easy chairs at the table and I was invited to sit, not on one of the chairs, but on a specially decorated stool. The guard of honour consisted of about twenty little girls and a few boys all dressed in white, waving little flags and singing a chorus of welcome. There was a small band, that is someone with drums and a harmonium and they too played me some music. I was introduced to the schoolmistress, also the schoolmaster, who seemed to be a very fine man. He then escorted us out of the school grounds, through the village to what I understand was his home; a rather poor home, but it was well arranged. The principal spoke to me about a stack of beds. I thought he was joking with me but it seemed quite true that these were part of the dowry for the bride. These Indian beds had been stacked up. I'm not sure whether they are used or kept later for an increased family. Around the walls there were beautiful bronze bowls, quite a lot of china and then on the one side a pile of wooden containers and bowls, which apparently are used to store grain. I was able to take a photograph of this. All the students, staff and I were invited to sit down for a light meal there. They brought us a very nice cup of tea but I didn't have much to eat.

After the refreshments we returned to the school. I was invited to go in alone and as I entered through the gate all the children threw flower petals over me. I then walked up the sand-decorated path and took my place. Others followed and then the choir sang and music was played by what you might call a "skiffle" band and then a group of girls stood and recited the Ten Commandments. After a few words and a prayer by the headmaster, I was invited to speak. Arthur James interpreted for me. I took the text from Matthew 19:14 – "Let the little children come to me, and do not hinder them, for the kingdom of heaven belongs to such as these."

The children and many parents (a good number of women had joined them, sitting at the back), and as I looked around, every available vantage-point on walls, gates and doorways was occupied by people from the village. We were in the shade of a large tree in the school grounds. It was as usual a cloudless day, with temperatures I think in the 70s Fahrenheit. We were glad of the shade and I told the children how the tree had not come through the gate, it had in fact come in when it was very small and had grown, and their lives too would grow and they needed to grow for Jesus. I talked about giving their hearts to the Lord and following him.

I then illustrated this with the story of Joseph from Nepal, the little boy whose parents died and who was eventually alone in Darjeeling and then, in a farmer's house saw a picture of Jesus and went looking for him. Later this little boy became a pastor in Nepal. I think the message came over fairly clearly and it was well received. Of course, I took them greetings from England, thanked them for honouring me and for inviting me to their village. At the end of the meeting I took photographs and then was invited to meet the village headman.

Later I heard that some of the local residents had objected to the Christians using a PA system. In this country we hear Muslim PA five times a day: from very early in the morning to late in the evening. Christians are not allowed to do very much at all. However I was pleased that Iqbar, the principal, had spoken to the headman and said they had every right to do this as there was freedom of religion in Pakistan. This politician was very friendly to me and accepted the response. The boys set off on their bikes and we made the hour-long car journey through the dusty Pakistani roads and the crowded villages and towns of Gujranwala. Then back to the college, where I was invited once again into the principal's house for a cup of tea with them. A most splendid and exotic day. I would not have missed this for anything!

This evening has been a very humbling experience. After a short break during which I recorded the previous part of this tape, I was called for by the principal's son, taken back to the home and then we drove out to a small town about half an hour's drive. We parked the car and then walked down the narrow lanes of this town. It was dark and it was good that someone had a torch to lead us. Eventually we arrived at the home of one of the believers. We were invited in for a meal. I had been warned that we were going out for a meal. At first I thought we were going to some restaurant, but then I discovered that it was someone's house and I was a little bit apprehensive regarding the kind of food we would be given. Several of the men sat down to the meal. What a surprise to find that these dear people had gone to great lengths to provide an English meal − at least there were peas, carrots, cauliflower, potatoes and a few other things cooked the English way, nothing spicy. Then there was bread, jam and tea made especially for me. Being cautious, I refuse to drink the water as it is. They were very friendly people. Half way through the meal the electricity went off, as it does from time to time in this country. We were in total darkness until candles arrived. At the end of the meal the host led me with a torch through the lanes to a church. It was a fairly large one, which I understand has been built by the people themselves, without any foreign financial help. The custom here was to take your shoes off as you go in and I went down to the front and onto the platform in stocking feet.

There were just a few people in the hall at the time but as we sat there and the boys began singing and the customary drummers and harmonium-players began to arrive. The singing continued. The pastor led us in prayer, then the students sang a specially prepared piece which had been broadcast on Pakistan TV on Christmas Day. (Apparently one half-hour Christian programme was allowed.) The music was very good and then I was invited to preach. Arthur James read the scriptures for me; I chose the end of Luke 18 (the healing of the blind Bartimaeus) and the beginning of 19 (the story of Zacchaeus): "The Son of Man came to seek and to save what was lost." I preached on the topic, "Things which change and things which do not", beginning with God doesn't change, the message doesn't change but we need to change and we can change the world. There was a very good response. I told the story of the Brazilian burglar who was converted.

Afterwards people queued up to shake hands with me. By the time we had finished, the church was absolutely packed. There must have been at least 300 people in the room. The meeting had been scheduled to start at 7 p.m. We didn't get there until nearly 8. People were still coming in at 8.45 and we finished the meeting at about 9.30. This time I have had quite a good talk with Dick Bad and also Arthur. They seem to be much more friendly. For a long time I have felt really isolated and they were very stand-offish. There were so many problems here. But tonight we seem to have got through the ice. They were very friendly. The students really warmed to us too. I shall be sorry to leave this place now.

When we got back to the compound I was invited into the principal's house once again for a cup of tea. There I was surprised to find they have a colour TV and video recorder. I mentioned that I had some videos in my case, which I was taking from London to Bombay. One of them is called "Thief in the Night". Immediately they asked if they could make a copy. They have access to the necessary equipment, so the principal's son came back with me to collect it.

Thursday 4th February
This morning was our last day in the seminary at Gujranwala. I spoke at the devotional service in the chapel to the students. I was pleased to see that the principal was there as well as Arthur

James, who interpreted for me. My message was on Philippians 3:13-14, "Forgetting what is behind and straining towards what is ahead, I press on towards the goal to win the prize for which God has called me heavenwards in Christ Jesus." I asked the question, "What is the most important thing in your life?" At the end of the service it was clear that the word had been very much appreciated. The principal thanked me very much. As Arthur James was about to go to Lahore it was clear that I would probably not see him again. We shook hands and then he embraced me. This was quite a victory, because at the beginning of the visit I felt very distant from him. He had seemed to be rather cold towards me, but his attitude had changed very much.

One of the students came to see me. Javed had been playing the harmonium during the meetings. I was surprised when he told me that he had already spent about seven years in Abu Dhabi in the United Arab Emirates and that he had ministered in a church there. I am not quite sure if he had actually started the church, but he has been in leadership there – in a church which has a congregation of 600-700 people. It appears that he has been sent to spend three years in the seminary and he completes his training at the end of this month. He spoke very warmly concerning the messages that he had heard from me and had been very much helped. He seemed to indicate that when he went back he would possibly suffer persecution. I asked regarding Arabic. He said he didn't speak it. The church consisted of Pakistani people and he was addressing them in Urdu and Punjabi. He has invited me to visit him there if possible in maybe a year or so when he has settled back into the church. A very fine warm young man, who apologised that he couldn't speak very much English. He is here with his wife and two daughters, though I haven't met them.

At about one o clock, I was called for, to be taken by car to the village of Quilla Dida Singh. This was a lovely experience. The people were expecting us as usual and we first went along to the pastor's house. I had met him the previous night and he seems to be a supervisor over a number of churches. I asked how many congregations like this there were in the area and he said 42. They had constructed the church building themselves.

We had a good meeting, which soon became quite crowded. I took a photo of the church. We had a nice time with the family, where we had lunch. There were obvious preparations for something special, bunting around and some of the ladies were very well dressed in special clothing. It transpired that during the service we were to hold 2 infant baptisms. In fact there were three children and this was quite a splendid occasion. The service was conducted by Iqbar, the college principal. I was not very pleased at first because everyone else was taking their shoes off and I went to do the same, but the principal said that I should not. Having got to the front I noticed that everyone had removed their shoes and I insisted on doing the same. When I insisted he took his own off and carried the shoes back to the entrance door. I am not sure whether I pleased him, but I am sure it was the right thing to do. The Lord gave me a good message and it was well received. As soon as the meeting was over and I took a photo of the outside of the church we were escorted back to the car. I thought at this stage that we were to return to Lahore. I knew I had a long journey to make. But I was told no, we had another little village to visit. So we went out into the country along dusty roads until we came to Haripur. This was a very small village just off the road, reached by a very dusty track. Some donkeys were tethered at the entrance. The whole scene was so reminiscent of the Bible stories. We went into the small yard of the house. There was an outside staircase leading onto the flat roof and the children were playing up there. There was just this enclosed yard where we were first greeted with some simple food, which was brought – tea and biscuits and rounds of toast. The student team from the college were there again. Each day they were travelling. On the previous day they had cycled everywhere but on this occasion I think they were too worn out. They had come by bus. They always managed to make it somehow. We took piles of Christian literature in the back of the car and the students ended the meeting, as on other occasions, by giving these out to the people. Once again we had a good meeting, quite a lot of singing to Indian music, then I would be invited to preach with an interpreter. It was a very moving, beautiful evening, and as we left the sun was setting. I couldn't help but stop to take photos; I wanted to remember this.

Return to Lahore

After the meeting we were taken by car to a place where we would pick up what they call the "flying bus". This really was an experience. It is intended to be a 12-seater Toyota minibus, I suppose. In fact there were 18 people in the vehicle and this is the one that "flies" to Lahore. It has a special screaming siren, like a police siren, and it really moves very quickly. I would imagine that there is a limited life expectancy for the drivers of these vehicles. We in fact passed one that had obviously had a serious accident. It was a long, fast journey, through the night, although always full of interest: always people, cycles, tongas, bullock carts, cars, trucks, and everything you can think of! The shops are dimly lit with crowds of people around them and always the bumps on the road, though the road to Lahore does get better and eventually becomes a good fast road. When we arrived we saw the magnificent tower, reminiscent of the Blackpool tower, but it was in fact the floodlit monument to the signing of the constitution of the Pakistan nation. On the other side of the circular road there is a great red fort, and also a beautiful mosque, which I would like to see in daylight. There are some very fine buildings in Lahore. Eventually the bus arrived. I was so pleased that I had accepted an offer for someone to travel with me. In fact it was a pastor, whom I hadn't met and I don't know his name. He spoke very little English. He was obviously a fine man. He stood with me all the way and when we arrived I was so glad he was with us because the coach just pulled into a crowded area, obviously not the bus station at all, and I would have been completely lost if I was just there with my two pieces of luggage trying to find my way in the dark with all the mass of people and tongas, horse and carts carrying loads of metal and all sorts of things. We were behind two trucks loaded up with sugar cane. It's a regular hobby for children to jump on the back of it and pull out sticks of cane to eat for themselves – a very dangerous thing to do. In this crowded situation we were so glad to find a rickshaw, and we soon set off to our destination, Empress Road, which is the OM base.

How pleased I was to arrive there. The Chinese cook was like an angel. She immediately fussed around us, made us a coffee and prepared an egg on toast for me. It was very refreshing. Then they made us comfortable. The OM half night of prayer had just begun, so I was invited to talk first about the work of BCM so they could pray for it, then after further prayer I was asked to take part, so I shared about the visit to the seminary and villages. They were very supportive. I was then put in the charge of Robin and Cathy. Robin was the mechanic in Lahore and Cathy was a secretary to Mike Wakeley. Robin is Australian, Cathy Canadian. They took me with them to the place which is serving as home in the vicarage of St. George's church, about a quarter of a mile from the base. It has two rooms. There are three beds. I chose the double, which looked the most comfortable.

Friday 5th February

It was good to be back to a measure of English civilisation; this morning there was a knock at the door at half past six and there was Robin with a cup of tea for me. I rose and had breakfast with them and then we went down to the base office, where I conducted devotions, speaking on Philippians 3. I had to finish by 8.45 because we had to travel. Melvin (the Pakistani boy, guide and interpreter) was to go with me. We went to Batapur, which gets its name from the shoe factory. It took just over half an hour in a minibus. That is another of these vehicles that should take 12 passengers but carried nearer 20. There seemed to be large numbers of these minibuses around. They are run privately and vie with each other for business, the drivers calling out to people on the road asking if they want to make a trip with them. The fares seemed fairly cheap too.

We were on the road to Amritsar, within three miles of the Indian border. We called first at the pastor's house, picked him up and then went on another bus to a church, a Pentecostal church. The congregation usually grows as the service continues. There were about 50 in the end with many young children. The service lasted over three hours, which included the communion, and they asked me to preach, which I did with interpretation for nearly an hour. Afterwards I took some photos and then we walked leisurely along the very dusty path, not more than a track, to the road. The women were dressed in very colourful headgear and the traditional Pakistani baggy trousers. Again we bussed it back to the pastor's house, where we had lunch, consisting of rice, some meat and chapati if you wanted it, dhal followed by fruit. There was also the usual cup of tea. We left there at about 3 p.m., so it was a long morning.

We travelled back to Lahore by bus and there I spent some time talking to Mike Wakeley, who was leaving for Karachi. He gave me the rest of my programme in writing and we spent some time talking about some of the needs of the work. I asked him how I could help. He said, send some more workers. There was then little time before a meeting I was to attend in the evening. I barely had time to return to the house for a wash and hurry back. Then unfortunately the meeting was entirely in Urdu. A professor was giving a lecture on the foundation of the Bible and answering Muslim criticisms of our Bible. From the way the people were questioning it seems there were some Muslims present. It seemed to be quite a good meeting, but fairly meaningless to me and it went on endlessly, I felt. I was relieved to be told that Cathy and Robin were ready to leave. I went with them; we had a nice evening meal together, sat and talked for a while and so finished the day.

Saturday 6th February

This morning it was officially the OM rest day. Robin and Cathy said they would have a lie-in so I got my own breakfast and then spent some time in Bible study and prayer as I had been invited to give a lecture to the OM Bible School students. On my programme it had said it was from 2 till 4 p.m., but as usual this was a mistake; it was actually 4 till 6 p.m. This gave me opportunity to spend some time first talking to various members of the team at the OM HQ. I had a long talk with Nigel Hallett, who was once a student at Westhill Training College, Birmingham, doing community studies. He knew Tim and Joy Farrell, and Liz Eades. He is living here in Lahore dividing his time working with OM and with some blind people. He believes in friendship evangelism. He was encouraged by our conversation as I shared some of my experiences with him and assured him of my prayers. I also talked to Mark Lees, who was on the base HQ and was responsible for the Bible School. He was a young man from Sheffield and attended St. Thomas's church. He took me with him as I had asked to see Lahore Fort and the large mosque there. We went by rickshaw through the busiest part of Lahore – according to Mark, the busiest part of Pakistan. We were jostled and pushed around in the little auto-rickshaw. Somehow we got through. The fort is a magnificent place, as is the mosque, and I took a number of photos. We then contended with the traffic to get back in time for me to speak to the students.

I was asked to speak about my experience. I dealt with the matter of guidance and talked about some instances of guidance we had experienced. There were questions and someone asked, "Will you please come to my church and preach tomorrow?" Mike Wakeley had left a note that I should preach in a church at Garichahoo. Nigel told me earlier that the meeting was cancelled, so I was free and will go. After that we had a light meal together and I talked to a few people, including the boy who interpreted for me, Peter George, from Gujarat. He knows Dr. Bryan Drever quite well. Dr. Drever knows his father and this boy wrote a note for Dr. Drever in my book. He has applied to All Nations Bible College, and a former student who was here in Pakistan has been able to acquire 50% of his support. The college has accepted him if he can find the other half, so he is asking for prayer for this.

Robin and Cathy invited me to go out for a pizza but I declined, having already eaten with the team. I was glad to have a time in the house on my own to write letters and read.

Sunday 7th February

Arrangements had been made for me to be collected at the base at 10 a.m. We were having breakfast in the house when the brothers arrived at 9.10 to collect me, saying arrangements had been made. I had to dash to get ready. I had simply agreed to speak at a service, which I thought was a Sunday morning service somewhere in Lahore.

We first walked, then took a minibus to another part of Lahore, walked a few yards, and then took another bus, which travelled for some distance. I had been told that it was possibly 200 kilometres. I felt more like 1,200! Eventually we arrived at a small town and walked a while, then haggled over the price of a tonga. I was suddenly asked to climb aboard the high step and sit beside the driver under the canopy. My Pakistani guide sat facing the rear. So here was I, sahib, facing down the lanes with crowds of Pakistani people gaping at me. It was a very busy area, dusty, with donkeys, buffaloes, ox-carts, people, blaring horns of buses and motorcycles. We went at a leisurely pace through the crowds and eventually came to the church. We were then as usual invited into the pastor's house and sat for a while. My guide disappeared so I was left with the pastor and his family. There were no formal introductions; they could speak very little English, and I could speak no Urdu. However, somehow we communicated and soon I was brought a cup of tea and biscuits.

We waited possibly an hour and then were escorted out again for another walk, through narrow lanes, having to step over the open sewers several times, rubbish everywhere; a very poor, dirty, smelly area. This, I am afraid, was the Christian quarter. We came to a house which was a bit better than the rest and stepped into another reception room and I was asked to sit down. It proved to be the home of a city councillor, who was also a member of the church. He came and we spoke a little. We sat and waited, and then lunch was served in real Pakistani style: rice and what they call spinach, which is difficult to describe, and meat of some kind. If it was chicken, it was very old chicken. I just put a small piece on my plate. My host immediately put another piece, the leg. That was sufficient. It was quite hot, the food that is. I was offered water but I also refrain from drinking Pakistani water unless I know it to be boiled or filtered. However they came along with another cup of tea which was very welcome. While I was eating my meal I had the leg of chicken, actually taking a bite from it, holding it in my hand, when suddenly I was attacked by a cat, which snatched the chicken-leg straight out of my mouth. In fact my lip was cut. However, it was all passed off as an amusing incident and after sitting and talking I was then escorted into the women's quarters.

I had no indication whatever of what I was supposed to do, but soon discovered that I had just been taken to say thank you for the food, which I did in my best Urdu, saying "Salaam shugria," which is "Thank you", and then I was escorted out of the house again and back to the church. Once again I sat in the pastor's best room. His wife was there with a baby, a few months old. They were very friendly. The pastor also had a daughter in her teens and their son was on the OM team. In Pakistan you can never tell who are the parents or the grandparents, who belongs to whom. There are no proper introductions – you have to guess it all!

Eventually I went into the church, removing my shoes first. There was a small company of people, not more than twenty. I sat up on the platform. The pastor began by praying and then there was quite a bit of singing. Gradually the people began to arrive. The singing went on for half an hour or so, and by the time the service proper was beginning, the church had quite filled up. I think there must have been 70 or 80 people there when it was my turn to preach. Mark Lees had joined us later. They had started the journey – he as my interpreter – but had left us to visit a contact of theirs. Apparently this lady had been converted. She is married to a doctor who treats her very badly, so they went to see her to encourage her in the Christian life.

There had been a delay in the service, because of course the interpreter wasn't there, and it had been very embarrassing for me not to be able to talk to people. Eventually Mark was asked to give his testimony, which was translated. Then after more singing, I was introduced, and preached on Psalm 1. I had been warned that many people in the church were purely nominal Christians. There were many problems in the church. So I preached on the secret of the happy life – not walking in the counsel of the ungodly, standing in the way of sinners or sitting in the seat of the scornful. This had to be spelt out very simply, during which I quoted from the Ten Commandments, and also got them to respond and taught them the simple words of Psalm

23:1 – "The Lord is my Shepherd", which in Urdu is only four words – they have no definite article. Everyone repeated it, and then we got the children to say it as well. This seemed to be a success because they knew very little scripture. Many of the people cannot read, and they seemed to own only a few Bibles between them. I then continued to preach on the two ways – the wide way – the broad road, and the narrow way. I believe that the message was well received. After the service, several people came to me asking for prayer and healing. There were sick children, a man with a twisted foot, and an old man who wanted prayer for something else. And so we went around laying hands and praying over them. They were very warm and hospitable. It was a lovely hot day. I took photographs of the church inside and outside and the pastor insisted that I took a special picture of him and his family. We were then escorted back to the councillor's house where Mark, who had missed his lunch, had something to eat and a cup of tea. Time was getting on and it was almost 5 p.m. when we set out back to Lahore. That journey took well over two hours on a bus, after walking to the bus stop at the railway station. The bus was very crowded, with many passengers standing right from the beginning. I stood for a little while, but people at the back of the bus insisted on making space for me and I sat down. They also then made space for Mark, who sat beside me. Everyone wanted to talk to us – Mark, speaking some Urdu, got involved in a conversation which led to spiritual things. There were some students from Lahore University and he was able to pass scriptures to them and tracts. The journey was extremely noisy and very dusty. At one point I thought that there was a cloud of smoke billowing in. In fact it was dust. These roads are so dusty if they have to move to one side to let another vehicle pass, clouds of dust come. They are so dense that vehicles put their lights on as they drive through them, to be able to see oncoming traffic. It was quite dark and we eventually stopped near the base. We were very glad to have arrived.

Geraldine, the Chinese cook, is a real angel. She immediately came out, offered me beef burgers, made a nice meal, a cup of coffee and made us very welcome. I was quite exhausted. I sat afterwards and read an English-language

Pakistani newspaper, picking up a little bit of news from abroad. The only item from Britain was a photograph of a nurses' demonstration in London with police holding people back. Quite clearly it was putting Britain in a bad light. I then exchanged some views with Mark and with a Canadian girl who is due back in Canada at the end of February. She would like to visit Northern Ireland. I gave her my address, so that when she comes she can perhaps call on us in Birmingham. And so I have returned alone back to the house. I found that Cathy and Robbie had already turned in for the night although it was only nine o'clock, and now here I am making my report.

Monday 8th February

Today we began with team devotions at the OM base in Lahore. After speaking there and having a time of fellowship, I went to see the workshop. Robin showed me the equipment they have there. It was a smaller unit than the Kathmandu workshop. They seem to be very efficient. They were mainly maintaining Ford Transit vans. This is a much more economical way of dealing with vehicles than using other makes. I took a photograph of the workshop and Robin.

We then went for a tour of part of Lahore, escorted by Benjie. I took photographs of a number of buildings in the old British sector and a photograph of the famous Kim's gun. We returned in time to take tea, say our goodbyes and reconfirm the flight to Bombay, and then we made our way first by rickshaw to the coach station and were able to get comfortable seats on the "flying bus" from Lahore to Sagoda.

Sagoda

The home at which we were staying was a large, well-built, very clean and well-furnished home. The family are very hospitable. We were soon made aware of a very serious situation however. The lady of the house has three brothers who have been arrested on a charge of murder. Apparently a Roman Catholic boy was killed in a fight. These three lads had nothing to do with it, but had been to visit him and were wrongly accused and arrested, and have been in prison awaiting trial. The situation is so serious because it is quite possible that they may face the death penalty. Capital punishment is practised freely in this country. It also appears that there is a great deal of police corruption. Bribery is commonplace and it is very difficult to change the course of their rough justice. We had prayer for these three boys and we await news of the outcome.

Later, we were taken to a small church for their evening meeting. It was a typical Pakistani fellowship, where the congregation sit on the floor, the women at the back, the men at the front. There was a small platform. The pastor, who speaks good English, interpreted for me, the subject again being Philippians 1. This is a passage which has been a real burden to me for this country. By the time all had arrived, there were about 60 adults and a number of children in the meeting. There was a good response. People were listening very attentively. They sang very well, and we had a good meeting overall. Later I was introduced to a number of the elders. The leader of the church is a man called Emmanuel. I was introduced to his wife also.   It turned quite cold and we came back in the back of a Suzuki pickup van and stopped at a small restaurant for some food before returning to the house. This was a long, fairly busy day but one that I will remember for many years.

Tuesday 9th February

The earlier part of today was somewhat frustrating. No instructions had been left by the pastor in whose care we were. So my guide, Benjie, and I, having had breakfast, sat in the garden. It had quite a good-sized lawn, a little bit worn and a good flower border with what we would call African marigolds but growing to the height of about two or three feet with some smaller English marigolds interspersed, and lots of English stocks of various sorts, all in full bloom. The house has a large veranda. It is very fine to look at, a good substantial building with large rooms. The floors are tiled and cool to the feet. It is a single-storey building with many large rooms, two bathrooms, Indian-style with Western toilets and a shower. The guest room which we share is about 12ft x 15ft and there is a large lounge about twice that size beside us, well furnished. We are next door to a small workshop which I think is a source of funds for this family. They manufacture heavy farm equipment – ploughs, seed-sowing machines, and other implements which are towed by tractor. They are hand-made: we watched them welding and working at these implements which are painted and then put on display outside the workshop.

The delay gave us opportunity to talk together. Benjie is a Pakistani boy whose mother is Tamil and therefore he has a darker skin and a Tamil build, which is somewhat different from most Pakistanis. He comes from Karachi. He has been with OM for two years and has one more year to go. He is praying that he might be able to join the OM ship, MV Doulos, but requires financial support for this. He speaks quite good English and he is able to translate and is a tremendous help on this tour. He told me quite a bit about the problems of Pakistan and especially their work with OM. He has been on the travelling teams which go into the bazaars selling gospel packets, and usually in the evening show the Jesus film. They have had many good opportunities of reaching the people with the gospel. He is now working at the base in Lahore, helping in general ways.

He told me of one rather horrific experience which illustrates the problem with the police. An American OM-er had had his camera stolen. Someone must have just walked into the base and picked it up. In order to claim the insurance, he needed a signature from the police. So he went to the police station, explained what had happened and tried to get a signature. They said they couldn't understand what he wanted and in his frustration he returned, asked Benjie to go with him so that he could translate. As soon as Benjie began to tell the story, the police immediately arrested him and dragged him by the throat and threatened to beat him. He screamed and struggled and shouted, hanging on to Simon, the OM-er. He told me that many had been beaten and beaten again, to the point that they lost their reason. He didn't want to go that way. It took a great deal of persuasion to cause the police to release him. He felt very relieved indeed. Apparently the police are quite capable of arresting people for no reason at all. The story goes that one man went to report that his house had been burgled and was immediately arrested and accused of the burglary. This is a police state under martial law. There is much evidence of police activity and the people rather fear having anything to do with them.

At about midday the pastor arrived. I thought he was going to take us away. He talked to us for a short time and then said he had to go to collect the children, but he would be back. To try to express my frustration and desire to be released from this kind of quarantine, I asked what time he would be back. He said about 3.20–3.30 p.m. We waited. Eventually he arrived at about five o'clock, explaining that he had had a problem with his Suzuki. I think we could have walked there and back several times, but we have to adapt to the pace of our hosts. However, he then immediately said "Bring your baggage – we are going!" and I suddenly realised that we were no longer staying in the guest room of this lovely house. Benjie and I packed our things and put them in the Suzuki and we drove to the pastor's home where I am now staying.

This is quite a different situation. It is a typical Muslim-style house. There is a courtyard with an outside gate, and rooms built around that courtyard all facing inwards. The pastor there has eleven children and he therefore needs the space. There is a room for the boys, a room for the girls, a room for him and his wife and a kind of lounge. Toilet facilities are primitive in one corner of the courtyard, and a washing place in the other corner has the usual water pump. They have a few chickens and a dog. The children are happy, dressed in colourful clothes, very bright and cheerful, and the older ones speak quite good English. The pastor speaks good English too, and the children are receiving quite a reasonable education. One of the older boys is studying statistics for a B.Sc. degree, some of the children are married or working away. One is a girl working in the Pakistani Air Force, another is a nurse in Karachi.

In the evening we went for a walk down to the nearby village. By this time it was dark and we were glad that the stars at least gave some little light, for there was no moon. The track down to the village is not metalled, and one has to avoid the ditches, the open sewer, and as the pathway goes around a couple of pools, there are plenty of mosquitoes about. We called at several small homes. Apparently this area has a number of Christian families and we went into one after another where people were sick. We were called in to pray. Most of these homes were so small, and consisted of just one room about 12ft x 15ft in size, just a little courtyard outside where they did some cooking and where there were primitive toilets. The wooden beds, with webbing bases, were stacked high. Some of the children were sleeping in them. Everywhere we could see extreme poverty and quite a bit of sickness. But we were always warmly welcomed and were asked to pray for those who were sick or for those in the household. It was an enchanting situation – these invalid homes were very cosy, and the people very friendly and appreciative.

"Come and hear the Englishman!"

Eventually we went to the church. This particular church was just one room, about 12ft wide and maybe 18-20ft long. At first, only a few people came in and the pastor decided to take a ladder and climb on to the flat roof. From there he shouted as the Muslim clerics shout, but calling people to the Christian church. When he came down, I suggested I did the same, so I laboriously climbed this home-made ladder onto the roof and stood there shouting at the top of my voice, "Come and hear the Englishman tell you about Christ. Come and hear him show you the way of life!" and various other such slogans. This certainly drew attention. The pastor came straight back up the ladder and joined me, interpreting for me. By the time we came down, quite a crowd had gathered, and soon as the meeting started, people were filtering in until the room was packed with between 70 and 80 souls.

They sang very well. They had the usual small, old, decrepit harmonium and the cymbals, which are long pieces of steel fixed together rather like a spring, and are just clapped together. There was the usual tambourine, and someone on the drums – the native drums which are played by hand but do give a good sound. The people certainly sang well. I complimented them on their singing, telling them that they would make the Top Ten.

After much praying and singing, I was invited to speak. I had the scripture read – we read from Philippians 2 and I preached on shining as stars – "among whom you shine as the stars in heaven and in the midst of a crooked and perverse generation".

Certainly that is their situation. There is a great deal of darkness here, and much ignorance, dirt, sickness and sorrow. Above all, Islam grips this country like a vice.

This Christian community shows that they are a rather poorly treated minority. The people are poor, their houses are poor, and they own little. There is much pressure put upon them. Nevertheless, they were happy, and as I looked around I saw many bright faces. Some of the boys looked quite intelligent and keen, and some of the women were quite beautiful with their coloured dresses and headgear, and they seemed to have great joy. Few of them seemed to be able to read. There were very few books around, and so I spoke very simply.

I began by teaching them the English chorus "This little light of mine, I'm going to let it shine". I used my forefinger as an object lesson of the candle and with the other hand struck the match and lit it. They were quite amused, and I got them all doing the same thing. Then I actually taught them the English words "This little light of mine, I'm going to let it shine, let it shine, let it shine, let it shine..." They all joined in the singing, and had a really good time with that, especially when it was "Shine all over Punjab" and "Shine all over Pakistan". I then talked to them about my arrival in Pakistan and the sight of Karachi from the air − a beautiful sight in the midst of such darkness, the city all lit up, explaining that it was lit up because of tiny bulbs. There was in fact just one bulb in the church, and that gave the light to the whole room. I think they got the point that if one person shines for Jesus, all have light, and if they were to shine together for Jesus then Pakistan would have light too.

We returned very happy. I thought it had all been worthwhile. Feeling a bit hungry by now, and we came into the pastor's house and soon food appeared − chapati, rice, dhal and a few other things, vegetables and salad and, I think, some meat. We had just started the meal and there was a commotion and who should be there but Rupert! Rupert had at last made it. He had had a difficult journey, difficulty in finding it but at last he had arrived, accompanied by a Roman Catholic priest, for in order to find the way he had seen a cross on a building and decided that that sounded Christian and he went in and asked.

Fortunately the priest knew the pastor where we were staying, and brought him here. It was ten o'clock at night. You can imagine that we settled down quite late. I should mention that he brought letters from home. How important letters from home are to our missionaries and workers in foreign lands!

Journey to Peshawar
Wednesday 10th February

We were awakened early with the sound of the cocks crowing and the usual noise of Pakistan, together with the bustle of a family on the move, for some had to go to school or college or maybe work as well. We stayed where we were until it had quietened down a bit and then at about 7 a.m. we emerged to look for a place where we might wash and prepare for the day. We discovered one problem, in that Rupert had understood that today we should drive to Peshawar; that is why he made the journey yesterday. I had also understood that, but the pastor had thought that we were to stay with him today and leave on Thursday. When we compared notes, it turned out we had received conflicting information in letters from Mike Wakeley: to one he had said we would be travelling to Peshawar on Wednesday and to another we that we would be available to stay in Sagoda on Wednesday. The pastor had in fact arranged a meeting for this evening and therefore that was a cause for concern. I wanted to get off, so did Rupert. However, we realised it would cause embarrassment, not only to the Pastor but could bring some difficulty on the work of OM and the Lord's work generally if we were to disappoint the congregation. In order to clear the way we drove back to the house where we had spent the previous night and were able to use their telephone and ring the leader, Gordon Magney, in Peshawar, and ask what arrangements had been made. Fortunately, we were not expected to preach until Friday, although he was expecting us today. We explained that we would be a day late but would make an early start on Thursday morning. This also gave Rupert an opportunity to ring Janet and the children and explain we would not be calling in as originally planned.

Making a telephone call is an event! We had to make a special journey by car to this house. There are no public telephones to be found in the Punjab and there are few phones that work even if you have them in a house. We were most fortunate to be in this house where for the sake of the business they had an efficient telephone. However, there has to be a great deal of talk and a cup of tea and prayer time etc. We were in the house for two hours!

Eventually we left the house and took a tour of Sargodha, transporting the pastor and his wife and going to collect the children from school. We returned to the pastor's house. Then Rupert and I took the opportunity to go to the village where I had been preaching the previous night. We took some pictures of the village and various wonderful things we could see in that area. We were followed by a crowd of children – soon feeling like the Pied Piper! We took some pictures of them too. Wherever we went people came out of their homes to greet us and invite us into their homes for tea which, because of time and for good health reasons, we declined.

We also took a walk along a nearby road and discovered a small cotton mill. There were some old machines which we noticed were made in Oldham and dated 1903. They were still in good working condition and the few men working there were sorting out the cotton and the machine separated the seeds and prepared it for further treatment. We were given a warm welcome when we entered and again were able to take some photographs.

In the evening we went to another village near the small mountain range we had passed on the way from Lahore. We arrived in the dark and went to a very primitive village, well off the track. There was no electricity in the place. We were led by someone carrying a lantern – very much the "light to our feet, a lamp to our path". We visited one simple home, a very small room, and felt obliged to eat the food prepared for us. The people were very friendly. As we left we were again surrounded by children and escorted to the little church, which was indeed very small. Having given the invitation to the services from the rooftop on the previous night, it was suggested we do this again. This time, however, there was no ladder and the pastor suggested I was too old to make the climb without one. Rupert, however, did so and the two men were up on the roof shouting and soon a crowd gathered. The room was lit by a Tilley lamp which kept nearly going out and was quite a distraction. However, the singing was good and again I had a great opportunity for preaching. An invitation was made and there were hands raised in response. As we concluded the meeting a number of people wished to be prayed for regarding sickness or special needs. This is a common occurrence at the end of these meetings. On the previous night about a dozen women had come forward with young children asking me to bless them and pray for them. It was so like the story of Jesus in the Gospels.

On our return to the pastor's house we were confronted by another problem. Apparently the pastor's son had run away with a woman who was already married and had children and he had had two children by her. He had now returned, repentant, to the family home. It had been a disgrace to the family. He now had a little boy with him and was trying to bring him up by himself. Because of his behaviour he had lost his job and was threatened with being sued to repay money for a course he had dropped out of. This young man was very distressed and wept when we prayed with him. His father had been quite severe towards him. I counselled him as well, asking him to forget things behind and go forward and have compassion upon his son and bring him back into the family. It was late and we were tired and eventually turned in.

Thursday 11th February

Today it was time to leave Sargodha and travel to Peshawar. We rose very early. It was still dark. It was difficult to wash in these circumstances because the washing place was a small brick cubicle in one corner of the courtyard and there was no light, just a pump and a bowl. The water of course was cold; there was no roof to this cubicle so I washed by moonlight. We were asked to have breakfast which consisted of a cold fried egg and two slices of sweet bread. The tea had been warmed up from the night before and was made from aniseed. I really couldn't drink this. I thought it was good for colds but hardly a substitute for tea!

We said our goodbyes to the pastor and to the son who had had so much trouble. They embraced us warmly. We set out on the long journey. It wasn't easy to find the way; there are few signs and they are all in Urdu script. However, we made good progress. We came up over the salt range, very rough mountains with winding roads, lots of rock and scrub, a very forbidding area. Coming down the other side we had a problem with a truck that was straddling the road. Evidently the clutch had broken. There were bricks under the wheels to stop it rolling backwards. We had great difficulty getting past and at one time we thought we would be there for the rest of the day. However, we were able to scrape through in the end. We continued along the way and gradually the road improved as we joined the grand trunk road to Peshawar, a good dual carriageway. We developed a fault with the motor horn, which is a serious problem in Pakistan as you have to sound the horn each time you pass a vehicle, or see approaching pedestrians, cycles, bullock carts, vehicles in the middle of the road and a thousand and one other things. Horns are being sounded all the time. If you suddenly lose this it's like driving blindfold. We had to be very careful. On one occasion an elderly man walked into the road. We could see what was happening, he looked in the opposite direction and kept going. Rupert applied the brakes and we stopped within a yard of him. He looked very scared, but we too were very nervous as we entered the Peshawar area.

What a busy city! Much traffic: camels, horses, auto rickshaws, as well as many modern cars. It was very strange to see the modern Peshawar. It wasn't easy to find the way. We stopped at one point and were amazed to find an Englishman standing there with a tourist map. He spoke to us and directed us matter-of-factly as if we were in Stratford on Avon. We went on and found it difficult to find the place, having to retrace our steps two or three times. Eventually we found the address of the headquarters. What an oasis in the wilderness this place is after having lived in the villages and through Pakistan for the last two or three weeks, feeling very dirty, tired and generally out of touch with civilisation. Suddenly we arrived, backed the car into the very crowded courtyard, stepped out of the car and heard someone say, "Oh it's Mr. Orton". Dot Wade was there yet again. When we went to Lahore she was about to leave with her husband and family. They had the two girls with them. Again, it was the same situation. She welcomed us in, showed us the room which they had been using the night before and there was her little note of greeting once again. She had been told two people were coming but didn't realise I was one of them. They made us very welcome. We had a lovely meal together, just like a family. This place is spotlessly clean, very modern, well furnished, and here in this room there are two beds where Rupert and I will be staying, and they even have electric blankets! There is an abundance of hot water and I had a lovely warm bath for the first time since leaving England. It was a really good soak, beautiful! And that meal which included ice cream with chocolate sauce and nuts, unbelievable to have such a welcome as we found in this place. Before the Wades left they sang a song, with Grace Magney playing the piano and her husband Gordon playing the trumpet and the Wade family and the rest of us joining in and singing Christian words to Edelweiss from the Sound of Music. It was a beautiful time and we were sorry to see the Wades go, but they had to depart to catch a train at six o'clock that evening.

The rest of that evening was spent relaxing, talking to some of the folk, hearing more of the work of SERVE (an association of Christian workers in this area). While we were talking the telephone rang. There was a message to say that a Pathan leader, with whom Gordon and Grace had been the night before as they visited the American Embassy, had been shot dead outside his home just an hour before. He was living in an apartment just below an OM couple. This was a shock as they had seen this man up until very recently. We had a little time of prayer for his bereaved family, realising again how important this work is in reaching these people for Christ while the opportunity exists.

It was good to get into a nice warm bed. We even had electric blankets to keep us warm. However, it was an unusual setting but before we had been in bed long we could hear gunfire of various sorts, machine guns, rifles and other small arms. I discovered later that it was not that we could hear the battlefront in Afghanistan, but simply there are often skirmishes in the vicinity of the nearby university.

Friday 12th February

This morning I woke refreshed in this beautiful home – such a change after being in Pakistan and in the primitive villages and the poor surroundings. Rupert was with me and brought me a cup of tea in bed, bless him. After a breakfast of toast and strawberry jam we dressed and I put on a suit as I had been invited to speak at the fellowship service.

This was held in the schoolroom of St. John's Cathedral. About 100 people gathered, Western people mainly, a few Pakistani people. It was a lovely time of worship, plenty of good singing, use of an overhead projector, good music. There were several times of open worship and then I was introduced and invited to speak. I first asked Rupert to give a little report of why he was in the country and relate that to an incident in the Bull Ring when he had had contact with an Afghan who spoke warmly of what he had observed Christians doing for the refugees in his homeland. This had given Rupert an opening to speak to this man about Christ and give him some literature. I think that was an encouragement to the people who were present in the service. After that I preached from Philippians 3, the Lord giving me real liberty. One of the leaders in the service had been very moved as he had mentioned the death of the Afghan leader the night before. They had known him quite well and clearly it had shaken people. I therefore sought to put the whole thing in perspective, talking about priorities in Philippians, mentioning Paul's situation at the time of writing and how he considered the possibility of being put to death but that his eyes were on the Lord. The Lord really blessed us at that time and I felt God had given me real anointing. The ministry was followed by a beautiful service of communion. As we went out into the sunshine at the end, many came to speak to me and I felt really encouraged that I had been privileged to be used in this way today.

We returned to the SERVE house, where we had a good lunch and then were free. Rupert and I changed and then drove to the SERVE headquarters, where we left the car, and then walked a little, went on a wagon which functions as a Pakistani bus, to a point near the old city, and then took an auto-rickshaw into the bazaar. We had a lovely time walking around

Madrid City Mission Centre, Spain

Daravi Slum, Bombay (Mumbai), India

With Hilda Baker in Mysore, India

Rural cottage, Nepal

Bangalore, South India

Edwin and Dorothy at the Taj Mahal, Aggra

Brindavan Gardens, Bangalore

Dorothy wearing her sari in India

Dorothy teaching at Logos Bhavan

Preaching at Entebbe, Uganda, 1993

Mwanza Service, Tanzania

Charles and Val Kadalie on Table Mountain, Cape Town

Devine and Mrs Ammatey, Ghana

Trinity College, Accra, Ghana

On the River Volta, 1994

With the Christian Union leader at Cape Coast, Ghana, 1994

Birmingham Silver Jubilee, 1991, Start of the CMWA

CMWA at Vietnam Memorial, Washington DC

CMWA Leaders, Kansas, 2009

Edwin and Dorothy in New York

... and at the Niagara Falls

Dorothy at the Arctic Circle, Finland

... and Sydney, Australia

With Elizabeth and Arturo, Mexico, 1996

Avenue of the Dead, Mexico, 1996

Shelter Ark Boys' Orphanage, Mumbai, India
with Bethela Thasiah and Gabriel

Janet Chisholm at Good Shepherd Seminar, Lucknow

Good Shepherd Seminar, Hyderabad

Mahadeb, Rita and family

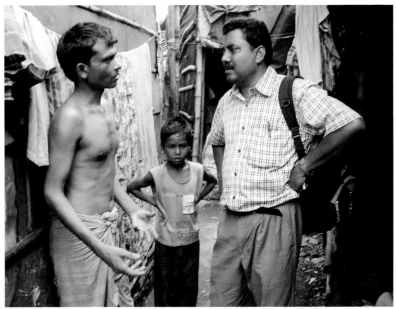

Mahadeb at work in a Kolkata slum

Pastors' Training Seminar, Bangalore, with Chelladurai
and Singaporeans, 2009

Shaji Amos and family (Kolkata City Mission)

With Shaji on a motorcycle

Henry Nerella and daughter, 1982

taking photographs and purchasing a few items for home. We took a picture of a man selling pelican medicine. He had a live pelican chained and two dead ones wrapped up and these little bottles of oil which is made from the pelican which he was trying to sell as medicine. We found the people of Peshawar to be very friendly. There were no signs of the Bhutan image of the man with a bandolier and always carrying a rifle. There was evidence of weapons, plenty of toy guns about. The Police tended to be armed with rifles or pistols and in one little shop we noticed a Russian machine gun and Rupert had a word with the owner and took a picture of him holding it. We had quite a bit of fun. We were able to go to the fort. I tried to take a photograph near the entrance to it but there were soldiers there and they waved us away, refusing to be pictured, so we had to console ourselves with taking pictures which were not the best angle but nevertheless we did get something of the fort. It was a good afternoon.

We returned to the house for a short break before leaving with the Swedish girl and Grace, Steve driving and Rupert with me and the other young American to an Afghan restaurant. We squatted on the ground to eat our food which was rice and bowls of spinach with some sort of meat in it, together with the distinctive chapatis, beautiful bread and then the kebabs, which were delicious. We each had a bottle of Coke as well. It was a thoroughly enjoyable meal. We talked at length and I was hearing of some of the problems which the Afghan refugees faced. I was surprised to find that Steve had in the past been visiting refugees in very difficult areas and had had to have an armed guard with him in the van. They make distributions of quilts and clothing and cooking oil to the refugee camps, helping them in various ways. Grace told us quite a bit about Peshawar and life in Kabul where she and Gordon lived for ten years. They have now been in Peshawar for eight years. They therefore know the situation very well, speak the language fluently and clearly have a real heart for the people. I found that out when I made a remark which she rather misunderstood and felt that I wasn't quite in sympathy with the refugees and she was very defensive about it. Her heart really is with these people.

After the meal we took a photograph of the interior of this restaurant, also another one outside and later we drove along to a Kashmir chai shop where we had a special kind of tea with almonds in it. It was served in china cups which were brought to us as we sat in the car. It was really delicious. A beautiful end to a lovely day.

Saturday 13th February

This morning began with devotions at the SERVE office at 8 a.m. I was able to share with them from Philippians 2, the humility of Jesus, linking it with 2 Corinthians 8, the grace of our Lord Jesus Christ.

After a short break we were escorted by Ron, the leader of the SERVE office, around the various departments. We were shown the offices; they have up-to-date computers, good financial control and modern equipment. There are several offices. Then we were taken into the nursery where they are growing young trees which can grow very quickly. The Afghan refugees need wood for fuel. I think they use it for other things as well. Where the refugee camps are there is sparse vegetation and it is used up very quickly. These young trees are presented as gifts so the refugees can begin a new kind of life. Within the nursery there are all kinds of plants, seedlings, and all kinds of things they're developing suitable for crops for the refugees in the very barren areas which they have been given. They are put in areas where there is little or no vegetation, just rocks and desert and these seedlings are developed to grow in the poorest kind of soil. Also in the nursery they had a lot of chickens which Steve Craig is responsible for. Apparently they were given several hundred of these chickens and they are being reared so that again they will lay eggs and be suitable for the refugees. Having a relevant background, Rupert was very interested in this nursery. He was asking many questions and clearly could see the value of this work. The staff are Afghan refugees themselves.

We were then taken into the carpet factory, where we watched refugees making their own special rugs. The designs have been handed from father to son for generations. It appears they are very ancient, for some of the designs clearly have

Christian elements to them: crosses and fishes. It seems that prior to the Muslim invasion of Afghanistan there was a Christian church there and some of these designs date from the time when Christianity flourished in Afghanistan. The designers are quite young boys and they work long hours. All the carpets are beautifully made by hand and we watched them finishing them off, cutting off loose ends and stretching them and preventing them curling up by watering them and fixing them on a frame. The manager of the factory is a fine Pakistani Christian, an elder in the Bible Church where I am to preach on Sunday. He also speaks good English. I was able to purchase some small items from the factory to take home to England. They have a showroom and it is possible to send orders from the UK to Peshawar and SERVE people will send them back. The cost to people in England is about double the cost that they would charge in Peshawar. This is due to duty and carriage.

From the carpet factory we also inspected the solar ovens being manufactured. These are rectangular boxes with a slanted roof. The box is made of fibreglass and the roof of glass and mirrors and by the mirrors being used through this glass they produce intense heat, enough to cook a meal. You can put two or three pots in each of these ovens. We saw quite a number of them awaiting distribution. They are sold very cheaply to the Afghan refugees. Again it helps them very much with cooking if they have no fuel. We had a solar meal later and that was a beautiful, delicious meal, each dish cooked within its own juices, a sort of waterless oven. The solar project is at present at a standstill due to some government regulations. It is hoped these will be lifted so that manufacture can go ahead, therefore employing more refugees and also benefitting them in the camps. If the go-ahead is given it is hoped that a new unit will be opened in Quetta, meeting the needs of Afghan refugees who are coming to that part of the country. Little is being done for them down there.

Following our inspection of the SERVE facilities (their centre occupies several acres of ground) we then went for a trip to one of the refugee camps. This took us on the road towards the Khyber Pass and we passed a checkpoint. The camp consists of hundreds of small mud houses enclosed in mud walls. We drove into the camp, being advised not to take any photographs. There were Red Crescent centres, also distribution activities, social work, sponsored by Arabs, but also we saw a work under the sponsorship of a society from West Germany. The Christian work goes alongside all this and it was interesting to see all these Afghan refugees. This is just one of many camps. The poorest camps are for those who have just arrived and they are in tents and with very little. SERVE people go out and supply them with quilts, cooking oil and essential clothing and other things they might need. A certain amount of medical work is done amongst them.

At the conclusion of our visit to the camp, we visited the Eye Hospital. This is a remarkable place. There was a crowd of Afghans and Pathans and all sorts of people pressing to get in through the gate. They are only allowed through in small numbers and are searched before they enter. Apparently there have been threats to put bombs in the place. The work is run by Dr. Fresan and his wife Ruth and their son, all of whom were at the meeting on Friday morning where I preached. The son showed us around the place. There are many rooms; operating theatre, inspection centres and several small wards with people in bed having had operations on their eyes. There were people coming for spectacles and eye tests, also a typical optician's chair and all the different lenses and eye-testing equipment. Dr. Fresan, an ophthalmologist of tremendous skill, is a very gifted man. He has set up this hospital in the last few months.

The Eye Hospital is part of the work of SERVE. Overall, the funding for SERVE is adequate. They receive finance from World Vision, Tearfund and a number of other agencies. This enables them to have some very good vehicles and food and equipment. The workers are supported by their own individual agencies and their funding does not come out of the funding for SERVE. Altogether the work of SERVE is one of the finest Christian efforts I have ever seen.

In the afternoon it had been planned that Rupert and I should go to witness some games held by the Pathans. These are fiercely wild games with riders on horseback. It is the forerunner of polo, it would appear. The idea is to get a calf into a certain circle and they just thunder round the field, chasing this and pulling it between them. It sounded rather bloodthirsty and violent. In the event, there was no one to take us to see them and I was not disappointed.

In the evening, from 4.30pm onwards, the SERVE prayer meeting was held at 5 Mulberry Road.

In the afternoon session we were pleased to have Rosemary Weston from Sutton Coldfield to speak to us. She is an amazing lady who has spent many years in Afghanistan. She has learned several languages and is now working in Attock and is very effective on a personal level, reaching certain language groups among whom very little work is being done. She told us some enchanting stories including one of a person who had come to Christ in that area. There are many homes open to her and she is serving the Lord in a wonderful way. We had a light lunch together and then the evening session where many more people arrived. It was, however, a very tense situation, for on the Friday night a Pathan leader had been shot dead outside the house of Ron and his wife and two children. Other members of SERVE had been introduced to this man. Some knew him quite well. Also his wife and daughter were interested in spiritual things and had good contact. The whole team was very shaken by this, particularly Ron's wife. There was a time of real intercession for the Afghan people. Several were in tears. There was a sense in which people were rather fearful and I was most concerned at the distress I was witnessing. I led in prayer and tried to lift the situation, but others were telling stories of their concerns and their apprehensions about the possibilities for the future. The meeting went on for some time and I wondered when I was going to be invited to speak. When I did, I was much helped by the Lord. I spoke on Epaphroditus in Philippians 2, the Messenger of the Church. I endeavoured to be objective so that they could see themselves in the context of the world church. I was able to use a little humour and the atmosphere was lightened as well as their being encouraged and comforted. It was a very moving meeting and I feel the Lord had put me there at just the right time. Several spoke very appreciatively. One girl came and hugged me. The fact that I am older than the rest seems to be of value as they respect me and see that I have much experience. There is a difficulty in a group whose age is very similar.

Sunday 14th February

We awoke refreshed this morning, having had a good sleep. I had taken the advantage of the nice hot bath the night before also, realising that soon I would be leaving this beautiful home. Rupert and I had breakfast together and a short time of prayer, and soon we were out to the service at the Bible Church. This is an Urdu-speaking church. We were not sitting on the floor but had some small stools, made locally. There was a time of worship and the small group, I think possibly 40 people gathered, were very warm and friendly, and full of praise to the Lord. I was invited to speak, with the carpet factory manager interpreting for me. I spoke from Philippians 2 as well as 1:6 and 4:19. The Lord gave me much liberty, and together we enjoyed the time, which was much appreciated. We had the Lord's table following this, and at the end of the service people came and spoke warmly to us, two women asking us to pray over them, one for healing and one for help in other ways.

Before attending the service, we were escorted by an Australian called Jeff, who is out there on his own doing language study, studying Urdu. I had my camera with me, and as we were earlier than we had thought, we stopped at the British cemetery and looked at some of the graves. It was interesting to see that there had been many who had died at about the same time that my father had been serving as a soldier in that area. I thought perhaps he would have known some of these men. There were some women and children too. Some people had died of fever, of heat stroke, but others had been killed in action. One, it said, had been shot by a fanatic. I was sorry to see that a number of the graves had been desecrated. Many Muslims don't like to see crosses around, and the crosses had been smashed off the tops of the tombs of quite a number of them. I took a couple of photographs. We noticed that an orange grove was planted around them, and there were still some oranges on the trees.

We had packed our belongings and put the cases in the car before setting out for the service, so when it was over we made our way, being led by a couple of young men from the church, who had also played music for us in the English fellowship on Friday. We soon found the grand trunk road, which is a good dual carriageway where we could do a reasonable speed. We were pleased that on Saturday we were able to get the motor horn replaced. It had been very difficult to drive without one on our way to Peshawar.

We made very good headway, stopping at one point as we crossed the River Indus. I went to take a photograph from there. A policeman blew his whistle and ordered me not to take any photographs. After Rupert came out of the car, and some haggling over it, I was allowed to take a photograph of the river. We hopped in the car and started off. He blew his whistle again and was waving to us, but we ignored him and just drove off. It was a good drive but we made it in tome to be early to see Janet and the two children and have lunch with them, and make a phone call to Britain. There was no reply at Wheeley Moor Road as Dorothy was in Sheffield, so we rang Ian and told him how we were getting on. It was nice to hear his voice and that of Helen and Jamie. I also had some post. Two letters arrived while we were there. It was then a drive to the airport and our final goodbye to Rupert, Janet and the children. It had been a lovely time with them. I was sorry to leave.

The flight was to Lahore at first, and there we waited on the runway for an hour and a half because of a violent thunder storm. This meant that I was late arriving in Karachi. I was very pleased to see David Moulden waiting for me. He drove me back to the house where I am now.

We have had a nice meal together and have been out shopping. I have been able to re-arrange my luggage because I have some gifts from the Mouldens to take to their relatives, and I praise God for a good trip to Pakistan and India.

I should mention that arriving here at the house the girls' leader of the OM team in Karachi was there. She has some fellowship with Sarah. She told me that today the boys' team, which consists of four fellows, had been distributing literature in the centre of Karachi, and that they had been attacked. One of the Muftis had attacked one of them and grabbed him by the throat. It seems that the others had been beaten too, but there were no details. However, I was told that they had given out over 6,000 leaflets before this happened. Praise God for these OM-ers doing such a good job.

Monday 15th February

Today I was able to rest up. I had been exhausted from the long journey and the preaching tour, and so it was delightful to spend time in bed, and at my leisure to get up and have a warm shower and generally relax. David's two children are a delight. I spent a little time playing with these two young ones. Later David returned from his teaching work, bringing his little girl with him, whom he had picked up from school.

After lunch I asked David to take me into the city. I needed to confirm my air tickets to Bombay. We went to the Pakistan International Airways office and left the car outside for about five minutes. It didn't take long to see to this confirmation. In fact, as they checked the tickets I was told that it had already been confirmed. However, when we came out of the office we were amazed to see David's car disappearing in the distance. It was being carried away by the police because they alleged that it had been parked illegally. Actually I noticed later many cars parked in similar situations. It seems that they have a forklift truck that just goes around picking up any car that they decide to, and carry it to the pound. We were there for about half an hour, as David remonstrated with the officials, eventually having to part with 50 rupees in order to get it out again. We watched this forklift truck; the man was just going in and out picking vehicles up. There was no question of waiting to see if someone had overstayed or giving them a moment's grace, but just bodily lifting the cars up and bringing them into the pound. No receipts are given for these fines, and it is quite clear that this is a racket. There is much corruption in Pakistan.

We were then able to go to Air France and confirm my return flight to England. Following that, we went to the bazaar and I did some shopping. It's always a fascinating experience to go into an Asian bazaar and see so many different goods and haggle over the prices. In fact, we did quite well. I was looking for goods which were typically Pakistani, made by the people in their own ingenious way.

After supper with the children, we spent time relaxing and chatting, and having prayer together. It is so important to listen to our missionaries and understand the problems which they have. Especially it is noticeable that they react strongly to things put in letters. We must encourage people at home to write frequently, whether or not they get answers, but also to be careful what they put in letters, remembering that this is all they have out there, and one sentence which may be a little critical can reverberate and become a source of annoyance or hurt for a long time. I packed, and had an early night, because I had to rise early in the morning.

Tuesday 16th February

The alarm went at 4.00 a.m. and I rose quickly, packed the last few things, and got myself ready for the trip to the airport. As I was the only one with an alarm clock that worked, I need to knock up David, who quickly was with me. We drove to the airport and said our goodbyes. I was so grateful to David for escorting me, having to rise so early. He tells me that he often has to do this, either to take people or to meet them. This is clearly an important role which David occupies with OM, for most people have to come through Karachi. I don't think he realises what a blessing it is to be met at an airport and to find friends and a comfortable bed to go to.

8

Excursion to Bombay

Leaving Pakistan through Karachi airport was not a pleasant experience. First, there was the long wait just to enter the airport. There were queues of people trying to go through the international barrier. That was because they are only allowed through one at a time, and each person was checked to see that he or she was holding the correct ticket and a passport and a visa. These were to be inspected several times before we got to the plane. There were the usual searches – the body searches, the baggage going through radar screens, and many questions. Then much stamping of tickets and checking that they had been stamped, and the wait before eventually going out on to the tarmac and being taken by the airport coach to the plane. I was glad when at last I found my seat. This happened to be at the front of the main Economy section. There were just two seats on this one side, and the one was already occupied. I sat down, to be greeted with an American saying "Hi there".

Soon we were in conversation – a conversation that continued throughout the flight. This man is an itinerant evangelist preacher. He lives near to Billy Graham in the United States and knows him quite well. His wife died a year or so ago and he is now free to travel. He has a large family, and he tends to visit his sons who are abroad, all in Christian work. He had been travelling for over twenty hours, and therefore was very tired. We had some good fellowship, sharing news and experiences, talking about the Lord and His keeping power and answers to prayer. I very much enjoyed the fellowship. As we neared our destination, he let me know that he didn't know where he would be staying, and he had never been to India before. I therefore told him to stay with me as we went through immigration, baggage collection and customs to get out of the airport. I wasn't sure who was going to meet me. I had notified OM and hoped there would be somebody from the base to meet me, but also there was Dr. Greenrose, my main contact here, but I wasn't too sure whether he could meet me or not. However, there had been a phone call to Rupert Abbott in my absence. Dr. Greenrose had rung to say he would look forward to meeting me at Bombay airport. On our arrival therefore, it was delightful to see him and two other brothers, all ready and waiting to meet us. They were dressed in white, they had smiling faces, and greeted us warmly. We were then advised to book our taxi back inside the airport, which was a much better arrangement, avoiding the usual Eastern haggle over the price of the taxi. Soon we were all in the taxi, or rather, in two taxis, because my companion had luggage too, and we were speeding into the city centre of Bombay.

It was lovely to be back in India. It is in some respects very similar to Pakistan but there are noticeable differences. I was pleased to see the absence of weapons. Pakistan is now under martial law, but there is no sense of that in India. Also the dresses and the appearance of all people was different, particularly the Indian saris of the women with all their colours and the usual Hindu mark on their foreheads. The city of Bombay seemed to have improved a lot since I was last there. The roads were better, much more traffic about, but not nearly so much as in Pakistan. In India there is still a restriction on imported foreign goods which includes foreign cars. Vehicles on the roads are usually manufactured within the country. I noticed a number of Suzuki cars, and learned that Suzuki have a plant in India.

We were taken to the Methodist Centre in the centre of Bombay. This was a large, square building with several floors, square around an open courtyard – open to the sky – and in that courtyard there were various palms and quite tasteful shrubberies, and an area where one could sit and relax, a large lounge and dining area. Our room led off that ground floor, or it appeared to be the ground floor. In fact, we had gone up two floors before we started. We had Room 7 and that room was shared with four people. My American friend was fortunate in that there had been one spare bed. My bed had been booked by Dr. Greenrose and his group. The two other occupants were unknown to me. One present throughout my stay was very shy and we had no communication. The other man was from Kashmir. He spoke with what seemed like a Germanic accent – I thought perhaps Swiss – but in fact he was Kashmiri, a very pleasant fellow who runs a trekking centre up in the hills and invited us to send young people there and that they would make all the arrangements for them. My American friend was utterly exhausted after his long journey, and spent the rest of the time resting. I hardly saw him again, except that our Indian friends called for him at 5 o'clock the next morning and took him to the airport to get his next plane to Hyderabad.

After an hour or so rest, my host called for me and I was taken by taxi to another place about half an hour's ride away, and there, up a very dark staircase onto the second floor, there was an apartment in which they have their base. It is also the home of an elderly couple. As I stepped into the room, I saw that it was occupied by about 14 or 15 people, a dozen of them men and the others women, and that they were seated on a prayer mat on the floor. I removed my shoes and took the seat offered to me at the other end of the room. This was their worship meeting and Bible study, and they had been waiting for me to arrive. They sang well and praised the Lord, had a time of open prayer, and then I was invited to speak.

Once again I spoke from Philippians 3 on the subject of "our citizenship is in heaven". The man who interpreted for me quickly entered into the spirit of the meeting and this was a good time. Dr. Greenrose led the meeting, and afterwards led them in prayer. I was given a light lunch and invited to stay where I was in that room while the others disappeared to hold open air meetings, and I was able to take a welcome rest.

At about quarter to seven, I was called for again, and we left again by taxi some distance away. By now it was dark. We went through a very poor quarter but the place teemed with people. It was as if a large football match had just turned out its spectators, but this was a normal evening – people strolling about, doing their shopping, going hither and thither; lots of bicycles, cars, many taxis, lots of noise of all sorts. We arrived at a place which was rather like a small park. It was well lit up – the team had put special lighting there – and they also had microphones on tripods, with a general PA system. There were mats rather like sheets of canvas spread out on this rough ground, and quite a number of people were seated cross-legged on the ground already, the men on one side and the women on the other. The team were singing and playing music and it was already attracting quite a lot of attention. Testimonies were given and a prayer time, and eventually I was invited to speak.

The audience grew. Soon the mat was completed covered with people, and not only so, we could see from houses all round that there were people in the alleyways, and up on the balconies, and standing here and there listening to the Word. I was glad that I had a good interpreter and I felt great liberty as I preached once again from Philippians 2 "among whom we shine like stars in the heavens" linking that to the claim of Jesus Who said "I am the Light of the world". The Lord gave me great liberty as I preached an evangelistic message, first talking to the Christians about their need to make sure that their lives were shining for Jesus as they should.

It is not often in these meetings that I have felt led to make some sort of an appeal, but on this occasion I did. I felt that God was with us in such a way that I led them in prayer with translation, and then asked for those who had really prayed in their heart to raise their hands. Quite a number of them did. I asked that they should later come forward for counselling. I handed the meeting over to Dr. Greenrose, and he spoke for a while, emphasising the points which I had been making and then leading them in prayer. After this quite a number of people came forward, I think perhaps twenty. Some had clearly made some response to the gospel. There were two Hindu women, there were one or two Hindu men. Quite a number of Hindu men had in fact joined and listened in the meeting. My hosts were quite pleased with this because there are many nominal Christians in the area and they mainly reach them, but to find so many Muslims showing an interest was greatly encouraging.

And then people came with their children for prayer, people who are sick, and I spent some time just praying over this one and the other one.

At the end of the meeting, I was disturbed by a woman who was brought to me with a young child about 2 – 3 years of age. I was told that they lived in a nearby house and that they had been listening to me, and to the meeting, and this child had fallen from the balcony onto his head. The child looked very poorly, and was very sleepy, and I was very concerned that he might have a fractured skull. I could do nothing else but pray very much. Later I asked others to make this a matter of prayer, not only for the child and its mother, but also for our situation, for if the child were to die, or be seriously ill, it would be a very serious thing for us, for we had announced that we would go to the same place the following night and hold another meeting there. It was a very tense and exciting time. I will never forget this meeting.

We were taken back to the elderly couple's home and there a meal was prepared. By this time it was about 11 p.m. As I had flown from Karachi that morning, having left at about 5 a.m., I did feel extremely tired, and I was glad when they took me back to the Methodist Centre where I was to spend the night.

Wednesday 17th February 1988

I did not sleep too well. There were no coverings on the beds except sheets, and the fans were going. There was no mesh at the windows and no mosquito nets, and so the fans were our only protection from mosquitoes, and though it may have been a warm night outside, it made it rather cool inside and I felt cold. The Kashmiri man told me that he had not slept too well because he had been pestered by mosquitoes himself. I did not appear to have been bitten.

Breakfast was at 7.30 a.m. We joined a group of Americans in the dining room. Apparently they were a party doing a three-week tour of India. This was a scheme called 'Ploughshares', which looks into other cultures, and especially Christian work here and there. I soon formed the opinion that they were not evangelical people. There was little fellowship – one or two seemed to be rather kind, but most of them had very little to say to us. This was my first meal in the place. I should have had lunch on our arrival but after the rest, I had got up and gone to the dining room and was surprised to find everybody clearing things away. I was not offered any food. It was later that I discovered that there is a half an hour's time difference between Pakistan and India, and not having adjusted my watch I had been half an hour late. Today my watch was corrected and I was glad to have the simple breakfast that was prepared. Everything was very clean and quite acceptable.

Yesterday I attempted to make contact with the OM base. Eventually I got through on the telephone and spoke to Alfie Franks. I told him that I had brought two videos from the UK for him and also would like to be at the base and have some fellowship. I thought perhaps I might be asked to speak at their devotional meeting. We discussed the proposal and he said I would be called for at about 8.00 or 8:30 a.m., so today I expected him to arrive. However, when I got in late last night, I discovered a little note pushed under the door of our room and found it was addressed to me. It said that an OMer would call for me at ten o'clock this morning. Unfortunately I had promised Dr. Greenrose that I would be available for them by 10:30 a.m. So when the OMers arrived at ten o'clock, the Indian boy was ready to take me; he had a taxi waiting outside with two English passengers. One was going to the airport first and then on to their base. Clearly there was no time. So I gave them the videos, which they were glad to receive. The one man is the new head of STL. I sent my greetings to Alfie Franks and assured them of our prayers, and returned to the centre.

At 10.30 a.m. I was called for by the elderly brother, who took me into a taxi, and again I was off to their house, and the team were already waiting for me. After worship, I was invited to speak to them. On this occasion I spoke chiefly on Philippians 4:19 – "My God will meet all your needs." I had decided this before I had arrived, and was encouraged to see as I stood up to speak, facing me at the back of the room was that very text on a large poster. I shared with them some of the experiences that I had had, specially the incident with the Mission in the provision of the filing cabinet, for there in the room was a filing cabinet very similar to the one that had been brought to me in answer to prayer. They were encouraged, they said, to hear that I was not a wealthy person and that often I had had to really seek God for small things.

Immediately after our meeting, we proceeded to an open air meeting in another part of the city. This was to be in an area described as the "red light district". It was a poor area, in fact slum conditions, with a row of hovels either side of a narrow path. We found a place about halfway along, where the team began to sing, using amplification which they carried with them. One of the young women then began to speak. She was a powerful speaker. I didn't understand her message, but she was clearly speaking with great conviction. All down the one side women appeared, made up, and dressed in bright clothing. They were the prostitutes of that area. Their keepers seemed to live on the opposite side. The women listened carefully to the speaker. At the same time, two or three of the fellows were going up and down this street passing out Christian literature. Then I was invited to speak, which I did with a great caring concern for these poor people. I understand that many of these women have been kidnapped from Nepal and other parts of India, and some from overseas, and they are forced into prostitution. There were a number of very small children around with them. The conditions were pitifully poor.

I noticed suddenly that they seemed to disappear – these prostitutes went indoors. I thought perhaps it was because of my preaching. However, at the conclusion of the meeting as we slowly moved away down the street, I was amazed to see two men attack some of these women, slapping them about and pushing them into the building. I thought these men must be their keepers, but I was told to keep moving because they were police – CID men. These women were breaking the law, and occasionally were attacked by these men. I had enquired whether I could take a photograph, but was warned that this would not be appropriate. It would be thought that the girls' photographs could be handed over to the police, but there may have been other reasons as well. There was an adjacent fairground, with a Big Wheel, and then soon we came out into the bazaar. We were near the railway, and I was able to climb up the stairway to the bridge over the railway and take photographs of the whole district.

It became very hot, and I was glad that they took me back to the house, where I had something to eat and could lie down for a while. The rest was short-lived because there was another meeting for me to go to. This time we were going to the Daravi slum area. Dr. Greenrose didn't come with us, he said he had business to attend to. We therefore went this time in a very fine vehicle. Apparently we had been loaned this minibus (Suzuki) by a businessman who had been converted through the work, and he was a great supporter of this team, and supplied the driver as well. And so we were able to go to the slum area. First I was taken to another bridge across the railway, so that I could see the extent of this place. I was told that it was the largest slum in Asia. How they come to know that I don't know, but certainly it was of great extent. They said a third of the population of Bombay lived in the sum area. If that is so, it holds over three million people.

We went into the narrow streets among these single-storey hovels, built by the people out of any material they could get. Some of the alleyways were no more than a yard wide, with little open sewers that one had to step across continually. There were children playing in all the filth. The place really was a disaster area. It smelt very bad. Refuse littered the ground and you had to watch where you put your feet. Dogs lay around. Yet there were no people begging. They were all trying to make some sort of an existence. I was impressed that here and there, there were small clinics with red crosses on them, and when we came to a wider area, we held an open air meeting. There was the usual singing. This time we had a drum, and that attracted quite a bit of attention. I was asked to stand in the shade, because it was very hot. When I wanted to take photographs, I had to step out into the sunshine, and I was surprised that one of them produced an umbrella and kept it over me all the time I was in the hot sun.

I was invited to speak for a short time, and it was a delight to be speaking to these very poor people in this district. I used the Red Cross on the clinic as my lead-in, explaining what that really meant, how Christ died for sinners and he brought us hope in whatever situation. Again much literature was given out, and then I was escorted all round these alleys just to see some of the privations of these people.

I was suddenly surprised to be taken into the home of one of these slum dwellers, where some Christians were living. The woman had been sick. She said she was Pentecostal, or I was told she was Pentecostal. The interior was quite clean and had been painted up. The woman was obviously very pleased to have my visit, and I prayed with her, asking the Lord for healing, and with a greeting and blessing moved out again.

Eventually we came back to the vehicle, and then we went for a circular tour around this district. It is immense. The widest roads in this area could just about take a vehicle. On one occasion we were confronted by another vehicle coming the other way and we had to reverse quite a distance so that we could pass. The tour ended at a small works where some sort of bean was being processed and put into packs. This was the factory of the owner of the Suzuki we were travelling in. They were very friendly towards us. I was offered a seat, and sat in the shade whilst someone went and brought a bottle of mineral water for me to drink. We were facing a several-storeyed building which looked rather grim, and I was told that this was a government school. There being five major languages spoken in Bombay I was told each floor of this school is used for a different language group. We could hear the children. It was in a very poor area. There were hovels made of kind of matting, sacking of experience. The young woman who had preached so well earlier in the day, came and asked me to pray with her. We said our goodbyes, and embraced several of them, and then I was taken back to the Methodist Centre. The Kashmiri fellow was in there, and he asked me what I had been doing. I spent some time going over the whole day.

Thursday 18th February

This is my final day in India. Last night I was glad to have a good shower, although it was cold and late at night, I felt clean and refreshed. I rose early and packed all my belongings before I went to breakfast which was at about quarter to eight. I had time to read the Indian-English newspaper, not much news from home however. Breakfast I took on the end table, which I think was probably the women's table – it mainly consisted of women, several Indians and some far Eastern. There was one man there however and I asked if I could sit. This conversation was dominated by an American woman – I rather think she is a missionary. However, I had a little conversation with the man, and the Indian woman with him, who could possibly be his wife. I was pleased and surprised to hear that they were from the Ludhiana Medical Centre and that they were attending special meetings in Bombay. They seemed very pleasant Christian people, though very shy.

After breakfast, having sorted things out and got my luggage into the lounge, I sat and waited. Eventually Dr. Greenrose and Mr. and Mrs. Thasiah, the elderly couple, arrived. They had a great difficulty in getting to me because of traffic jams. They had a taxi waiting and soon we were on our way to the airport. What a lovely couple these elderly people are. This man was once a member of a Bakht Singh assembly in Madras. He has lived in Bombay for over 40 years. His wife is a radiant Christian. She has been to England and I hope that we will see them again. Dr. Greenrose has proved to be a fine man. I am sure that he is worth encouraging. I should say that when he is preaching in these evening meetings he dresses in green – special green robes – he is quite a sight! But in spite of this kind of thing, he is a man with a real burden and vision. It would be good to see his work among the Muslims. They saw me into the airport, and after checking in I went to the bank and exchanged some travellers' cheques, and gave them a gift, which I had promised. They also gave me a gift, a round small stool or table, beautifully decorated on the top with elephants and other figures. I must look at it carefully to see what it is all about.

Return to Karachi

There was the usual hassle through the airport at Bombay. Whether it was because we were travelling to Karachi or not, I don't know, but it seemed as if they were particularly awkward. It took so long to get through the one barrier where we simply needed to show the passport – we were leaving the country, not entering it – but the man spent a considerable time (I think we were there between half an hour and three quarters of an hour) to see just three people, and even then he put the passport on the side and made no attempt to give it to us. The next man was impatient and we were told to take the passports to another desk where the man would check it with a computer. If we had gone to him in the first place, surely it would have been much quicker! It was as if they were deliberately being awkward with us. We were searched several times – it certainly was the last straw when as we were just about to enter the plane, we were made to go through the whole process again, this time opening my baggage and searching through it to see if there was anything we shouldn't have. This had already been through the X-ray machine and had been opened before. I was glad to get into the plane. There were quite a number of Indian young men. It was a noisy trip. I think they were going on to Nairobi; obviously they were all together. There were one or two things about that trip which were not very pleasant. I was glad when eventually arrived in Karachi.

To my surprise, entering Karachi was a very simple matter. My visa said it was a single entry and therefore I was concerned that I would not be allowed to enter the country again, and maybe have to spend several hours in a transit lounge. David Moulden had invited me to go back home with him and said he would be there to meet me. So coming through the immigration section, there was a queue waiting to show foreign passports, I being included. I waited for a few minutes. I would think there were 30 people in front of me. There was no movement. It looked as if we were in for a long wait. Suddenly a man appeared from another area, and he came directly to me and asked me what passport I had. I said I had a British one. He said "Come this way." I was through in less than two minutes! I entered the baggage collection area to see my suitcase immediately in front of me. I grabbed it quickly, put that and my other bag on a trolley, and walked out towards the customs area, looking for the green 'Way Out'. It wasn't very clear. Often one has to be searched again, or fill in some form, or give some explanation, but I had stood looking at the open doorway and a man in uniform came to me and asked me if I was ready to leave, and there, behind him, was David Moulden to take me home. Surely God had sent His angels to help me.

PART III: STEPS INTO AFRICA

9

Encounters in Uganda

The daring raid by commandos to release hostages from the hijacked Israeli plane grounded at Entebbe in 1976 came very much to mind. Now, seventeen years later in January 1993, I was about to enter this place of drama and heroism. The invitation had come in an airmail letter with a Uganda stamp from someone I had never heard of before. Letters were exchanged and prayer was made before the offer was accepted but the final note containing details of who would meet me or where I would be staying had not arrived.

It had been a night flight from Heathrow and we disembarked in an African dawn. The airport looked much as it appeared in the famous film of the Israeli raid. Actually much had been demolished and rebuilt since then. At the arrival hall we showed our passports and visas then collected our baggage and queued at the customs desk. Everyone was being told to open their luggage and it seemed we were in for a long wait. At the desk a policeman asked to see my passport and then queried, "Mr. Orton?" followed by "Please stand there!"

Within seconds I was joined by a large black lady with a huge smile on her face. Later I learned that this lovely Christian woman was a senior customs officer at the airport. She gave me an enthusiastic welcome, picked up my bags and escorted me right out of the airport building, avoiding any further formalities and into the bright Ugandan sunlight. There awaiting us was a large group of African Christians who waved, clapped and sang their welcome! I was at home.

Two of the young men took me by car to a five-star hotel. This would clearly be costly, but more importantly, it was very different from the accommodation which the believers were accustomed to. As I was very tired I agreed to stay one night but insisted that they find me a much simpler room for the rest of the visit. This they did the next day and it was in a pleasant African guest house, modestly priced but with caring local staff, some obviously Christian.

My arrival day was not yet over. It was very hot, but not overpowering, as Uganda is near to the equator but Entebbe is on the banks of Lake Victoria, which cools things down a little. After allowing me a short siesta my hosts returned to take me to my first engagement. This was in a small church in Entebbe which was still under construction. The meeting was held alongside the structure in the open air. Before the service I was taken into the prayer room, separated from the congregation by a large canvas sheet.

Half a dozen people were already awaiting prayer. A young mother and her child were brought in first, with the information that both were suffering from AIDS. This was my first close contact with the ravages of this terrible disease which afflicts much of Africa.

Having prayed for these people I was escorted to the meeting place which was in the open air outside the church being constructed. I was introduced to a tall, intelligent, godly man who was to be my interpreter from English to Luganda. As we discussed the address which I would give I realized that we were on the same wavelength and that he would give a faithful translation. Such men are very precious and vital to the success of this kind of ministry.

The area soon filled with happy, smiling Ugandans and the singing was loud and exuberant with clapping and the playing of African drums. The warmth of their welcome and their love for the Lord were apparent, making it easy for me to preach to them. They responded well and by the expressions on their faces, "hallelujahs" and laughter in the right places, the message was understood and appreciated.

Following the time of worship and Bible teaching I talked and prayed with many individuals until I was taken to the home of the pastor. This was a very simple structure which spoke of poverty and sacrifice. He certainly was not in the work for the money.

The whole vicinity was poor and it was obvious that they did not have many foreign visitors like me. I felt very privileged.

At the end of the day I was glad of the comfort of my hotel bed and didn't take long to go to sleep on my first night in Africa, far from my home in Birmingham but very much at home in Entebbe.

Next morning I moved my things from the Victoria Lakeside Hotel to the African guest house with more primitive washing facilities and one simple room. Later I was taken for a drive to visit several families in the district. As in India I was invited in to pray with them. They were all very friendly, especially the children. Their homes were very simple and I was impressed that the pastor's home was one of the poorest I have seen.

Everywhere was luxurious vegetation, banana trees, and beautiful flowering trees in reds, yellows and purples. The ground was obviously very fertile in which almost anything would grow. Along the roads were sellers of all sorts of fruit and vegetables, and many people walking.

Kampala

The capital of Uganda is about twenty-five miles from Entebbe. On this my first visit I was taken to the tombs of kings, an encampment of large African huts, with a huge building which was thatched with very low doors. This was the palace of King Metessa who lived there when Alexander Mackay, the British missionary, began his work. Mackay's work is one of the great missionary achievements of African history. He had much trouble with this very powerful king. Inside the palace were pictures of Metessa, and rows of spears and other weapons, and a large stuffed leopard which had once been the king's pet.

In the city centre we went to meet a number of Christian friends of John Paul, the young man who had invited me. One was Michael, president of the Sapphire movement of which Omega Healing Centre is part. The movement is rather like the New Life group, Pentecostal but indigenous. I had good fellowship with Michael who is a former school headmaster, an intelligent, godly man.

Having spent time with others of Paul's contacts we raced back to Entebbe to the church I visited the night before. There we found a fair-sized gathering already assembled. The pastor had complained that I had finished speaking too early. Considering I'd flown all the way from England into a completely new situation, missed a night's sleep, had booked into my hotel, just about had time to change, been counselling people who needed healing and then preached for an hour I thought I'd done pretty well! Today I was asked to preach a little longer and I decided to do it in two sections. I gave two messages, the first on Blind Bartimaeus, which also included details about BCM and our concern for the cities, and the poor. There was a break for more singing and they kindly provided me with a bottle of pop again. After an interval of 10-15 minutes I was invited to preach again. This time I gave a message on Philippians 2:15: "You shine like stars in the universe as you hold out the word of life." The people were very receptive and I continued until 6.30 p.m. That was a long stint – I suppose I preached for two hours that evening. We stayed to talk to a number of people.

On another occasion we passed through the chaotic main bus station, crowded with people and minibuses. Within the confusion I noticed many street children, such as are seen in other great cities in India and South America. I enquired about them and suggested that local believers consider starting a Kampala City Mission aimed at reaching children rendered homeless by conflict or disease such as AIDS. The suggestion was well received.

The next few days passed very quickly with meetings in churches in Kampala, the capital, and at the Christian Union in the university. It was there that I stayed one night as a guest of one of the lecturers, Jeffrey Kisule, whose sister, Catherine, was on the In-service Training Course at Birmingham City Mission. Sadly, after leaving BCM she went to live in London where she became ill and died. Her family was glad to meet me and hear of her time with us as she had not returned home since leaving for England.

The night I stayed with the Kisules became very special. It was dark and after a well-attended meeting on the university campus the keen Christian students were full of questions. I was then taken to the nearby lecturer's bungalow where his wife made me very welcome and prepared a sumptuous meal. While she was serving I could not help noticing that she was very pregnant so when they asked me to pray I included her and prayed for her health and a safe delivery. In the early hours of the morning while it was still dark I was awakened by a disturbance next to my small room and then the sound of a car being driven away. Being still tired I went to sleep again until I got up in a very quiet house. While I was dressing my host arrived with the exciting news that his wife had given birth to a lovely little girl. They were sure that my prayers had made a great difference and that she had gone into labour, which was short and uncomplicated as a result. Therefore they wished me to name the baby! I thought for a while and then suggested they name her after my own daughter, Esther. Today, somewhere in the heart of Africa there is a young lady who bears her name.

Next day John Paul arrived on time with others. We went directly to the airport for it was time for me to confirm my flights by Air Tanzania to Kilimanjaro and Mwanza. We were charged at a check point for permission to take the car into the airport area and were dropped at the entrance. It is a far cry from a British airport. It looked rather like a run-down parcel office from the outside! Unfortunately there was no Air Tanzania desk at the airport. There was something of a post office and we thought about making a phone call from there or even post the letters there but there was no-one in charge, the place being deserted. Fortunately there was a very fine Christian lady called . Alex (the one who met me at the airport when I arrived) and John was able to find her. She looked at my ticket, took the instructions and went away. I think she must have used the telephone. She came back in ten minutes to say it had all been confirmed and all was well. We then walked back to the car but it had disappeared. However, we could see in the distance it had been stopped by the police and Alex was quite sure the driver had been arrested and there was some trouble. I said, "Let's lead the way and let the Englishman talk our way out of it!" I think they saw us coming but by the time we arrived the policeman was all smiles and there was no difficulty whatsoever. We just got in the car and drove off.

Omega Healing Centre

The people were already singing as we arrived. The Omega Healing Centre is an uncompleted building. The meetings are held outside. There is a large very moth-eaten tarpaulin sheet which serves as a sunshade. Today there were more people than ever. I told them I would be bringing some gifts for the children and the children came in dozens. First, we had a short time of prayer in a room and they brought me a cold drink. They asked first that I speak to the young children. I decided to teach them the chorus, "God is good to me". We went over the song several times until they had learnt it with the actions. The instrumentalists formed a kind of backing and they sang it until they knew it. I then persuaded some to come out and they sang as a little choir. When I gave them some bookmarks as a reward for being there suddenly the choir increased in number! We had a good time and I believe they learned something and enjoyed the time. Of course the parents too were listening. I was then asked to speak to the young people so decided to tell them the story of Joseph, the pastor in Nepal. This wasn't too easy to do through an interpreter but it is easier for Africans to understand than the British because they are aware of the rural situation and the difficulties of being orphaned in a country without a social safety-net. They were very receptive and listened intently right to the end, and then applauded. I was able to bring them the challenge again to go out and reach others for Jesus, particularly the street children in Kampala. In this kind of ministry I felt even led to talk about a Kampala City Mission. As the day has gone by this seems to have crystalized and now there are several of the brothers who are talking about it and feel such a thing should happen. Some however are saying, why not a city mission in Entebbe, and I suppose there could be one.

After the message to the young people John Paul gave a testimony as to how he came to be in touch with me. It is quite remarkable. Apparently a Christian man had asked John Paul to get rid of some rubbish. While doing this he came across a booklet in which I'd written an article. He read it and was so interested in the vision I had shared he wanted to know more, hence his reason for writing to me. He said he didn't really expect to get a reply and was surprised and pleased to receive one. When he had written again giving me the invitation, he didn't think I would accept but had been overjoyed when I had. These people have really taken me to their heart. You should see their shining faces. The pastor is a quietly spoken man whose English isn't too good but he is a lovely Christian. The interpreter is another pastor whose face really shines and he enjoys the ministry. Apparently he does a lot of preaching himself but he is quite at one with me and appreciates the ministry.

Departure from Entebbe

In the morning I packed my things and before I was ready two or three members of the Fellowship at Entebbe were there to help me along and escort me to the airport. Here was a long wait and there was no sign of Air Tanzania. I was very pleased when the customs woman, Alex, arrived. She took control. Eventually the airline people arrived. I had to pay an airport tax in order to leave the country (23 dollars). Alex saw me through customs etc. I said goodbye to John Paul, Alex and Margaret and another brother who is the assistant to John as youth minister for the Omega Fellowship. This episode had been yet another step in my journey of following the Lord. He has not failed. It has also been a wonderful experience of seeing God at work and to meet his people.

The flight, amazingly, left on time. As we were waiting to get on the plane an American man of my own age came and sat beside me and immediately started to talk. He was a university professor but represents the World Bank, and is involved in financing charitable works around the world. He was Jewish and we had a very good conversation and I was able to witness to him. He is married to a Protestant woman who seems to be a real Christian.

The plane, to my surprise, didn't go directly to Kilimanjaro but first went to Burundi – we almost passed over Mwanza. Kilimanjaro was my problem because I had no arrangements for anyone to meet me. However, when I enquired people were helpful and there was a man who seemed to take charge of the situation. He escorted me to a place where I could exchange money and also suggested I confirm my flight the following morning which I was glad to do, especially when the next day I saw the plane was full. He then took me to a small minibus and gave instructions to the driver who drove me to a tourist hotel in the city of Ashura at the foot of Mount Kilimanjaro, the highest mountain in Africa. Ashura was obviously where mountaineers and trekkers kitted up for their safaris. It had a similar atmosphere to that of Kathmandu in Nepal with the exception of the trappings of Hinduism. However I was not there long enough to explore as I needed to be up at 4.00 a.m. to get my flight to Mwanza.

Dawn was breaking as I arrived at the airport and again people were helpful. When I'd been coming through customs entering Tanzania the officer had insisted on opening my case and had seen a copy of the BCM magazine. He immediately asked if he could have it, and I said he was welcome to it. On my return this man called me by my name and thanked me for the booklet. He said he had read it and would like to write to me sometime. He then stayed close to me for a while. He had apparently been to England on one occasion and had also visited Germany and Sweden. When we got on the plane I sat beside him and found him to be quite a helpful and reasonable person. I was surprised he was also a passenger on the plane, but I am sure the Lord had a purpose in the encounter. At Mwanza I lost him.

10

Adventure in Tanzania

FROM MY DIARY

We arrived at Mwanza at 8.15 on Monday morning. There was a real fight for the luggage – no organization, carousel or trolleys. I then began to look for Bishop Ndimi, who hadn't appeared. I waited until all the other passengers had found their luggage and left. The airport personnel were now insistent that I went somewhere so I looked through my belongings, found the itinerary and my letter to Bishop Ndimi in which I had said I would be arriving at 10.15 a.m. This was the arrival time given to me by our travel agent. Eventually Bishop Simeon Ndimi arrived, promptly, and gave me a warm welcome. He and his companion made me very much at home. Bishop Ndimi said he had only just arrived from Nairobi by road, so he was tired.

They took me to a small hostel in the centre of Mwanza, just a short distance from the main post office, called The Diocesan Hostel of Mwanza. I had a small room, with electricity. It overlooked a courtyard where they clean and throw out waste food from the restaurant, which wasn't a pleasant sight. There was a mosquito net and just along the corridor was a shower and toilet. There they allowed me to rest for a couple of hours.

First Week in Mwanza

Throughout the next day I found my room became the base for all sorts of callers. The idea was that I could talk to the pastors, so I spent quite a bit of time showing them the literature I'd brought from BCM and explaining the different ways in which we worked. We had some good fellowship together. I was shown a timetable for a conference next week but this week, I am told, things are more relaxed and we're just meeting and talking to people.

After a rest we went by taxi to an outlying part of Mwanza where we were to meet another "bishop". It was a remote and poor area. We went as far as the car would take us and then started to walk. We turned off the road and began walking up a steep hill on stepping stones from one rock to another. It was very difficult. It was very dirty with rubbish here and there and the little houses were very poor indeed. We walked for some distance and then Simeon asked me to stand still and he disappeared. I think he went to some kind of public toilet. As I stood there a young man passed by and greeted me in English saying "Praise the Lord!" He said he was a Christian, then disappeared. We then arrived at a village and found one hovel with a cross on it, obviously belonging to a Christian. This was the home of the "bishop". This man called his family in and the young man I had met earlier was in fact one of his sons. They asked me to speak and I gave a short message on following Jesus and then prayed for them. They were a warm, friendly group. The interior of the house was not very large. They seemed to have two rooms. There seemed to be a lot of cats around and I noticed one in the kitchen stealing scraps of food. (In the hotel where I am there are also cats – I counted 12 in the courtyard below.) All around the room there were texts from the Bible and pictures, quite clearly a great deal of Christianity there. It was a very poor place; little covering on the floor, a kind of settee and couple of armchairs. The head of the house sat on an armchair, rather like a throne – perhaps that's why he's called a "bishop". However, he was a very friendly person. I talked to him about my family. He then told me he had ten children, and more than twenty grandchildren. After our little time together they posed for some photos.

On Wednesday we were taken by taxi to a very large Assemblies of God church. It is quite a good building by local standards. They tell me they get 600 in their congregation. The pastor was a young man, about 30 years of age. Several other young men were with him. They seemed bright and intelligent. I had quite a talk with them, especially the pastor. He explained they had had a split in the church which had done them a lot of harm. However, they were keen to continue and the church was being blessed. We had a good time with them and I shared a piece of scripture with them. By now the sun was out and it was quite hot. We were able to return in the taxi to Mwanza and then took lunch in our hotel. This was a new experience, so I let Meeshak order and was surprised to find bananas cooked like vegetables. It was pleasant enough and we had some fish with it. Meeshak and his wife Grace were full-time workers in the Anglican church in Uganda and we had good Christian fellowship.

After a rest we prepared for the main event. Again we took a taxi to the east of the city and as usual soon left the tarmac road then had to leave the taxi and walk some considerable distance uphill along these narrow footpaths strewn with rocks.

Eventually we could hear singing and we came to a wide clearing with a large tree in the midst. Seats were positioned under it. This was a church under a tree. A pulpit had been set up, a table with a cloth, and four good chairs for us to sit on. Grace gave her testimony and Meeshak said some words also. There was an excellent choir. A very tall young man conducted and led in prayer. It was a good meeting with a real sense of joy in the Lord's presence. I then preached, taking John 7:37, "If anyone is thirsty, let him come to me and drink." I talked about the Indians who saw the River Thames in London when they visited us. They had asked if the water moved or was it still. The challenge was not to be static in our Christian life. Simeon translated for me and the message was well received. About eight or nine came forward at the conclusion for prayer. It was a very touching time.

We all walked back to the minibus and the ride back was very bumpy. When we arrived in the town it was decided that, as it was dark, we should have dinner somewhere else. Last night we had chicken and it was so tough I couldn't get a knife into it and eventually eat virtually nothing of it! We found quite a good Indian restaurant and had a good meal. I had beef but again it was very tough – I'll have to stick to fish in future! The fruit salad I'd ordered eventually arrived just as we were going, much to everyone's amusement. I paid for the meal for the four of us, which worked out to about £5 – food is quite cheap here, though I was still smarting about the price of the telephone call and fax, which cost more than £10!

On Thursday at about 10 a.m. Bishop Simeon Ndimi arrived to tell me a seminar was about to begin and I was the speaker. He produced a programme. It looked very complicated, but he wasn't keeping to it anyway. I very quickly made arrangements to go down to the seminar, not knowing what to expect. I had to wait for some time as people were still arriving. Eventually there were twelve people. Each was a pastor, and I believe they are key people. Some had obviously travelled a long way. During the meeting one of them fell asleep – I don't think it was my fault, I think he was just exhausted by the journey! I began an introduction to city missions, doing a biblical background and adapting it to the needs of the people. I had the use of a blackboard, which was useful. I wasn't able to use the transparencies I brought as no overhead projector was available. I therefore drew the outstretched hands and described various parts of our ministries.

We had a short break and began again. On the second occasion two of the people disappeared, including Simeon, who didn't come into either seminar. At first in the second session I didn't have an interpreter. However, one young man offered to do this, although he was a little slow. This time I dealt with the basic nature of man, with the tripartite body, spirit, and soul, and the need to have each element right. There was some discussion and the feedback was that they had appreciated my talk. I have just been told there will be more seminars tomorrow (Saturday), so it looks as though our trip to the Serengeti National Park will have to be on Sunday. There seems to be nothing definite in this place and even if it appears to be so it is changed at the last moment or they haven't communicated their information! Simeon is always saying he will leave me for five minutes which means half an hour! He says similar things to other people. However, we get into the pace of the people and it is not unpleasant. I thought that in the circumstances I had done quite well: seminars throughout the morning, taken a late lunch. I went to my room for a rest but a few minutes later Simeon appeared and informed me we were due to go to a church where I was to preach. I quickly prepared, despite feeling tired. Simeon did not come with me and I was accompanied by two pastors, neither of whom spoke much English. It was a long walk and eventually we got on a very crowded bus. We travelled a few miles out into the country and eventually left the bus. After another walk we arrived at a school room consisting of a large room with blackboards at either end. From the figures on the board it looked as though they had had almost 100 children in that place during the day. There were not many believers present (15 in all). However, they were enthusiastic. One of the pastors gave a greeting and another member gave a testimony. I spoke to them on Matthew 18, "the hands of Jesus". They received the message well. I gave a real challenge about giving themselves wholly to the Lord based on Romans 12:1.

By this time it was well after 6 p.m. and the pastor then invited me to his home, which was at the top of the hill. I had to be firm and decline on this occasion. I could see the weather didn't look too good; also I was very tired, having been active all day without any proper rest. We also had a journey back to Mwanza by bus and on foot. It is very dry and dusty here. I was glad to be in my room by about 7 p.m. Again, I hadn't been there long before Simeon appeared again saying we were to go for an evening meal. I had no idea where we were going and told him firmly he would have to wait while I got ready. Suddenly there was an enormous explosion. I could hear people shouting and heard pieces of rock falling on the roofs. When I investigated, people were looking across the lake where a huge pall of smoke was rising. Quarry workers had apparently been blasting the mountain rock for the granite. I should imagine the whole dynamite dump must have blown up.

Accompanied by the Ugandan couple and Simeon we made our way towards the Red Cross hostel where the Blundells are staying. We collected them then walked on for half a mile and came to the home of an African family with six or more children. Most of their sons are mechanics, one called David, another Martin! We entered the home and there was some conversation. I prayed for the family. We were then escorted out to a quadrangle where food had been prepared. There were six of us altogether. It was a warm, beautiful evening. Unfortunately the meal was chicken, and again it was very tough! We also had rice, tomato salad etc., also red bananas. Later they brought tea which was very milky with a sort of antiseptic taste which wasn't very pleasant. As we were leaving I was relieved when the eldest son offered to drive us back in his Toyota minibus. It is usual at the conclusion of the day for everyone to come into my room for a time of prayer and short conversation before turning in for the night. I have been keeping quite well apart from a few mosquito bites. I've been taking my daily Quinine and Paludrin, and also my fortnightly dose of the other medicine.

Saturday 23rd January

The meeting was held downstairs in the conference room, which was fairly roomy though poorly equipped. There were about 17 or 18 people, all pastors and leaders. I decided to continue with an Introduction to City Missions, talking about the principles of city mission work. I had been able to adapt this to the African situation and it seems to be well received. Through translation it took some time (over an hour). I then asked for a break and they brought in bottled soft drinks.

Soon they were ready for me to begin again. Simeon had arrived this morning with a fairly expensive cassette recorder. When we were having the break he switched it on – an American speaker was being translated into Swahili. I took it he was the next speaker. I stayed there for about 15 minutes, decided I'd had enough, then left and came to my room. Fifteen minutes later Simeon appeared and said everyone was asking for the teacher to return. I rejoined the meeting to discover others had joined us. This time I invited questions on the talk I'd given earlier. A lively debate followed. One man who had a burden to work among orphans asked how they could do it as they had no money. I spent some time sharing how the Bombay City Mission operated and how they found what they could and worked within their culture in a small way. That it might be possible for them to receive some help from the West but they shouldn't become dependent on it. Another question was regarding the type of people they should help. I turned them to the parable of the Good Samaritan and asked them if they could answer their own questions from that. They took the point quite well. One interesting question was with regard to literature. They seem to have very little in the Swahili language and it was a matter of there being so much in English, which not many people speak. I talked about the difference between production and distribution. I suggested there was a need for more Tanzanian authors. Later the man who asked the question told me he had written a couple of book manuscripts but had been unable to get them published. I gave him some advice. I also talked about distribution of literature – to get it out to the people and not stock it up.

Sunday 24th January

At about 10 a.m. Bishop Ndimi arrived with two other African brothers and he told me I was to be escorted to a church in a school where I was to speak. We made our way there. I had risen to the occasion by putting on my tie and jacket so as to be formally dressed. The service was well attended. At first there were about 40 people there but as the meeting went on the numbers increased to twice that number. The pastor is a fine man, though doesn't speak much English. He is a tall, black man and was wearing a pin-stripe suit. They provided me with an interpreter. A number of people had come from different churches in outlying districts. The visitors were invited to go to the front and bring their greetings. There was a choir of ten and they sang some fine songs to the accompaniment of a drum and there was much clapping. The women make a high-pitched call as a means of praise. I preached again from Matthew 18 – Jesus putting his hands upon the children. I brought greetings from overseas. Pastor David who accompanied me gave his testimony and greetings and showed everyone a picture of his family. When I preached I also followed suit. It was a good service and they allowed me to preach for an hour. Afterwards I had to stand at the door shaking hands with everyone as they left in single file. Once outside they then formed a large semicircle so that I could take a photo.

It was a beautiful sunny day, quite hot, and after all that, we had to make the journey back. They gave me no drink but fortunately I still had some of my fruit pastilles with me.

There was no-one around when I returned to my hostel as the restaurant is closed on Sundays. I needed a drink and some rest, which I took. At 2 p.m. Simeon arrived, informing me they had had lunch at the Red Cross hostel and had in fact seen me as they were travelling in a car and were wondering why I hadn't gone there. He then took me to an Indian restaurant for lunch. Having arrived back at my room after lunch I was rather exhausted; it was very hot and I had walked back alone from the restaurant. The reason was that after the morning service where I was preaching some distance away, I came back with an escort of two African brothers. The service was held in a school quite near to the Red Cross hostel where the two Europeans are staying and two Ugandans have been having fellowship, but I did not see them.

Dark Days
Monday 1st February

You will notice there is a gap of one week since my last diary entry. This is due to sickness. On the day following my previous entry I developed malaria. On Sunday night, 24th January, I had a very hot restless night. I was due to take the devotions for the pastors' conference the following day. When I awoke I felt very ill but forced myself to get dressed. I went to the conference room but found it empty. One of the pastors arrived, spoke to me quite sharply and told me to follow him. I tried to keep up with him, it was a fair walk and very hot. However, I managed and came into another conference room, a place I had not seen before. It was in a new building. I had not been warned about this at all.

There were not many people in the room. Derek Blundell was in charge. I went to the front and opened my Bible and he simply informed me they were doing without devotions today. I could hardly believe my ears. I simply said, "Thank you very much", turned away and walked out of the building. This time I had no guide, I hadn't taken much notice of the way I'd come but somehow managed to find my way back to my own room and flopped on the bed. Thus began my illness. I had little water. At first no-one showed any concern. I asked for more water.

Tuesday was just as bad and I felt quite neglected. This was the day I was supposed to have gone to Serengeti but that was now out of the question. One helpful thing was that Prosper

Maringa who is the travelling secretary/treasurer of the Evangelistic Assemblies of God in this area came to see me and encouraged me. He is a fine young spiritual brother with a degree in horticulture. He could clearly see through Ndimi and has very little to do with him. I sent him with a message to Don Baker at the AIM (American Inland Mission). He delivered this and brought the missionary to me on Wednesday.

It was later on Wednesday that Derek, and the Ugandan, came to see me. They were worried as the Ugandan immediately recognised the symptoms of malaria. They insisted on taking me to a doctor and after some waiting about he took some blood and told me I had malaria. I was given medicine for it and returned to my room. It was then decided I ought to go into hospital. They took me in on Thursday although I don't remember much of that. Actually the hospital was worse than being on my own. They put me on a drip, but that was all! It is a hospital where the doctor makes his diagnosis and prescribes the medicine, and the nurse simply administers it. There is no care whatsoever. I'd been taken to the hospital as I stood and put on to a trolley in the same clothes. I lay there under a mosquito net in the heat, with thirst discomfort and delirium, not having been washed, sponged, or fed. Fortunately the Lord was with me. During my delirium I had illusions of huge flies crawling overhead. I had a feeling that my life was under threat and I cried out to the Lord for his protection. In the night three Catholic sisters from the nearby school came in. They didn't do very much but smiled, prayed and encouraged me. I had a terrible thirst but there was no food or drink in that hospital. I believe that night I was the only patient. I overheard the sister complaining to the other nurse that if I was a missionary I should have gone to the Mission Hospital. They made no attempt to help me. They forced the tablets down me but that was all. Then the nurse got on to a bed and went to sleep.

The first sign I had of the Lord's intervention was when a young boy came in and I recognised him as having been at the service where I was preaching on Sunday. He was pleased to see me and I asked if he could get me a bottle of mineral water. It soon arrived and, in a sense, saved my life.

I began to think that if I was to survive I must take my discharge from the hospital.

On Saturday I staggered out of the hospital just as one of the RC sisters was passing by. This was God's provision as she could speak English and when I asked if she knew any nearby hotel where I could stay she offered to take me to it. It turned out to be the New Avenue Hotel near to the hospital. This was in fact where the others from the conference were staying, and I discovered my things had been moved to this accommodation. I was now installed in new quarters which were very hot and noisy with poor food plus mosquitoes around and the awful atmosphere of Mwanza.

I find it difficult to believe that English people can treat others from their own country in such a way as I've been treated here. On the one hand they have proved to be kind friends and they did a lot for me, but on the other hand they were very stand-offish, aloof, seemed to resent my presence and almost tried to come between me and the Ugandans. Grace, the Ugandan lady who is a very fine noble spiritual woman, clearly sensed the difficulties.

I now heard more about Ndimi. Apparently for some years he has been inviting Westerners to Mwanza and then neglecting them, trying to extract anything he can from them, having so-called conferences and churches which do not exist. I heard about one couple (I believe they were from Holland) where the man became desperately ill and nearly died and his wife was found wandering looking for help. Ndimi had organised or invited the Blundells of the African Pastors Fellowship as well as myself. Neither knew of the other's existence. There were no plans; the halls had not been booked. Pastors were invited and had been told that they were being sponsored. In fact they were sent out to find food on their own and even had to find their own accommodation. Some spent the first night sleeping in bus shelters! They hadn't been fed. Some had brought their wives with them. It was a terrible situation. Ndimi had received money in advance, which he seemed to have spent. Each day he seemed to have a different outfit. He had a fairly expensive radio/cassette recorder which he insisted on bringing to my room even during my sickness. He seemed to use my room as a base. There was no consideration for me or my comfort.

On Sunday I felt somewhat better. I was not strong enough to go to church but the others did. Ndimi was still around. I sat on the veranda for a while and he sat some distance from me. I avoided him. I then went to my room and he followed me. This time I took the initiative and told him severely what I thought of him and pointed out his need to repent. He apologised and sought my forgiveness but I said he should ask God for this. I said I would forgive him on one condition; that he utterly repented, never invited Western people here again, that he renounce the title "Bishop" and never use it again. Moreover I told him if he was in my country I would call for the police and have him arrested. I said if I ever heard he had invited any more Western people and treated them badly I would speak to my own government, who in turn would speak to the Tanzanian government, and he would be dealt with according to the law.

When I told my companions what I'd said they felt it was probably the reason for my being there. Apparently he had done a great deal of injustice to a lot of people for some time. I pray he may turn.

During the day I began to think more clearly about the next step. During my sickness my friends decided I would be quite unfit to travel on Friday and therefore had moved my belongings to this place. They had changed my air tickets and I was now flying to Dar-es-Salaam on the following Friday, going on direct to Johannesburg on Saturday. This meant I had another week in Mwanza; also I would miss the conference in Cape Town. I asked about the possibility of the MAF and to my astonishment learned that Derek Blundell had been talking to one of their pilots. He said I could probably charter a plane down to Zambia. However, this would cost around £800. I mentioned Nairobi as I felt if I could get there it would help as this is the main route down to Africa. I was informed that the MAF had scheduled flights from Mwanza to Nairobi each Monday. I finally managed to talk by phone to the pilot's wife who told me to be at the airport for 9.15 although she couldn't guarantee I'd have a place. I was excited and packed.

The following morning I rose, had breakfast, then made my way alone to the airport. There were crowds of people at the airport and I had to fight my way through and hang on to the man carrying my cases. I was taken into a small customs office and was told sharply to leave all my baggage there, including my passport, money etc. and go back into the crowd. I refused, saying I was sick. The woman officer eventually softened and indicated another lounge area where I could sit. As I sat there I could see the airfield and to my delight I saw a small plane landing. Shortly afterwards an English pilot of the MAF walked into the room and I was able speak to him and he agreed to take me. I waited until 1 p.m. and eventually I was able to check through and board the plane. I was so weak I couldn't carry my luggage.

There were thirteen people on the plane. We took off and I then learned we were going south to Dodoma first. We eventually landed at Dodoma and were told it would be a further two hours before we would take off again for Nairobi. When we arrived at the small airport building a member of the MAF staff appeared with an air-conditioned car and took three of us to a beautiful bungalow/guest house, very clean and modern and fully equipped. It was heaven on earth and I was able to have a shower, make some tea and have a rest etc. The Lord certainly met my need that day. I felt much refreshed when they called for us again at 4 p.m.

Arrival in Nairobi, Kenya

We finally arrived at a small airfield in Nairobi and one of the MAF staff saw us through customs. I wasn't able to change any currency there, so was without money. I was standing alone with my luggage, not sure where to go, when a car suddenly appeared and the driver asked if I needed help. He offered to take me and as we drove it turned out he was a missionary from Australia. His speciality was "urban mission"! His name was David Omalia and he was working in the slums of Nairobi. We had a short conversation and he gave me the name and telephone number of an SIM missionary who is majoring in urban ministry in this area. It seems this is why the Lord has brought me to Nairobi to discover what goes on in the largest city in East Africa. What a difference between that and Mwanza!

We went to the Fairview Hotel, but discovered they had no vacancies. My spirits dropped. However, I was able to change some of my money there to Kenyan shillings. I asked where the other hotel was and one of the staff took me and carried my bags. Eventually we came to the SPCK guest house in Bishop Road. At first the receptionist said they were full but I stood my ground and eventually a room was found. I was told another person would be sharing my room and would be arriving in the early hours of the morning. I just had time to change before going down to dinner. I sat at a table beside an elderly English lady and two Australians who also knew the young man who had brought me and came from the same missionary society. I'm at home and where God has put me.

Tuesday 2nd February

Today I awoke to find that the person who was supposed to have shared my room had not turned up. I was still feeling somewhat exhausted as it was taking a long time to work through the weakness from the malaria.

After breakfast I decided I must try to sort out a flight to Lusaka, Zambia (to pick up the original itinerary disrupted by my illness). There was no-one about downstairs so I asked for directions to the city centre. I'd read in my guide book to avoid walking through park areas alone. The directions given in fact led me through a park. It was not a pleasant experience as there were a number of unsavoury characters around. Somehow I managed to find my way to the main avenue which leads into the city.

Nairobi is a modern city with many high-rise blocks and yet it is fairly pleasant with a good deal of greenery about. The streets were busy, with numerous bookstands; there are also beggars and con-men trying to sell things all along the way. I was concerned about finding a travel agent and suddenly came across Mary Dark, an elderly Christian lady whom I had met earlier. She was more than pleased to find me because obviously she was at a loose end and I had no one with me. She knows Nairobi reasonably well so was able to come along with me to the travel agent. I went through all the formalities. However, they would not allow me to purchase my ticket by VISA. Eventually I persuaded them to tell me where the Kenyan Airline Office was. It wasn't too far away and I was told they would accept my VISA card there. We went along there and I was able to obtain a ticket from Nairobi to Lusaka for the following day.

Other developments during the day proved useful. I was able to make a telephone call to Rev. John Shane, of SIM. He runs an urban ministry support group. He very kindly came round that afternoon and took me out for a cup of tea. We talked for about an hour. He knew my friend Michael Eastman of Frontier Youth Trust and had heard of my name and ministry through Michael. I gave him a copy of my book. We talked about urban ministry around the world. John Shane is certainly the contact for anyone interested in urban mission work in eastern Africa. He seemed to be well aware of what is going on and was doing a considerable amount of work in this city.

There was also an Indian evangelist here with whom I talked at mealtimes. He was there to do some research about work among Somalis. He works with the United Nations and has various contacts.

I talked to the manager of the establishment, a disabled man. He asked me to come and share about my work but I was too exhausted to do this.

This was a very interesting tour. It was very tiring, but I believe I was still in the will of God.

The following morning I rose early, packed my belongings and was ready to leave from the SPCK guest house in Nairobi. They very kindly put on an early breakfast for me and the woman who had been rather difficult was quite helpful in the end. Another woman arranged for transport, which turned out to be her own car. As always, the Lord had provided.

11

Recovery in South Africa

Yesterday (Thursday 4th February, 1993) I flew from Lusaka down to Johannesburg. The arrangements for the journey from Nairobi to Lusaka the previous day worked well and I spent Wednesday night in a hotel in in the Zambian capital. The taxi fare to the hotel amounted to about £10, which was quite expensive. I arranged for the taxi to call for me again the following day and the driver was there promptly.

The plane, South African Airways, was better than any I'd seen so far on this trip: new aircraft, spotlessly clean, plenty of room with excellent food. As we flew down to Johannesburg I saw what a barren country South Africa appears to be from the air: miles and miles of rocky desert. Johannesburg is a huge city, reminiscent of Sydney from above (which I visited in 1988). Clearly many of the people are quite affluent: looking down I could see swimming pools in many gardens, some had tennis courts. I was treated well at the airport and there were no problems on entry. I made my way to Domestic Departures and came by Flights Star down to Cape Town. I saw lots more of this very red, barren country on the way with little sign of habitation.

Caring Encounters

On arrival it was lovely to be able to walk through Customs and meet Bruce Duncan. He drove me to my accommodation, at the home of a lovely Christian couple, Charles and Val Kadalie. They have given me a beautiful room with a single bed with duvet, built-in dressing table/wardrobe, comfortable settee, everywhere is fully carpeted. It has an en-suite bathroom. The window is a patio door which leads to a swimming pool. They have two daughters and a little boy, Jason, 5 years old. Today I heard his story. He was actually a victim of serious domestic abuse and neglect, HIV-positive, and left to scavenge for food. Val found him and she and Charles were able to take him in as foster parents. He is now coming on well and is a lovely little boy.

This morning, after a welcome rest and good breakfast, Val took me to see the elderly care home where she is the matron. It was a beautiful place, well equipped, like a modern hospital with computers and all the latest equipment, everything spotlessly clean and specially designed for the elderly. I was invited to have lunch there.

It was then decided that I should see a doctor this morning as my malaria had caused considerable anxiety and I was still very weak. He was an Englishman, a Dr. Evans. The surgery was spotlessly clean, smart and well ordered. He asked me all about it and I showed the documents I'd been given by the Hindu doctor in Tanzania, and told him the story. He gave me a thorough medical examination and also took a sample of blood. In the meantime he decided to give me another new malaria remedy. It must be a very powerful drug. There were three tablets, which I took earlier today, and he thinks this should settle it.

In the afternoon a young man, Trevor, the youth leader of Cape Town City Mission, took me in a car to see some of the estates in the coloured areas ("coloured" is the term used in South Africa for people of mixed race or Asian descent), where there are many gangs. Apparently each area is controlled by a different gang. It can be very dangerous. Trevor is obviously well accepted and a number of people greeted him. I also saw a site for a new child care centre which they hope to build.

We called at a centre which deals specifically with child abuse. It was incredible, so well equipped, with a beautiful room for the children containing lovely toys and furniture. It is all monitored and recorded on closed-circuit TV, enabling staff to observe what is going on. They have two full-time social workers and other staff, all Christians. It was a beautiful building, with lovely grounds, and they have sufficient space to build another centre on the same site.

I came back to my lodgings and had a good sleep this afternoon. After an evening meal, Bruce Duncan came for me. This evening has been wonderful: I was taken up Table Mountain and all along the coast and into the city. It was a beautiful night, with a full moon shining on the sea and mountains. Table Mountain is actually floodlit. From the hill road the city of Cape Town was a magnificent sight. It is a finely ordered place and as we drove along the coast the lights were reminiscent of the Blackpool illuminations.

Old Cape Town is an impressive city with beautiful housing. I saw the church where Andrew Murray, whose devotional books I have read, used to be the minister. We drove near the government buildings, where there are many fashionable boutiques.

Val's sister has just returned from a tour of Europe and they collected her from the airport this morning so this evening they've had a family get-together. These people are so kind, warm and friendly; it's like being at home.

I should mention that I was taken on a short visit by Charles to visit an elderly couple, a man called Pat Kelly, who ran an evening Bible College. Apparently they have done a tremendous work with thousands of students in the past, training people at very low cost. He is a godly elderly man who has now lost his sight. We had a good time of fellowship together. He spoke very highly of my late friend Dr. David Rigby and his wife Beryl, who served in another Bible College in Cape Town following his retirement as principal of Lebanon (now Northumbria) Bible College in England.

Saturday, 6th February

Once again I have had a magnificent day. My hosts are so kind. We had breakfast on the little terrace upstairs looking out at Table Mountain, a splendid view from the house. It is a glorious sunny day.

After breakfast Bruce Duncan took me for a long car ride to the west and south, along a wonderfully spectacular coastline with beautiful beaches. Eventually we came to the most southerly point of Africa. At a gift shop, Bruce bought me a video and a certificate to document my visit! After a cold drink I attempted to walk towards the point but had to give up after a little way as I was exhausted. We were able to take a bus instead, though I still had to overcome some steps. The view was lovely, reminding me very much of Land's End in Cornwall. I enjoyed the visit very much. We came across the monument to Bartolomeu Dias, who discovered the Cape.

After lunch (fried octopus and steak) along the coast we visited a colourful bird sanctuary, advertised as the largest in Africa. It was very hot and I began to feel faint and had to sit and rest at frequent intervals. Eventually Bruce escorted me out. I declined his offer to find me a doctor.

I rested for a few hours on our return. I had a little chat with Charles, and gave him a copy of my book. I was able to give Lisa, their daughter, and Jason a couple of Bible-story books which I'd brought from England. The older daughter, Robin, had gone out to a carnival. We had a lovely meal together and Val has done some washing and ironing for me today.

Today I also learned a little of Charles' story. Apparently they had initially invested money on a site some distance away but were swindled and lost their money. They then heard about this site but had insufficient funds for a deposit. However as it was the last day for expressions of interest they decided to enquire. Charles was told he didn't need the full deposit because he worked for the same company who owned the ground. They built a small three-bedroomed house on the site to begin with; the rest has been added as they've gone along. At first they had no wall or protection. On one occasion during the night they had a horrific experience when burglars entered. One put a huge knife to his throat, demanded money and ransacked the place. He told me how calm they were able to be, how the Lord protected them. These three men had escaped from prison and were murderers and rapists, very violent people. The man with the knife discovered that Charles was a pastor and began to ask him to pray for him. This seemed to be their deliverance. Though the criminals escaped, taking Charles' car and all they could fit in it, a few days later the men were discovered; the man with the knife was shot dead and the others taken back to prison. In total they have been burgled about seven times in this place. Hence the burglar alarms everywhere. This is a tough area, although it doesn't look it.

Sunday, 7th February

It has been a busy day. I rose early and prepared for my sermon. I was called for by Mr. Kadalie, my host Charles' father and Chairman of the Cape Town City Mission. Mr. Kadalie took me to his church, with a congregation of around 200. I was received very well and had liberty in my preaching.

Following this I was taken to the home of one of the believers, where we were given refreshments. I also met some of the leaders of the open air team. I prayed with them and then moved on to another area. We saw some of the extensive shanty towns of Cape Town, built by the incoming Africans, whose numbers are growing weekly. When the government builds better housing for them they are then moved on. However, I heard tales of the way they had originally been moved from certain areas which were declared white years ago under apartheid. I even learned that Mr. Kadalie himself, an intelligent, well-respected man, had lived there and brought up his family there for a number of years. Apparently a high-ranking official came by in a black limousine, and made some enquiries when he saw the non-white and white children playing football together. He asked who the non-white people were and Kadalie stated that this was where he lived. A few days later they were given two weeks to quit, without compensation.

The Kadalies' home today is very beautiful, large and luxurious. I was treated to a lovely meal there at lunch-time.

The second service took place in one of the poorer areas. The City Mission has one of its centres there. They are working among needy children and families. It is very much poorer than their other properties but is being used for rehabilitation (a real care centre). There is a small Xhosa-speaking church there. I preached on blind Bartimaeus, with an interpreter. It was well received.

I was then driven around the area a little. They showed me districts which had burned down in the midst of tribal fighting. On one occasion Charles Kadalie had been caught up in a riot and was glad to escape with his life.

After lunch we were taken to the elderly care home where Val works. A church pastored by Charles meets within the centre. A good number of people were present. A couple from the Africa Inland Mission were there with a display and shared about their work. The congregation split into four groups for prayer. I then gave a word, which was well received.

Monday, 8th February

Today my hosts left early for work. I was collected by Joe the driver at 11 a.m. We had to go and deal with another driver first who was having problems with his vehicle. We entered Cape Town on another beautiful day.

I had received a message from Martin Hone, from Birmingham, to say he was also in Cape Town and wanted me to have lunch with him at his hotel. We had a good time together reminiscing about the BCM Jubilee celebrations which he had compered. He was in Cape Town making arrangements for the Whitbread Round the World Yacht Race.

Following this Val and George came for me and we went for a drive to the beautiful Botanical Gardens on the mountainside and saw the Cecil Rhodes Memorial. This is an amazing place. It dominates the whole landscape and from there you can see the whole city, bay and port. Eventually we found a place to eat before returning home.

Bruce Duncan arrived, bringing me letters from home. We had a short discussion until Mr. Kadalie senior came and took me to Baker House, a hostel for young women. It can take up to seventy girl students. There is also a place for battered wives. One deaf-and-dumb girl had made some beautiful dolls. Mrs. Kadalie is in charge there and is teaching the girls needlework. There are compulsory meetings for residents, and we had a short time together with them in the lounge.

Tuesday, 9th February

I started the day by going with Val to Starck House and speaking at their morning devotions. There were quite a number of elderly people coming into a kind of day centre and I was asked to speak to them also.

Later Bruce took me on a tour of some of their centres. I saw several where they have special care facilities for children. They have residential quarters for street children who are being brought in, rescued, found a home and sent to school etc. The homes were quite numerous; a number of the rooms had six beds, typically clusters of four rooms with a central lounge area, TV, and small recreation rooms. The standard of cleanliness and care was very high indeed.

One place had a creche for local children, allowing their mothers to go to work. I think there must have been at least thirty little tots having their sleep when we arrived.

Another Home called Bruce Duncan House is the oldest of the units. It is very much like our own City Mission Hostel in Granville Street; mainly twin rooms, some single. It is an older establishment but well looked after.

We also called in at a YMCA hostel, another older section, run by a fine Christian brother and his wife. They are having great difficulties financially. He refuses to accept money from the government. All these cater for the coloured community in Cape Town (no whites and no black Africans). The staff are very fine Christians who have very high standards of spirituality as well as the desire to care.

Each of these establishments is named after a benefactor. Val's care home is called Starck House. Others include Williams House and Bruce Duncan House.

We visited a number of the Mission churches and I have been very impressed. The churches are very well built, quite spacious and active, with pastors. There is a variety of emphases: some are charismatic, others are not, but each one shows the same care and the buildings are put to good use within the community.

In the evening we had a meeting for leaders here in the home. A number of the leaders of the Mission and Sunday School teachers came and we spent two or three hours together, during which they asked me questions. It was a good time of fellowship. I have certainly had a very busy time, meeting many people. I can't always remember the meetings I have been speaking at. It is very tiring being taken from place to place, but they have been very kind, providing transport.

I was very concerned about my return ticket. I had rung British Airways and reconfirmed the flight from Johannesburg on Monday, but when we called South African Airlines there was a difficulty. On Tuesday, Joe the driver took me into the city to find their office. There was a discrepancy between the itinerary and the ticket, and neither matched the flights. However, it was all settled very quickly and it gave me an opportunity of going right into the inner city. It is very smart, modern and clean with high rise office blocks, shops, and very quiet. There were parking meters, and everything was well organised. The traffic is never quite as bad as it is in Britain!

Wednesday, 10th February

I began my day again by conducting devotions at Starck House. Following that I was taken by minibus on a long journey, with much stopping and starting because we were going right into the local community. This is a district where homes have been demolished and people are being moved well away from the city centre into new estates, but with low-quality small houses. This of course caused quite a lot of resentment. The people have improved them and of course in some areas, like where I am now, they have made an excellent job. As I mentioned, Mr. Kadalie senior has a beautiful self-built house here.

We continued this journey around the area, dealing with stroke victims. Each one had to be helped out of their little house. Some were in wheelchairs, others with walking frames - all in real need. In some cases they lived upstairs and had to be carried in the arms of the drivers. In all we must have picked up about twenty and it took us most of the morning.

When we arrived back at Starck House and unloaded everyone they went in and sat in a circle. There is a white physiotherapist from the university who comes in each Wednesday to spend time with these folks. I joined the circle and they asked me to say a few words. I talked to them on Psalm 23. Then I sat and watched as they all went through their exercises. The staff certainly persevere with these people.

When I left them Charles and Val took me for the promised trip down into Cape Town and up the mountain in the cable car to the top of Table Mountain. It was a magnificent trip with panoramic views of the sea, city, docks, mountains and woodland. At the top we found a very nice restaurant where we had a good meal (including Cape Town brandy pudding – very nice!).

Later I was taken to see a man called Archie and others who were members of the Committee of Cape Town City Mission. He had a lovely home and provided me with a Chinese meal. There were chopsticks but I didn't attempt to use them! We had a very happy time there and I was able to share my experiences with them. One brother is a very able Bible teacher who has been to Britain. Apparently he preached in the New Testament Church of God in Wolverhampton.

I returned home at 8.30 p.m. to find a group of OM-ers here. These were folks preparing for "Love South Africa", on the lines of Love Europe, and also for the visit of the ship M.V. Doulos, which is due here in a couple of months and is to stay for quite a while as it is being re-fitted. They hope to do a lot of outreach and work with the churches. The leader has just come from the Leaders' Conference in Hyderabad, India, so I was able to have up-to-date news. They were pleased to hear of my connection with OM and some of the stories of the past. One of them was a young French Canadian who had been at the Birmingham conference in 1975 and had also been on the OM ships. They stayed until quite late.

Thursday, 11th February

This morning I was left quietly alone to sort out my things and do my packing.

They have been very good to me here. The hospitality and facilities have been marvellous, though I have not used the swimming pool! I have so appreciated this trip to South Africa after my time of sickness. The Lord knew, and He has provided.

12

Ghana Diary

African Challenge was a successful Christian periodical founded by missionaries of Sudan Interior Mission (SIM). After the independence of Ghana, West Africa, in 1957, Challenge Enterprises gained autonomy but continued with an effective programme of evangelization with a headquarters in Accra. My visit in 1994 was the result of my being introduced to the Director, Mr. Benjamin, by Kwasi and Joyce Okanta-Ofori, Ghanaian members of Kingshurst Evangelical Church in Birmingham. Challenge Enterprises invited me for ministry, arranging my itinerary and providing accommodation for me at the SIM Guest House. Joyce travelled with me to Ghana where her mother and family lived. Her kind and valuable help is gratefully acknowledged.

Devine Amattey arrived at Birmingham City Mission after studying at Cliff College near Sheffield. He was in need of food, shelter and experience in Christian service. For a few months we accepted him as a volunteer at our hostel for homeless men and then paid for his air-fare home. Before leaving for Ghana I contacted him, simply in friendship, but with surprising results.

FROM MY DIARY

Wednesday 1st March 1994

Devine Amattey met Joyce and me at the airport. We had a lovely evening together talking about the time when he was with us in Birmingham and sharing some of the good things that God had done for us all. I was pleased to be shown my room because I'd had a long journey, I suspect it is the main room in the house and there are two beds in here. There is adequate gauze netting at the windows and doors and I have been assured there are no mosquitoes in the room although it is quite hot; next door is a modern Western bathroom and I've taken a shower. As Ghana is close to the Equator it is very hot, they said it was 23 degrees coming into the airport, which was cool compared with what it might have been in the open air. They've had rain today, the first they've had for a long time and there were puddles everywhere. I told them I'd brought it with me from London. It is good to know that people at home are praying for me.

Wendesday 2nd March

I had rather a restless night after a lot of noise from outside. I thought they were geese or ducks, I've since heard that the noises was made by frogs as there had been rain during the day before and it had brought out all the frogs, and it is their custom to make noise after the rain.

I began the day by opening my birthday cards which I had brought with me from England, and also I was given one by Joyce who accompanied me. A lot of trouble had been taken to give me a kind of English breakfast, egg on toast, for which I was very grateful. We were taken by Joyce's brother-in-law, Kingsley, in whose house we are staying, to drop off the two children at their school by 8 a.m. and on to Challenge Enterprise office, where I met Mr. Benjamin, the leader who kindly invited me to Ghana. We spent a lovely time with him as he was telling us about their work. This consists of a bookshop and five mobile film units and a very busy office. From the office they administer a huge number of correspondence courses and follow-up letters.

Later a woman called Mrs. Roberts showed us around the compound and introduced us to the staff. I was asked to pray for them on two occasions.

N.B. There is a gap here in the diary so here are a few of my recollections.

One evening I was invited to travel with the Challenge film unit into the country. We arrived at an open area near two trees between which they attached a large screen. Music was played, and announcements made on loudspeakers. The films were projected from one side of a van, while the other side opened, giving access to the book display. Soon a small crowd arrived and began to sit opposite the screen. The people kept coming and by the time I had to leave there must have been more than 1,000 in the audience and more were coming. They were showing the *Jesus* film and selling Bibles and Christian books, and distributing literature adverting free correspondence courses.

Devine persuaded me to go with him one day to visit a village which he was trying to care for and bring them to Christ. On the surface it appeared an idyllic situation way out in the country. However, I learned the community had been uprooted from their former location because the tribal chief had sold their land, including their village to a property developer. We were warmly welcomed, especially by the women and children. Then I received a request from the village elders. When I went across to talk to them and asked them what the problem was they simply said, "Water, we need water". When I replied they must have water because no one can live without it they showed me a bottle of water which was a sandy red. They then invited me to go with them to see their water supply. We walked half a mile and found a large pool of this red sandy water. We were escorted by a number of women and children carrying bowls and pails. They explained that they used to go another half a mile further but when they saw a road being made nearer to them they asked the bulldozer drivers if they would leave the road and scoop up a hole to receive rain water. This small lake was now their water supply. The elders were worried about the health of their families drinking this sandy water.

Later that evening we held a wonderful meeting in moonlight with a backdrop of palm trees. Devine led us in singing and I preached the Good News of Jesus to the villagers while they listened intently. It was one of the most memorable services that I addressed during my visit to Ghana.

On my return to the SIM guest house I made enquiries about financial support for sinking a well for the villagers. I was told that World Vision was engaged in projects like this but they were fully occupied in the north of Ghana.

Next evening I was preaching at the Ridge Church and mentioned to the congregation the problem and my desire to help. I asked if anyone could suggest how we could bring relief to these poor people and that they should speak to me afterwards. Unfortunately no-one spoke to me on this subject.

The Ridge Church, Accra, Ghana

On Wednesday 9th March evening I was booked to take a series of meetings in the Ridge Church. It is called the Ridge Church because it was the main church built by the British when Ghana (then called the Gold Coast) was part of the Empire. For comfort they chose the coolest place, which was the ridge, benefiting from the sea breeze. When I was there the ministry was shared by three denominations in rotation, this time being Anglican, with an Anglican minister who was very kind and welcoming.

The Ridge Church is in the centre of Accra's business area and attracts professional people and office workers who come to meetings after work before travelling home. As they were likely to be a sophisticated audience I gave special attention to my preparation and as always looked to the Lord for guidance and enabling.

On the first day about 100 people attended the meeting. At first they were polite but uninterested, but gradually I sensed that their attention was aroused and they were responding. I always try to talk to them as individuals who have human needs, hopes and fears. It is my intention to lift up Christ as Saviour and Lord, and share my experience of Him. I also seek to broaden the believers' knowledge of the whole body of Christ and what God is doing through them in the world today. At the end many stayed to speak to me and expressed their appreciation.

On the second day I noted that the numbers had doubled and there was a warmth and enthusiasm for the message. I was greatly encouraged by the response of many able people who were clearly intelligent and hungry for the Word of God. Some were church leaders. The pastor of the church also was impressed and very warm towards me.

On the third day the numbers doubled again to about 500. Surely God was answering prayer. Many folks seemed reluctant to go and were full of questions and eager to talk. Finally the minister asked if I could come on Sunday morning. This had not been planned but I was happy to accept. I was invited to a Communion service at 7.30 a.m. followed by breakfast at the vicarage and a Family Service.

On Sunday I arrived at the Ridge Church expecting only a small congregation at an Anglican Communion Service. To my surprise there were about 1,000 people. The time was limited but I took the opportunity to share the gospel of salvation through faith in Christ. The people were warm in their attention and I felt privileged to be there.

Breakfast was held at rooms at the church and it was good to meet the minister's family and talk informally to him. It seemed to me that my visit had brought a special blessing to him, for which I praised God. I was then escorted back into the church where a further surprise awaited me. I had not realized that the walls were movable. Now they were open and the congregation was seated as far as the eye could see. There must have been several thousand but it appeared that all could hear as I shared God's good news. As so often the Lord had answered above all that I could ask or think, such as His grace is.

Cape Coast

My itinerary including engagements at three universities, the first one at the Christian Union in the University of Ghana, Legon, the second at the CU of the University of Cape Coast. A young man from the Inter Varsity Fellowship accompanied me from Accra. The journey was fascinating as we drove along the coast beside miles of magnificent beaches lined with palm trees. There were many gangs of fishermen wading into the sea and trawling huge nets full of fish.

We arrived at the 15th-century fort of Elmina, the oldest fort of the historic forts which dot the coast of Ghana. Beside the fort were many fishing boats and of course a strong smell of fish.

We met another young man from the university and the two of them gave me a guided tour of the fort of Elmina. These forts built by Europeans are the oldest buildings in West Africa. They were built to protect the Europeans' trade in gold. Their fort of Elmina ("the mine") was the first along the Gold Coast, designed to repel other European seafarers struggling for their share of the profitable Gold Coast trade. In due course, slaves replaced gold. Some of the forts, including Elmina, were also used for keeping newly acquired slaves pending the arrival of the ships sent to collect them.

It was for me a sobering experience to see signs for 'Males' and 'Females' and 'Exits' which were obviously one-way passages for slaves to the ships. What incredible suffering was inflicted on innocent fellow-human beings.

Cape Coast University Christian Union had a well-attended fellowship meeting which I was supposed to address that evening. I say, "supposed to" because their exuberant time of worship lasted so long that there was no time for me to speak! However, they were sorry enough to arrange a special meeting for me next day, Saturday morning. It was well worth it.

SIM Guest House, Accra
Monday 14th March

Sunday I was at lunch with Devine's brother-in-law. They kept me for some time and I think they would have gone on keeping me but eventually I had to ask them to let me go, Eunice Roberts had got a car and kindly drove me back here to the SIM guest house where I will be staying. It was well after four o'clock when I got back having set out from the house at 6.30 in the morning. They don't seem to realise how exhausting it is in the heat, the temperatures hovering in the 90s F.

I was asked to speak at the fellowship meeting here in the SIM guest house and the missionaries came. There were 15 of us and we had a pleasant time singing some of the really old hymns. We had a prayer time and we shared. I talked about Andrew, my nephew, whose wife is dying of leukemia and Jean his mother, who lost her husband in 1991, and their need for prayer. It was good time and I had liberty in speaking to them. They wanted something light so I said I wasn't going to preach a sermon; I talked about our holidays when we visited Ephesus. We looked at the passage in Revelation 3, the short letter to the Ephesians. It was very helpful for these people and it was appreciated.

We were saying goodbye because several of them were going to travel to northern Ghana next morning. I was amazed to hear what was going on. I'd heard references to "averting civil war" and things like that, but I thought it was a bit exaggerated when I'd heard that a policeman had been killed. However I learned other things; apparently there had been much tribal friction over land and so forth, and there had been a full-scale battle.

I was told about 300 villages were burnt and about 150,000 people were rendered homeless and we don't know what the casualty figures really are. The party going up was going to be involved in some relief work. They were taking provisions up there but also hoped to minister to the missionaries. Some had to pull out of the area and they were trying to get up there, so they could have a radio network. So this is a really serious situation and they'd got a long journey. They said that, if they went the long way round avoiding the battle area, it would take them 19 hours, if they could get through, so they were listening to the radios. There is a direct radio link between the different missionaries and they stand-by twice a day and get messages from around the country. They heard that it looked as if it was clear so they were going to take the direct route. This morning they left about 6 a.m. and they won't be back for a week. They've been loaded up with all sorts of gear and equipment. The two Canadians have gone too so I've lost my cook, the person to look after me, and I was sorry to lose them all. I don't know whether I'll see them again.

Maranatha Bible College

This morning we were off to Maranatha Bible College, outside Accra, and we had difficulty in finding it at first, along very rough unmade roads, but then we found a very pleasant college area. They have quite a large campus which we could drive around, with a number of bungalow-type buildings. I met the acting principal, a quite kind, fine Christian, and he showed me around. There was also a white man, an American in his late seventies, who was doing some building work, sawing away and working; by the time I was ready to leave he was still working in the heat, teaching a couple of African helpers. We called on his wife, who had been sick with malaria and didn't look too well. These elderly people coming to give their later years to help with practical things on the mission field are quite amazing.

I gave a formal lecture on city mission work to about 40 students, who were very receptive.

Who knows how these seeds will grow? Maybe in the future such work will be a means of blessing to many in this country.

Just as I had finished, a visitor arrived. It was Len, an SIM missionary who is the deputy leader for the whole of Ghana, and he told me that he had replaced Ira Mackie who was a friend of mine, a fellow student in BTI times, who became the director of the SIM. Len offered to show me the SIM office and we called in there, but as we drove in we met some Americans looking very sombre, and soon they were in deep conversation with Len. We were left to sit there and after some time Len's wife came and we chatted to her, but we weren't actually shown around the offices as there wasn't time in the end. Later we heard the story that the Americans were missionaries from another Society, and didn't know Accra at all. They had rescued a young man from the fighting in the north and had brought him down and put him in their base, but the Africans working with them belonged to the tribe from which they had rescued him. This had created a great deal of tension and danger. They had come to SIM seeking refuge for this young African, who was very frightened and had probably lost all his family.

Len fixed him up in the "boys' house" for servants. There is a young Ghanaian called Emmanuel who's been coming into the fellowship meetings, a very lovely young man but very quiet and they have found room with him for this refugee. I saw Len come here later and it was all fixed up. I decided to do a Bible study on the book of Jonah. The Challenge driver came with the little van, and it was a good thing he did because we wondered if anybody else was going to bring us. He took me to a church called Teshi Regular Baptist Church.

Teshi Baptist Church

Teshi is to the east of Accra and I was very interested to find we were driving along the coast road. We could actually see the beach but there were very few people there and those I asked said the beach isn't popular with the Ghanaians, they don't go there. However it did mean that we got some cool wind coming off the sea. As we were going just as the sun went down, looking towards the west it was a magnificent, beautiful red sunset.

We turned into a poor village area on a very rough road and soon we were at the church. We were there before anybody else, so we had to wait a while. I noticed quite a large construction site beside the church. The church itself was a low old building, larger than it first appeared. It reminded me of Stechford Baptist Church in Birmingham, but it was actually quite a bit bigger than that. Beside it was a new building project, which attracted my interest. Piling work had been done for what looked rather like a factory or block of offices. Everywhere you go in this part of Ghana you see unfinished buildings. I was told that people have to begin building quickly on land they have purchased, otherwise somebody else may claim the land; hence the many half-built buildings. However, the construction work on the Teshi site, I was to learn, was for a new church building. When it is finished it will be an enormous building. They are constructing it themselves in stages, praying in the money as they're working.

The pastor, Ashley, is a young man, who is very keen. I was told that the meeting was just for leaders and Sunday School teachers and that they wanted me talk to them about evangelism, so I put my notes aside and we just talked about evangelism. I gave them a few models of how we do things and we had a question time about "soul-winning", tract distribution and that kind of thing. They were very receptive and appreciative. At the end I went and shook hands with people and went into their little vestry to meet the deacons. There were just four deacons and the pastor. They very thoughtfully provided me with a bottle of cola. I asked the deacons what they did for a livelihood, and it was interesting to hear that one was a management consultant, another an electrical engineer and another a quantity surveyor. I've forgotten what the profession of the fourth was, but these were very capable people and they're all involved with this building project and raising the funds. They are preparing for an Easter evangelistic thrust, which is why they wanted me to talk to them about evangelism.

I arrived back here just after 9.30, hoping that someone from home would phone. I can't make international calls from here, but I can be called; but I waited in vain. However, I cooked my stew and my potato and found that Marcia had left me a little pineapple in a bowl. I made myself a cup of coffee and here I am at midnight, about to turn in, but being chased by another mosquito!

Wednesday 16th March
Accra

Last night I had a bad night. I don't know what the problem was. Though the air conditioning was working, which is really quite cool, in the middle of the night I woke up in a deep sweat. At one point I had a terrible feeling of oppression, as if I had total weakness of my body and couldn't move. I was quite scared and struggled out of bed and could hardly stand. I got a drink of water and took some time to relax, but eventually I was all right and recovered. I was afraid I might be starting with malaria again. It may have been that I was fighting something. Today I've been reasonably fit. This morning I didn't have to rush around and for the first time had some conversation with the German couple known to me as Crystal and George, who are looking after this SIM guest house. There's an African woman who comes with a little child, to do the washing up and a little tidying. I intended to wash a pair of cotton trousers and she kindly took them from me and asked if that was all. I suppose I could have given her more washing to do but I'd been told that she would only do ironing.

Today I received a fax from Dorothy, telling me about the funeral of my nephew Andrew's wife, Lisa, which took place yesterday.

Trinity College

I waited as usual for someone to pick me up for I was due at Trinity College for three o'clock. A four-wheel-drive vehicle turned up at half past two. I almost got into it, but then discovered it was nothing to do with me. There's an American couple from another mission and I think they'd come to see a refugee from up north who is being billeted in the "boys' house". Eventually my own transport arrived; it was the Challenge minibus, the driver being very faithful. He took me to pick up Joyce before going on to the college; we were only two or three minutes late.

The college is in marvelous grounds, as all these universities and colleges seem to be, and there was a beautiful chapel. The principal was not there; someone else was acting for him. I can never make out who's who, but after the preliminaries I was taken to the chapel, where the students were already meeting. As I entered they struck up the hymn, "Rescue the perishing, care for the dying". I was soon introduced and with due ceremony went to the front. I commented that I couldn't have had a better introduction as this was a hymn written by Fanny Crosby especially for rescue missions. I gave a lecture on city missions generally and had a very good reception, with quite a number of questions, all in good humour. About 150 students were present. Joyce had accompanied me and after the service we went back to the offices. We took photographs of all the students coming out and shaking hands with each other. It was the last day of term and they were just leaving, though I wasn't told this until afterwards. With typical hospitality they supplied us with welcome drinks and biscuits. Our transport seemed a long time coming. I was due in Teshi Baptist Church by seven o'clock, so we just had time to drop off Joyce and quickly run in and wash and tidy up.

I went on with the driver and another young man from Challenge who comes from the Teshi area, and we made our way down to the coast road back to Teshi, arriving there just before seven o'clock. We went into the vestry and there I talked to Pastor Ashley. He was full of questions and we had a good time of fellowship. They'd appreciated the meeting the night before and several people indicated that they'd been blessed. Very soon I was on my feet again talking to the church and this time the church filled up. There must have been about 200 people in the church this evening. I spoke to them about the Master Soul-winner, the Lord Jesus. They're keen to do some evangelism this Easter and they wanted me to motivate the people so that they'd get on with the job. Again there were quite a lot of questions. Evidently many of them didn't speak English, so I dealt with the questions through an interpreter. It seemed to go very well and they were all very appreciative.

It was lovely to drive along the coast road later and to see a light on the horizon, out to sea. I think it was a lighthouse, with palm trees swaying in the breeze. There is usually something of a breeze, which is very refreshing; it has been very hot again today. I've put on the air-conditioning; it's really too hot to only have the fan. One of the difficulties in this guest house is that there's hardly anybody to see or speak too. There's a young American woman living here and I hardly ever see her. When I do, there is very little conversation. She appeared while I was getting my food ready in the kitchen. She just said, "Good evening." I said, "Did you have a good day?" and she said, "Yes, did you?" I simply said, "Yes, but I've been very busy." She said, "Ah, ah" and walked away, and that was that. I haven't seen anybody else tonight since I came in. I cooked my food and ate it. I browsed through the books and found an Agatha Christie, which is a slight diversion, and I waited, as usual, to see if there was a phone message but there wasn't. I wrote a letter to be faxed to BCM and I told Joyce about it, but when she'd gone, and I was on my way, I realised she hadn't taken the letter. I discovered today that the return flight is on Wednesday night, not Tuesday. Joyce had made the arrangements but it hadn't been clear to me that there was a day's difference.

Friday 18th March

I went to visit a school with Devine Amettey and his wife. We had a very good time there, and I left the headmistress with the sheets of sticky text I had brought. I don't think they're the best idea really but this was all I had left. I think that I have now given away all the literature that I brought from the UK. When we returned, they brought me water to drink, but I wouldn't touch it because I can't trust the local water. Fortunately I always carry a flask. I had filled it with mineral water from the fridge so it was very cooling to have my own drink in that hot place.

As usual we took our time. Devine had said that he had a meeting back in Accra at two o'clock. How he thought we could drive 40 miles there, take a meeting, drive 40 miles back and take a meeting at two o'clock I don't know because we left around midday. In fact they dropped me off here about ten minutes past three and I'd still got another drive to get into the city. In spite of the fact they'd been delayed we still had to wait about. I'd been told to wait in the car. We were ready to go so I got in and sat there for another ten minutes while they got out of the car and talked to this one and the other one, and when we were all back in the car the driver had disappeared! Eventually he came and we were off along this bumpy road, but these vehicles move quite quickly. I arrived back feeling rather sticky. I went and washed my hands and face, came into my room here, sat down and then went straight to sleep.

I awoke with someone knocking the door. It was about 3.30 p.m. and a little servant girl was asking me if I wanted some lunch. Joyce had come back from a shopping trip or wherever she'd been and she prepared me some sandwiches and got me a cold drink, which was very welcome. We had a long chat together. Time seems to go very slowly when we just have nothing special to do. I've had one meeting today and the rest of the time it's been waiting about and talking to people. The children were both back from school and we played with them a little while and then one of Joyce's three sisters arrived. She is very shy. She is married but her husband works away and she has no children. I don't know what she does with her time, however she came and we talked for a while and now they've both gone out shopping.

Challenge Enterprise

One good thing about this morning was that Benjamin Boateng, the man who'd invited me to Ghana who is the head of Challenge Enterprises, called in with a driver this morning at about eleven o'clock to arrange for me to go and see the Challenge office on Tuesday morning. I'm pleased about that and it does mean that I'll be able to give my report and say my goodbyes officially.

River Volta

Tomorrow was indicated to be a free day on my schedule; but Devine announced that he was going to take me out into the country. We were going to see the Volta dam where the river meets the sea. But he is uncertain: it may or may not happen. I asked him about it as we left the car today and he said that we may go or we may not, it depends upon transport. Joyce is a bit upset about this. She said, "Why can't we go on public transport? It is possible to do that." But he is saying that he will have to arrange it. I wondered if it was a matter of money and today I gave him some money to help with expenses. However, I said to him, "What time will you come if you are coming?" He said eight o'clock, but if this is like other scheduling here it could mean any time. This means we're rather tied. I've decided that if he's not there by ten we'll count it as not on and go our own way. I think I will try to see if they'll take me into the town shopping, but from what I can hear Joyce has plans of her own so it will be very difficult.

Saturday 19th March
A Day with Devine

Today has been a cultural experience, and a very amusing day in many respects. Devine Amettey had asked if he could accompany me. Although my programme from Challenge says that today would be free, Devine said he would take me to see the estuary of the river Volta, leaving at eight.

This morning eight o'clock came and went; I was ready to go. We were just beginning to plan what we would do, for we said that if he wasn't there by nine that we would cancel that arrangement and do something and Joyce was rather hoping that I would be going along with her. However, at 8.30 a.m. Devine appeared in a taxi. We thought this was the car we were to go with, so we got in and set off. We had been travelling for 20 minutes or so when we arrived at the beginning of the motorway which runs eastward. To my astonishment, we stopped here and Devine got out and asked me to come as well. He paid the taxi driver, who drove off, and then went to the "toll post". This is a toll motorway and Devine spoke to the man in the kiosk and beckoned me to come and to sit in the kiosk while this man was collecting tolls from the traffic going through. Devine then began to speak to various drivers as they were coming through. I gathered then that we were going to hitch a lift. He said that it was much quicker than if we'd have gone by public transport. This was quite embarrassing to me; we weren't doing too well, until we saw that there was a vehicle parked on the hard shoulder inside the barrier. We both went over there but they had no room and weren't expecting us to be there. We were standing on the hard shoulder for some time, Devine beckoning to anyone entering the road, seeking a lift.

We had been there about 10 or 15 minutes when a large four-wheel-drive vehicle pulled over and took us on board. Devine sat at the front. I sat at the back. The driver was a white man, smoking. Away we went. Soon there was a deep conversation. They all talk about the different people they know and it's amazing here in Ghana how almost everyone seems to have a mutual friend or acquaintance. This man was a Muslim and had been born in Ghana, as had his father, but his grandfather had come from abroad. The man had been educated both in London and in Egypt. He was clearly a successful businessman, and we talked about a whole range of things. He asked me various questions comparing Ghana with Britain. He seemed to know quite a lot about the Ghanaian economy, and he was saying that the future looked brighter, that things were beginning to pick up.

We travelled the whole length of this motorway, which is about 20 miles. At the end of it there's a large roundabout and the man turned off and drove up to a construction company called Tarzan Enterprises. We drove in through the main gate. People saluted, and we drove up to the front of the administration building. He invited us into the spacious, air-conditioned building, with a large reception area. We walked through and were ushered into his private office, a large room with a huge desk and all the latest equipment. He motioned us to sit down and asked if we wanted coffee, which I accepted. Devine asked if he could have tea! We continued our conversation, and he asked all about us, what I was doing, where we were going, and how we were going to get there. At the end of the conversation he offered us a car with a driver.

We drove down the main trunk road towards Nigeria, a very straight though rather poor road, with pot-holes here and there. I was astonished that we were being taken all the way to our destination. We travelled another 20 miles or more, stopping for petrol on the way. It was an interesting petrol station: a single hand-operated pump. I noticed that this managing director had given the driver money to purchase petrol as well. Eventually Devine instructed the driver to leave the road and we drove into a village as Devine wanted to visit one of his relatives! We called on an uncle of his. This was a small, remote village. Devine's uncle was an old man who welcomed me with an embrace and we talked for a while. He was on his way to hospital with an eye infection. We then continued on our journey, turning in at the Ada Foah secondary school.

This was a fine compound and we arrived outside a large assembly meeting building. Clearly there was a conference of some kind taking place. The older students were seated, possibly 100 of them, then on a platform at the far end were a row of people who were obviously giving lectures etc. Messages were sent to and fro and eventually the chairman came out to us. The story was that Devine had sent a message two weeks before to say I was coming. I couldn't see how it had all been arranged. However, it wasn't long before I was ushered in. The people on the platform moved off and gave place to me. Everyone stood as I was introduced by Devine.

I then had to speak and gave a simple evangelistic address. I didn't go on too long, as I felt we were interrupting their proceedings. I then concluded and handed back to the housemaster, a good Christian man who was enthusiastic about the address I had given. Devine always follows up my meetings and tends to repeat some of the things I've said. He then presses for some kind of response, trying to recruit people and take names so that he can send them correspondence courses. I really cannot see how he can be doing this, because I have seen his office and the way things happen. He is imitating what the Challenge people do, who do it very efficiently, but he has a lot to learn before he can do the same.

After this meeting they all stood as I made my exit. We then went and sat on a bench under a tree and were brought bottles of cola. The man who had brought us here had departed and we were now without transport. Devine said he had contacted the police inspector and that he would produce some transport. One of the students was therefore despatched on his bicycle to see the inspector at the police station. Fortunately as a kind of afterthought it was suggested that if this was not possible to ring for a taxi. We waited for half an hour and a taxi arrived together with the boy and his bicycle.

We set off and went for some distance, arriving first at the Adder Hotel, a very smart building, though there didn't appear to be many people there. The woman in charge seemed to know Devine and she took us on a tour of the building. It was very elegant and pleasant. It would make an ideal holiday or conference centre. I went up on the roof and took several photos. The sea, river and beach were visible in the distance. I could also see several chalets along the coast, so this is obviously a tourist holiday resort. I was told that people did come at the weekend, although today was Saturday!

We were introduced to the sister of the woman manager: an attractive girl who was a student in Accra. She was detailed to come with us in the taxi and escort us as far as the beach. Leaving the taxi, we walked down to the beach where some boats were drawn up. A period of haggling followed. I think it was intended that I should have a motor-boat but none was available. Eventually we obtained a paddle boat, a kind of canoe. I got in and soon I was given a paddle. It was very pleasant and calm and we went along the beautiful, palm tree-lined tropical coast, with fishing boats drawn up. We passed a number of luxurious chalets with boats moored and people fishing.

Coming to a new, very modern hotel, the boat was beached. There was a very large notice saying, "No landing here". However, we ignored this and walked into the bar area, where there were a number of people. Devine shook hands with the head waiter and spoke to him as if he owned the place. We then went and walked around and he offered to show me all the rooms. I emphasised that I didn't need to go into this hotel – I had really come to see the coastline. Then I remembered that at the school they said if we returned at 1.30 p.m. they would be having a meal and that I could say a few words with everyone gathered, following which there would be another meeting at two o'clock.

After some discussion we got back into the boat and continued our trip. I was glad I had brought my sun hat, glasses and flask of water as it was quite hot by now. We continued down the river Volta. I could see the sea in the distance, about two or three miles away. I was looking at my watch as it was getting on for 1 p.m. I was concerned about getting to the school meeting for two o'clock, so suggested we turn back quickly. Devine's response was to stop and talk to some women who had been catching crabs. He pulled in and negotiated at great length the price of the crabs and he bought some. These were put live inside the boat and we kept splashing them with water. Later I noticed they had been wrapped and were in his bag.

Further on we pulled in to another hotel, as Devine wanted a drink, while we waited. Progress was slow but eventually we got back to the beach and into the taxi and then on our way to the school.

This time the younger secondary children were assembled. Again, as we were led in they all stood. I was formally introduced, with Devine doing his bit as usual. The headmaster asked me to be brief. I brought greetings and told them a little about the places I had been to and the kind of work which goes on with the Christian church, encouraging them to train, work hard at their studies so they might eventually become Christian leaders and missionaries. I then gave a little word on the words of Jesus, "Come follow me and I will make you fishers of men". I did it in my usual simple way in such situations and they listened very intently. At the end Devine stood up and went over his ground again, this time making a kind of appeal, asking the children to raise their hands if they wished to become missionaries. He then got them all to stand and then went on to say if they handed in their names he would send them correspondence courses. I think there was a real response in some lives.

Following this the headmaster was very warm towards me and congratulated me, saying they had understood every word. He gave me a warm invitation to come again, not just for a meeting but to stay overnight and they would then put the whole school at my disposal so I could do some teaching with them. This was encouraging. The only drawback was that we were not offered any drinks and by now it was very hot. I therefore drank the rest of the water in my flask. It was a constant 35 degrees centigrade.

Our taxi joined us again and we then made our way to a point where we could get public transport, which was one of the rather old well-worn minibuses. They found me a seat at the front of the minibus and it was a very interesting journey. The driver kept leaving the main road, driving into small villages to pick up passengers or set them down. I really saw old parts of Ghana well off the beaten track. I think many of the local people hadn't seen a white man before. The roads were narrow and there was a lot of activity and people around. Chickens and turkeys were running about, and of course sheep and goats, but not many other animals. Most of the folks were on foot. The roads were rough and pot-holed. Every time we stopped we were surrounded by people wanting to sell us things: household articles, toilet rolls, soap etc. We stopped at one place where they had a large salt works and they were selling bags of salt. I was glad to purchase some cartons of fruit juice as I was now very thirsty and hot.

As we continued in the minibus it soon became dark and it began to rain. We passed through two or three heavy showers but by the time we were approaching Accra it was quite dark and then the heavens opened with a real tropical storm. Oddly enough, considering the delays we had had earlier on, Devine now spoke sharply to the driver, rebuking him, saying I was now very tired and he must get me back as quickly as possible. Duly chastened, the driver did not make any further stops.

Devine then told him where to go and said he was to look for a suitable taxi. The man was going out of his way in the pouring rain looking for taxis. Eventually we found one and we rushed through the rain. I don't know how Devine has the cheek to do these things! I was prepared to pay for this taxi but fortunately Devine decided it was time he paid for something himself which he did. I arrived back here at 7 p.m. I just had time for a wash before Joyce returned. She made me a drink and we had a nice warm meal. It has certainly been an interesting day – a true Ghanaian cultural experience. Of course my next concern was that I needed to prepare two sermons for first thing in the morning!

Sunday 20th March
Teshi Baptist Church

Today has been another cultural experience. The day began with my need to go to Teshi Regular Baptist Church. We had arranged I should be picked up at the Challenge Bookshop Centre. This was because I couldn't describe how to get to the house where I was living as there was no obvious address. The houses here do not have numbers and some of the roads have no names. There are road names and house numbers in some parts of the city, especially the Cantonment area where the British used to live, but there is no such system in this area. I tend to look for the primary school as a landmark, as it is right next door. It is a low, wooden building which I had originally thought was an egg factory. In fact the first night I was here I heard awful noises, which I was sure were produced by geese. Later I found the noise was made by frogs.

We arrived in good time for the Baptist Church and waited and continued to wait until it was 10.20 a.m. By this time I had given up, as the service was due to start at 10.30 a.m. and it was some distance away. However, at 10.20 a.m. a car arrived and I was duly collected.

The astonishing thing was that when we arrived the pastor wanted to know why I was late. However, the service commenced and I was taken into the vestry. I was amazed to find the choir of eighteen lined up and fully robed in bright blue/white academic dress with the girls wearing mortar boards. They looked very attractive. We then stood as the choir paraded in. It was a good service. The first hymn was Milton's "Let us with a gladsome mind"; the second was one I didn't know by Fanny Crosby.

I was then introduced and I delivered greetings from the UK, talked about different places overseas, encouraged them and then spoke on Romans 10:21, "the outstretched hands", based on the text in Matthew 19, when Jesus put his hands on the children and blessed them. I felt the Lord was very much with us.

The message was being translated into the local Ga language which I am told is the old Ga, a very ancient form of the language, mainly spoken in that locality, and there were a number of people there who couldn't speak English. The church was absolutely packed. When we were there the other evening there were around 200. On this occasion there were many more. Moreover I was astonished and pleased to see that the huge new building under construction next door (as described above) offered space for people to sit on a platform and listen to the message and enjoy the service, through loudspeakers. I guess there must have been several hundred there. The pastor, Ashley, a young man of around 30, is very good; he has authority and speaks with power, though he is also very humble. He very much appreciated my ministry. If he ever came to England I would certainly welcome him and he would certainly make a good speaker anywhere.

Perhaps I will return again and perhaps go and see their new building completed. There was certainly a challenge to ministry. I felt led to make a great call for people to become involved in evangelism throughout Ghana and overseas. However, it seemed there were some unsaved people present and the pastor made an appeal after my message and a number (around ten) openly confessed their need and came forward at the end and were counseled. God blessed us in a wonderful way.

After the service I was taken round to the vestry again and this time they produced soft drinks and biscuits. During this time I was informed that the driver had arrived to take me to my next service which Devine had arranged. Having said my goodbyes and having taken a photo of Ashley, I set off in this car to go to Devine's church in the city.

New Life Church, Accra

This time we actually drove through a part of the capital city I hadn't seen before. I saw the parliament buildings, the Independence Arch with its black star, and various other interesting public buildings and churches. Eventually we arrived at what appeared to be an old cinema. In fact it used to be a cinema though the part we were using was an upstairs gallery which would have been extra seating for the cinema. It looked down on the main open-air cinema which had a large screen in it. The open -air cinema would have seated around 2,000 people.

In our meeting, however, there were around 100. Again, I was warmly received and they sang well. I decided that I hadn't got a message because this was really the last meeting, at least so I thought, and on this occasion I simply gave my testimony and a kind of sermon based on Matthew 6:33. It was all very well received and again there was a challenge to commitment. As he usually does, Devine followed it up and made his appeal. A number raised their hands and stood for prayer. It was not the end of the proceedings however. I was now beginning to get anxious as I knew Joyce wanted me back as they had planned for the family to take me to the beach. However, it was now 1.30 p.m. and no way was it ended because it was clearly a special occasion and I was told it was a three-monthly meeting and many had travelled from some distance. One man had travelled 250 miles. This man has now offered to take us in his air-conditioned four-wheel-drive vehicle to Kumasi tomorrow.

At this point I was presented with a splendid Ghanaian costume and made an honorary "citizen of Ghana".

Photographs were taken by an official photographer. Refreshments followed with goodbyes etc. This took another hour. We then went to Devine's house, arriving there at 2.50 p.m. for lunch. It wasn't ready. He wanted to go on talking but I was so tired I just closed my eyes and tried to relax and rest. Eventually the meal was ready which was quite pleasant enough. Devine's wife, Florence, was there. I saw no sign of their children.

Having finished the meal of chicken, salad, yam and rice, followed by fresh pineapple, I was then informed I was to speak at their Sunday school, around 25-30, aged between 3 and 13. I taught them the chorus, "God is good to me" and told them the story of the man borne of four with my usual special teaching regarding it. They received it well and could all understand English.

After that they said they had a play to perform, which had been composed by the children themselves. It was a very prolonged affair and Iwas amazed at its content. It was about a mother and two daughters – one was very spoiled and the other was being bullied. The father appeared at one stage and spoiled the bad child. Eventually the bad child was mixing with bad company and the other girls, dressed up, were persuading her to go out with them. She eventually disappeared and later came back pregnant. The friends didn't want to know her anymore and there was a great scene. The play carried some lessons for them. It took a long time however. Finally Devine asked what time I had to go, and I made it very clear that I needed to leave straight away.

We returned to the driver who had been waiting all this time, sitting in his car. I arrived back at Joyce's place at 5.50 p.m.! Of course the family missed their trip to the beach and I think they were a little upset about it. However, as they already had a driver waiting it was agreed he should take me for a run. Joyce and I were taken around the city at night and it was a good trip, seeing many buildings floodlit.

Sunday 20th March

Today I spent quietly with Joyce's family and we made the trip to the beach which they had missed earlier. Her sister and husband Kingsley enjoyed a good swim. I could hear some pleasant music so went for a walk to find its source. I discovered that we were near a hotel and in its grounds were a troupe of performing artists. Their dancing and acrobatics were fascinating so I watched for quite a while and took photographs of their spectacular display. To see them all in national costume dancing to African music was a fitting conclusion to my visit to Ghana.

Monday 21st March
Kumasi

I was sorry to learn that my visit to the Christian Union of the University of Science and Technology, Kumasi was cancelled but I was persuaded to spend a day in this city. Kumasi is the capital of the Ashanti region and therefore of significant interest to me. Transport was provided for me and we travelled northwards into this wonderful tropical land, stopping here and there to examine local arts and crafts. I was intrigued to find the traditional Ghanaian stools on sale at the roadside. The Ashanti tribes still had their king and I was advised that if I could be in Kumasi by 11.0 a.m. he would be pleased to see me. Unfortunately it is a long way and we couldn't make it. Kumasi Fort is now a museum with many British artefacts. We were able to spend a couple of hours there and learned how British soldiers were sent to enforce the abolition of the slave trade but were surrounded by Ashanti warriors and besieged in the fort.

Tuesday 22nd March

This was my final day in Accra as a guest of Challenge Enterprise. My appointment with them at their offices was at 11.00 a.m. They overwhelmed me with their kindness. One special gift they gave me was an original painting of a Ghanaian woman carrying a huge basket of bananas on her head and a child on her back. It is signed by the artist, Sowetey Adjei, Ghana, 1993. I carried it in its large black wooden frame all the way home to Birmingham.

Our time of prayer and worship in the Challenge offices was very special and I really felt that I was part of their family.

Wednesday 23rd March

As it was my last day at the SIM guest house I was able to spend time with Crystal and George, the couple in charge of the centre. In conversation I discovered that Crystal was pregnant with her first child. As we discussed various medical subjects I found that they had been students at the London Missionary School of Medicine, just as I had been when our first child was born in 1952. This led to a surprising result.

Without telling me, Crystal wrote to the M.S.M. to tell them of my visit. They, in turn, wrote to me inviting me to speak at their annual meeting in London. As a consequence of this I was asked to become one of the trustees of the charity, and finally they honoured me by choosing me to be its president, which office I hold to this day.

PART IV: FURTHER STEPS AROUND THE WORLD

13

City Mission World Association

Nothing could better illustrate the step-by-step nature of my journey than the birth of the City Mission World Association. The General Secretary of the International Union of Gospel Missions (IUGM) had heard of my work and had asked to be put on my mailing list. A year after this was done I received a letter inviting me to a city missions conference in Houston, Texas. It was not possible to go that year but I replied saying that I would be pleased to attend the following year. So it was that in 1987 Dorothy and I found ourselves in Syracuse, New York.

Syracuse

The 74th IUGM Annual Convention was hosted by Syracuse Rescue Mission under the directorship of Clarence Jordan. It took place in the Sheraton Inn, Syracuse, with the final meeting in the sports dome of the university. Syracuse University campus is an impressive site and we arrived as guests amongst at least 2,000 people. We were surprised to see more than 200 people in wheelchairs in the large crowd. The reason became clear as the main speaker was the lovely Joni Erickson-Tada, a woman who had found a vibrant faith after suffering almost total paralysis following a diving accident and became a worldwide conference speaker as a result of her life-changing encounter with Christ and her joyful spirit.

After the meeting we were at the bus stop to pick up the shuttle service to our accommodation and standing beside us I recognised Steve Burger, a tall, John Wayne-like man, the president of IUGM and chairman of the meetings. As I looked up and spoke to him, my accent gave me away, "You're the Brit!" he declared. I admitted my guilt and, tongue in cheek, I said that we could do with one of these conferences in Birmingham and the seed was sown.

Stop-over in Toronto

On the way to the IUGM conference in Syracuse we stopped over in Toronto and there met with our friend Margaret Ogilvy, a remarkable woman who merits an excursus at this point. As I write (2012), this year would mark the 60th anniversary of our first meeting, when Margaret was midwife at the birth of our son David. Although born in Canada, she was in Britain, at Oldchurch Hospital in Romford, Essex as part of her missionary training in preparation for the Congo. Here she had been invited home by Ma Emblen, who features large in much of my story (as recounted especially in *Steps into the City*). After she left England to serve in the Congo, we corresponded and Dorothy and I were amazed, sometime later, when she turned up in Belhus Park, where we were establishing a church. It turned out she was taking a six-month course in motor mechanics at the Ford Motors plant in Dagenham to enable her to keep her vehicles on the road in the Congo. She returned to Africa but trouble in the form of the Simba uprising made life very dangerous and many missionaries were massacred. In fact she narrowly escaped the major blood-letting in the Congo as she had been called home to Canada to see her father who was extremely ill. Unable to return immediately to Africa after her father recovered, instead she worked with the Inuit people in northern Canada until things improved in the country of her first calling. As a speaker of French and a qualified nurse she was invaluable in the Congo, but health problems meant that she had to move to an area without mosquitoes and returned home. But not for long! She went on to work in the only medical facility in Nazareth, Israel but was so frustrated by the lack of opportunities to share her experience and her faith that she learned Arabic so as to be able to share basic health advice in the surrounding villages. Sadly, here her health broke again and she returned to Toronto where she was connected with the Yung Street Mission and was very effective in telephone counselling and in radio broadcasts. Near the end of her life she moved to a home near Niagara Falls and correspondence ceased. We learned that she had been "promoted to Glory", to use a Salvation Army expression which seems very appropriate for such a remarkable woman.

Sydney, Australia

In the year 1988 I attended an international conference in Sydney, Australia, this time without Dorothy. I arrived after a long flight via Colombo, Sri Lanka, not knowing anybody at my destination. I was relieved to be met at the airport by a woman from Sydney City Mission, who drove me to a small hotel in town. After a sleep following the exhausting journey I went for a walk and found Sydney Opera House. To my astonishment there were many flags and bunting and large crowds (I wondered how they knew that I was coming!). I had not realised that my visit coincided with the bicentenary of the Australian nation and the crowds were there to welcome a royal couple. Moreover many ships of the navies of the world were visiting Sydney harbour. Later, as part of the conference we were treated to an evening cruise around these ships which were fully decked out with flags and illuminated: a splendid sight.

Returning to my hotel I met the only other delegates boarded there: Lilla Reyes, a Philippine woman working among the very poor in Manila, and Bruce Duncan, leader of Cape Town City Mission in South Africa. Both were to become my good friends.

The conference was to be held in another large hotel nearby, but the first meeting was on Sunday evening. In the morning I looked in a directory for a local church and discovered that the nearest was George Street Baptist. When I entered I was astonished to find it was full, and the congregation mainly Chinese! I enjoyed the service, especially the preaching which was very sound Bible teaching and in English. However, I felt a complete stranger and left the church by myself. I did not enjoy my Sunday lunch alone in a MacDonald's!

The Australians at the conference were very welcoming and the Christian fellowship among the delegates, who were mainly American, was warm and friendly. Apart from the meetings we had a service in the historic Garrison Church, the oldest in Sydney, where the early British settlers used to worship. We were also entertained in local homes with traditional barbecues.

This coming-together of Christian leaders involved in city and rescue mission work was enormously important in laying a foundation for an Association which would potentially benefit millions of unreached and suffering people around the world.

For me, the most significant moment came right at the end at the closing banquet when I was asked to say grace and Steve Burger mentioned that Birmingham was to be the venue for the next conference. I thought he was half joking, but I decided to look into the possibility of using the newly built International Conference Centre (ICC) in Birmingham which was opened by Her Majesty Queen Elizabeth II in 1990. The conference centre manager responded very enthusiastically as we were the first event there that could truly claim to be international, but I still needed to convince the IUGM committee!

While in Sydney, Australia I took the opportunity to visit city missions in Adelaide, Melbourne, Launceston and Hobart in Tasmania, a mission founded by a London City Missionary, and saw much of their valuable work and was privileged to minister to their staff.

Presentation at Winnipeg, Canada

The Americans of the IUGM were generous in sending me an invitation (and the fare!) to Winnipeg, Canada, to their annual conference where I could present Birmingham as a possible venue. The ICC in Birmingham remained enthusiastic and even offered to send someone with me. I declined the offer but accepted their very professional presentation dossier and went to Canada armed with that. The only weak point in my argument for Birmingham as the ideal spot was that the building was not yet complete. Steve Burger and Charles Chambers, chairman of Sydney City Mission, agreed to come over to Birmingham and the three of us were to be seen just a few months later, in our hard hats, looking around Hall One and the impressive but as yet unfinished Symphony Hall. They were convinced.

Martin Hone

Although I knew that this was the way to go, I realised very quickly that I did not have experience in this field and could find myself out of my depth. I decided to consult a Christian business directory and rang up a man who, providentially, was tailor-made for the job: Martin Hone was a night club owner and entrepreneur who had come to faith but lost none of his acumen! He ran the "Opposite Lock" club in Birmingham – one of its best-known night spots and had been instrumental in introducing top-level international motor racing to the streets of Britain's second city (the Birmingham SuperPrix). (As mentioned in the previous chapter, I was to meet him in Cape Town when he was there in connection with the Whitbread Round the World Yacht race). Martin proved ideal in negotiating and the finances worked out perfectly (partly due to an oversight on my part, forgetting the income from ticket sales when calculating the budget!). We did not end up heavily in the red as had seemed likely.

BCM Silver Jubilee Celebration

It dawned upon me that October 1991 would be the 25th anniversary, the Silver Jubilee, of Birmingham City Mission and it was appropriate for the city to mark the occasion with a spectacular celebration in its new showpiece. The two events coincided perfectly. The Lord Mayor and two thousand people accepted invitations to the opening meeting at the Centre.

Birmingham International Conference 1991

It is not too big a claim to say that this was the first "World" conference of city missions, unlike previous conventions with that title. Delegates were introduced from every corner of the globe including city missions from India, Europe, South Africa, USA, Australia and Russia. The new International Convention Centre, Hall One, was a perfect setting for the combined opening meeting. The BCM Silver Jubilee celebration was compered by Martin Hone, with its Parade of Flags by BCM young people, the musicians from our own BCM orchestra, conducted by Alan Cutler, and the Birmingham Conservatoire of Music, and for the soprano soloist Anne Linstrum, who was well known to TV viewers. My newly published book, *Into the City*, was introduced, and the main speaker for the evening was Rev. Bruce Duncan from South Africa.

It was a memorable international conference in a host of ways. What excited me greatly was that the contacts made through Dr. Paul Toaspern and others had meant that we had delegates from the Eastern Bloc countries, including Russia, and the Baltic states. This would have been unthankable only two years previously before the Berlin Wall came down. We were indebted to men such as Raimo Sinkonnen of Helsinki, whose translation skills were invaluable and who was to feature strongly in the formation of the Association.

The conference lasted for a week with seminars and meetings of all sorts using the whole of the centre, including a banquet with Rev. David MacInnes as speaker. On the final day a business meeting was held in the nearby Christian Centre. There it was suggested that the World Association be formed and a steering committee was set up and Charles Chambers from Australia was to chair this committee with myself, Steve Burger and Raimo on board alongside Del Maxfield from Denver and Bruce Duncan from Cape Town. The office was set up in Sydney with the excellent Trish MacDonald as company secretary.

Washington D.C. 1994

The CMWA conference in Washington D.C. was memorable in many ways. On an earlier occasion Dorothy and I stayed in one of the two rescue missions and, although very close to the White House, it was in a very dangerous area with drug- and gang-related crime a terrible problem. The leader of the mission had, previously, been the curator of the Garden Tomb in Jerusalem and was a great lover of art. He changed the atmosphere of the district and his office and the buildings were filled with beautiful objects which inspired respect in even the most recalcitrant locals. When I asked him if he had ever been in danger he moved one of the pictures on the wall and showed me the bullet holes left from an attempt on his life!

The conference was held in the Ramada Old Towne Hotel across the Potomac River in historic Alexandria, Virginia. The theme was: "All Things Become New" – 2 Corinthians 5:17. The opening meeting in the historic Old Presbyterian Meeting House was addressed by Dr. Ray Bakke, professor of Global Urban Mission, known worldwide as a theologian, author and speaker.

On the second day we were addressed by Dr. Richard Harverson, chaplain of the United States Senate. He was a past chairman of World Vision, a retired pastor and well-known leader with a special interest in the rescue mission movement. I will never forget his self-description as "a servant of the servants of The Servant". Throughout the week there were many excellent speakers, seminars and programmes. My own contribution was small but on Friday I was honoured to chair a general session on the subject: "The Challenge of New Missions".

Delegates came from many countries at a significant time in world history. I have an informal photograph which I took beside the Vietnam Memorial in which are a number from former Eastern European Communist lands and some from Cape Town after the end of apartheid, talking to a blind Veteran with his guide dog. It was a privilege to be there at this crucial time.

Helsinki Preparations

The next CMWA conference was held to be in Helsinki, Finland. Raimo Sinkkonen, head of the city mission, accepted responsibility but it was an enormous task for one man. Owing to its international character communications and administration of this conference was difficult. The committee asked me to fly to Finland and report to them on progress. This resulted in two secretaries being sent from Sydney. They were invaluable in helping Raimo sort out correspondence, bookings and accommodation. Helsinki was, of course, ideally placed for the widening input from the East, leading to contacts with the Baltic States. It was Raimo who invited Maia Ehandl of Tallinn City Mission to attend the Birmingham jubilee celebration and we will always remember her in colourful national costume being introduced on the platform at the Birmingham conference, where she unfurled the blue and black flag of the newly independent nation of Estonia.

Later, Charles Chambers and the rest of the CMWA directors visited Finland. At first they flew to Stockholm where we met members of their city mission (Stockholm Stadsmission) and viewed some of their excellent ministries. One was an art centre, a former Abbey near the harbour, which now existed for the rehabilitation of prostitutes and drug addicts. The expression of their hopes and dreams in painting was a joy to behold.

That night a CMWA committee meeting was held on board a ferry taking them across the Baltic Sea from Stockholm to Helsinki. It was a beautiful voyage, for the ladies with us at least who enjoyed the rugged scenery of the Baltic coast. Our meeting was held in a stuffy cabin below deck and lasted all night!

In Helsinki we inspected the various aspects of the venue for the forthcoming world conference and met mission leaders. They too needed to be made aware of the implications of hosting an international event. We approved the purpose-built conference centre, right beside the harbour, and were satisfied that all would be well. Above all it was covered in prayer.

Helsinki City Mission had a wonderful lakeside camp centre for young people called Kelokaira in Lapland north of the Arctic Circle and we were invited to visit it. It consisted of several sturdy log cabins and a sauna in the silver birch forest. Apart from the mosquitoes, of which there are more than in India, we had a delightful time. One day we went by coach to Alta, Norway, near the area where the British landed during the Second World War.

At the close of this CMWA committee visit to Finland we were able to travel by hovercraft to Tallinn in Estonia where we met Maia and her fellow city mission workers. Dorothy went with an English-speaking young lady called Laura to visit some very poor elderly people in their homes. Their condition in a post-communist situation was deplorable and the mission's work is obviously very much appreciated.

Helsinki 1997

A successful CMWA conference was held in Helsinki in August 1997 when 120 delegates from 21 countries gathered. We were given a formal welcome by the mayor with refreshments at the city hall, and later by the bishop in the cathedral. The sessions in the conference hall beside the harbour were conducted in several languages with translation. Dorothy and I took with us several staff from Birmingham City Mission including David Torpey (my close friend from KEC and the City Mission) who went on to visit Leningrad, now St. Petersburg. I made a very good contact with Juhani Ojutkangas, CEO of Tampere City Mission, to which we all went on a day visit. The Helsinki conference ended with a bid for the next one from a Glasgow delegate, complete with kilt and sporran, and who carried the day. Unfortunately, although their bid was successful we never saw him again!

Glasgow 2000

In preparation for this conference I was asked to visit Graeme Clark, head of Glasgow City Mission, Glasgow being the place where David Naismith started the first city mission. We held a CMWA committee meeting in the city and viewed several possible venues but nothing proved satisfactory. Later, I went again alone by train and was surprised to notice George McIntyre, chairman of BCM, sitting in the same compartment. We talked and I mentioned my quest and said I would like to call on my friend Geoffrey Grogan, former principal of Glasgow Bible College. He asked if I had his phone number and then produced his mobile phone and dialled it. To my further surprise Geoffrey answered and said that I had caught him just as he was about to leave home, otherwise I would have missed him. He promised to meet me at Glasgow Central station and on my arrival there he was with his car. "I'm just going to see the new Bible College so you can come with me", he announced.

Within minutes we were inside the building which had been part of Strathclyde University but had just been acquired by the International Christian College. The vice-principal received us and invited me for lunch. As we chatted he interrupted, "Why don't you hold your conference here? It will be a week before our students arrive!"

In one step the Lord provided all that was needed, lecture halls and seminar rooms, with audio-visual equipment, kitchen and dining rooms. Residential accommodation was available for all in nearby premises. Our financial contribution was kept low but even that helped the new college in the Lord's work.

The Glasgow CMWA conference was a success but not without difficulties. The main problems were administration and programme leadership. The local mission was short-staffed and over-worked in their own activities. I was glad of the help from office staff form Birmingham and Sydney but as this was in Great Britain I carried more responsibility than I expected. But as always we proved that "My God will meet all your needs according to his glorious riches in Christ Jesus" (Philippians 4:19).

In all there were 220 delegates from 19 countries. A couple from Poland came for the first time. Prezemek Bartczak had been told of the event by a visiting American who gave him my name and address in Birmingham. He and his wife travelled there but I was already in Glasgow. However, Wesley Erpen, my successor as director of BCM, made them welcome, and took them to the conference. That was the beginning of a relationship between Birmingham City Mission and the new Ciechanow City Mission which continues to this day. BCM teams, Wesley and I have been there to help.

An Indian young man, Shaji Amos, received a sponsorship to attend the conference. He was an OM leader whom I had met many times in Hyderabad, Lucknow and Calcutta. He had been sent to do relief work during the Gujarat earthquake but now was seeking the Lord about his future. He was befriended and stayed with the ICC principal, Dr. Tony Sergeant. The conference proved a turning point for Shaji, who is now the founder of Kolkata City Mission, which is doing an excellent work in one of the largest and neediest cities of the world.

The conference concluded with a day trip to Edinburgh. Bill Chalmers, leader of Edinburgh City Mission, arranged for the mission to provide us with refreshments and he escorted us to Edinburgh Castle, where we were welcomed by a Scots Guardsman in full highland dress playing the bagpipes in our honour.

Sydney 2003

Australia is a long way for most people to travel. Nevertheless, Sydney City Mission, with the new chairman Ken Jarvis as leader, was keen to give us hospitality and put on a good conference, which they did. The meetings were held in the Congress Hall of the Salvation Army. It was encouraging for many to visit some of the services and projects of SCM. It also encouraged the local mission staff to see that they were in a wider community of urban workers.

The Australians have generally higher standards of living than much of the world so it was a surprise to the visitors to see the same problems of homelessness, alcoholism, drug addiction, prostitution and the like as they have elsewhere. Mission Australia, as it is now called, is tackling these matters in a very professional way and we were challenged to aim high. Perhaps some of us had reservations that in striving to be socially competitive we may not reach the spiritual goals of bringing men to repentance and faith in Christ.

By this time I had been with CMWA since its beginning and now 12 years on it was felt that I should retire from the committee. Conference gave me a good send-off and even presented me with a gold watch!

Kansas 2006

It seemed natural for us to return to the United States for our next CMWA conference and be hosted in Kansas, Missouri, by City Union Mission. Although no longer a committee member I was pleased to be asked to be one of the speakers. Our long-time friend Loraine Minor lived in Kansas so Dorothy and I and my secretary Pat Lambon were invited to stay with her. Loraine was a senior member of IUGM and spent years dealing with rescue mission clients and had much experience to share with others at conference level.

At Kansas there were 150 delegates from 20 countries. The teaching and fellowship were much appreciated and led to positive results. Steve Burger lived in Kansas and led IUGM from there for many years, so was well placed to make the conference a success.

Kansas, Missouri, is on that side of the river which became the starting place for the waggon trains taking settlers to the West which figure so much in Hollywood films. It was a grim reality and we were pleased to be shown around museums of Wells Fargo and Jessie James times. We also visited an old mission station which had reached out to Native Americans ("Red Indians"). The school rooms and other signs of missionary activity were there but sadly all those people have long gone from the state.

Wittenberg 2010

The CMWA held its 7th World Conference in Luther's city, Wittenberg, Germany in September 2010. Dorothy and I, though advancing in years, were pleased to be invited to attend. We all stayed in the Luther Hotel which is one of 10 hotels and guesthouses belonging to the Berlin City Mission group. It was the central conference venue for the world conference 2010. We were welcomed warmly by our friend, Hans-Georg Filker, director of Berlin City Mission and president of the City Mission World Association.

The title of the conference was, "The Spirit of the Reformation – City Missions Sharing Grace". Wittenberg is the place where Martin Luther nailed his 95 Theses to the door of the Castle Church on October 31, 1517. With these Theses he wanted to promote a discussion about the state of the Catholic Church. That is regarded as the beginning of the Reformation.

Parallel to the World Conference a Next Generation event took place for "juniors" interested in city mission work. Their leader, Alexander Garth, welcomed young people from different corners of the global village to their house in Berlin. Inspired by the gospel of Jesus Christ they were seeking how to be light and salt to humans living in material, intellectual and spiritual poverty.

The opening lecture by Herrmann Gröhe of Berlin was on "Challenges to city missions in a globalised world". That Saturday was Martin's Day – with a festival celebrated in the historic market place. We were entertained with cultural music and dance performed by local children's choirs.

On Sunday the Celebration Service with Hans-Georg Filker as preacher, was held in the Marienkirche, where Luther held his sermons. (On December 25, 1521 the first Protestant church service was held here – in German instead of Latin.) Later we were given a guided tour of the Luther museum, and on Monday we took a boat trip through the city of Berlin to the Berlin City Mission store and the mission church in Pankow.

During our stay we were also able to visit the Berlin City Mission base at the main train station and spend a few hours sightseeing. The Reichstag and the area around the Brandenburg Gate is now a major tourist attraction. How different from my first visit in 1977 when the sombre Berlin Wall was there. On this occasion it was a beautiful sunny day, and we left on a note of hope and joy.

14

Mexico Diary

It had never occurred to me that I should ever visit Mexico but here I am, dictating this in the home of Elizabeth and Arturo in Mexico City. It is 9 a.m. UK time, but here 3 a.m. and I am just about to go to bed!

I arrived after a long journey from Birmingham, having had a good flight to Chicago but then a long wait. The plane arrived early but the connecting flight was over an hour late leaving. It was 11 p.m. when I arrived in Mexico City. It took me some time to get through customs as they insisted on opening all my baggage. Eventually I came out and was met by Arturo, Elizabeth, Paco and his wife and two little boys. It was a joy to be welcomed by such good friends. Elizabeth and Arturo then brought me to their home. It is about half an hour's drive from the airport, north of the city. I had seen Mexico from the air - a huge pattern of light. I was surprised to see there is quite a large expanse of water on one side. Much of Mexico City was once a lake which was drained by the Spanish many years ago.

The city was quiet, and much more modern that I expected. Here I am, on the third floor of an apartment block. I carried the baggage upstairs and remembered when I soon got out of breath that the city is over 7,000 ft high, so you notice it when you make any special exertion. We have had some lovely fellowship already. I have my own room here with a single bed and everything I could possibly need. I am thankful to the Lord for His faithfulness and look forward to a useful time in this city.

Wednesday March 20th, 1996
Visit to World Vision

I began the day here in the apartment of Elizabeth and Arturo. They are a fine young, newly married Mexican couple. Elizabeth Camacho came to the UK two years earlier before she was married to Arturo Velasco Garcia, and stayed in our home.

A meeting had been arranged with World Vision but there was some confusion about the venue. We travelled some distance and arrived at a very fine office block. We waited in the upstairs reception area for half an hour, only to learn we shouldn't have been there at all but should have gone to the main office of World Vision. This entailed a journey of about an hour.

The streets here are wide with heavy traffic. However, it is not congested and the traffic flows smoothly. There are plenty of traffic lights but drivers are not too disciplined about using them. There is peaceful, easy-going air about the whole place. People appear to be cheerful and friendly.

Eventually we arrived at the World Vision office an hour later than planned. There was a seminar in progress with leaders from around the country. World Vision has a number of projects going on, not only in Mexico but also Guatemala, and the leader of that work was present.

Jorge Sandoval, who is the leader of the work here in Mexico, was present at the CMWA conference in Washington and I recognised him immediately. He is a very kind, capable and friendly man. After the seminar I was introduced and we spoke about city mission work generally. There were questions and answers and I was emphasising the spiritual aspects of prayer, which I think touched many hearts. I learned later that they were somewhat frustrated because the social concern had taken over from the spiritual and my visit had reminded them to get back on course.

I was shown around the offices of World Vision: very modern, with computers, fax machines etc., very well organised and it was good to meet the people we had been communicating with. I was able to send a fax home to let folks know I had arrived safely.

Later I was taken out to lunch by Jorge and another man who had been interpreting into Spanish for me. He told me he had been a pastor for many years, involved in a number of Christian activities, had gone back into business but was now working for World Vision. He very much appreciated the ministry and we had good fellowship. We had a tasty Mexican meal: pasta & chicken plus sweet and coffee.

Children of the Street

Elizabeth has been with me all the time and from the restaurant she took me by car to the headquarters of Niños de la Calle (Children of the Street). There are three dormitories accommodating around 20-30 children. They are not resident all the time; some simply come for the night. Various activities are planned. Some were making furniture. Upstairs they have their offices, which appear very efficient. One man was operating a computer, keeping records of the children: who they are, where they come from, their histories, drugs they have been on etc. I met some of the street children, mainly 14-year-olds. One, who had been a drug addict, was hanging around. He had been excluded because he continued to push drugs. They were obviously still befriending him.

I was then told I was to speak in a church that evening. By this time it was 5pm and I had not been prepared for anything. I was still in casual clothing and I therefore insisted that we go back home so I could change and prepare. When I arrived back I slept for half an hour, then changed and prepared hurriedly as to what I would say.

It was an hour's journey back to the church which is held in the upper floor of a large restaurant. Around 200 attend their midweek meeting. They sang well with guitars, drums & tambourines. There was a time for notices and prayer and I was then introduced. Arturo did the interpreting and the Lord helped me as I ministered from Acts 1:8. At the conclusion I met Elizabeth's mother, also the pastor and his wife. They were very concerned about doing outreach into the city and felt my message had been challenging and fitted in exactly with what they were looking for. I was encouraged. Pasco, who is the leader of the street children's work, was also there. Afterwards he took me home and I spent the rest of the evening with him and his wife and two boys. They are a very nice family. They had many authentically Mexican ceramics and other items on display. I was late arriving back to my accommodation and then Arturo was full of questions again so it was 1.30 a.m. before I retired to bed!

Evening Report

Today has been interesting, as it has become apparent that there is a communication problem. People often talk among themselves in their own language and they think others have understood all the plans. Therefore surprises are often sprung on them. This morning I got up before the others and had a quiet time and was waiting about but there was no sign of breakfast and the couple were still asleep. Eventually they came out and got dressed and as I was waiting around it became apparent we were not going to have breakfast. They told me we were supposed to be going to Arturo's mother's for breakfast. I learned that I would not be coming back here until very late this evening so I had to make hasty preparations and get my things together. Again, this meant I hadn't got everything with me that I wished.

Arturo's mother is a very intelligent woman. She speaks English well with an American accent. She has studied psychiatry and has been to university for several different studies and she is bright and cheerful. She is not a committed Christian but we had a useful conversation and she became interested in the kind of work I was doing. I left her with a copy of my book, *Into the City*.

First Day of Spring

The schedule indicated that we were to visit the pyramids. I noticed we should have been somewhere else at 8.30 a.m. so I just hope that has been changed and I am not disappointing anyone. I was told that today was a special holiday and about a million people would be visiting the pyramids. It is also the first day of spring, and the Equinox, which is a religious pagan festival, would be celebrated there. It was therefore decided that we shouldn't go today so I suggested we went somewhere else, perhaps in the country. This turned out to be a visit to a small town about 150 miles away. It was a long journey but a very good motorway with toll roads. The view of that part of Mexico is very much like the plateau of Spain with mountains in the distance and rough sierra – very dry. The small town we visited has a central plaza, with a small green park and open square which was surrounded by a market and the cathedral. We looked at the various handicrafts, a lot of intricate work in wood, basketry and pottery, with some brass work and jewellery. It is difficult to distinguish much of the stuff I saw there from what you would see in any tourist centre in the world.

We had a Mexican meal in a restaurant overlooking the plaza and were well served. It was very cheap and the full three-course meal was 27 pesos (around £2.50). Arturo drove most of the way and is continually plying me with questions about spiritual things.

Saturday 23rd March

As it had been decided that I should move from Elizabeth and Arturo's home, I was up early to pack my things. It was to be a key day in my time here in Mexico. We left there for the Niños de la Calle programme co-ordinated by Jorge Sandoval. This meant that we went to the place I had visited earlier in the week, the centre for the street children, but the room normally used for their sports activities had been turned into a meeting room with chairs and tables.

I was asked to present a similar programme from that which I was expecting to do in the evening but in reverse order. That is, the first session was the experience and methodology from the Birmingham City Mission ministry, and therefore we began with a description of the work we do, illustrating it from BCM with slides. They had been able to supply a carousel slide projector. The slides were put in rather hastily and I had no time to check the order. However, it came out well and I think the presentation was well accepted and a number of intelligent questions were asked. The audience consisted, not merely of the staff of the project or World Vision, but also from many social organisations, some humanists and Roman Catholics. There was a large, elderly man who smoked a cigar during the first session. He apparently is a priest responsible for several projects among street children here in Mexico City. He listened intently and asked some good questions at the end. The session was followed by coffee and we had a very warm time of fellowship.

After the break I was asked to speak from a biblical perspective. They listened well. Given the pressures of these occasions sometimes I find it difficult to recall the details. I know that I used the outstretched hands as a base for the message but I also ended with the illustration of the oil slick off the coast of Wales, likening the previous situation to the perfect world God had made and the oil slick to the disaster of sin which had infected everyone. Our work was wading into the oil, getting our hands and feet dirty in it, rescuing some that were covered and then gently removing and scraping off the oil, taking a long time for rehabilitation so that these injured birds might fly again. I likened this to the work we are doing in rescuing children. I noticed that the priest was particularly moved. I believe that the meeting was very significant for Mexico City. The response from everyone was most satisfactory.

I had packed my things in the back of Arturo's car so that after our session at the Niños de la Calle Centre we could go direct to the Royal Plaza Hotel. It took well over half an hour to get there. Upon arrival I was able to book in. I was rather sad to leave the accommodation with the young couple and move into a large hotel room. Here I am alone in it. I am afraid that the cost may eventually come my way.

A Wedding Gift

I should perhaps mention one little incident that happened earlier in the week. I had been concerned regarding Elizabeth. I could see they were not at all well off. One interesting thing happened first. Dorothy and I intended to send them a wedding gift and I thought an English lace tablecloth would be satisfactory and easy to transport. We had shopped around and eventually bought a circular one.

It was very encouraging to find that they had a round table in their flat and the only cloth they had on it was a blanket. They were delighted to receive the beautiful round tablecloth. Now later on in the week I have been aware of their needs and felt I should make them a gift. I had exchanged some money at the airport on arrival, just £50. Their exchange was 11–point-something pesos to the pound. I find the cost of living here is very low, as are the wages. I therefore decided to give Elizabeth some money. The wonderful thing was that on the evening I was speaking in their church I had been given an envelope and when I opened it was almost the same amount I had given away. That money continues to sustain me.

Development Christian Associations

I am now booked in here at the hotel. I had heard that Raimo Sinkonnen had arrived from Finland so I went downstairs and we had lunch together. When I returned to my room I fell asleep as I was still very tired.

We were called for by Jorge to go to the evening session that was planned. It was called a meeting with Development Christian Associations. Again, various bodies were drawn together and once more I gave a presentation. First, however, I gave a Bible address and felt that God was really speaking to the people. It was followed later by a presentation with slides and a short break. The people were very receptive. From the reports which came back it had been quite satisfactory. I think there were around 40-50 people present. It was held in a modern Presbyterian church. During the break we went downstairs into a large recreation room where refreshments were served.

A young American couple who were missionaries in the area were present and very interested. I think they originate from Mexico City. In the morning session too at the children's centre there was a young American man who was a missionary there. He is well respected, speaks very good Spanish and is doing a good work there. He was very pleased to have me there. It is very encouraging when Christian workers are present and express their views, which have always been positive.

After the evening session Jorge Sandoval arrived at the end and provided transport and took me to a large restaurant. It is obviously a very popular modern place with crowds of young people there. He treated me to a meal. He is a very kind man who reminds me in many ways of my friend Vic Parsons. He is the Director of World Vision here in Mexico. He confided in me some of his difficulties. He is a fine Christian man and we had some good spiritual fellowship together.

World Vision Project

This morning I had breakfast with Raimo in the Royal Plaza Hotel here in Mexico City. I did not have much to eat as it is quite expensive. We were to be picked up at 8.40am. I understood that Hans-Georg Filker from Berlin was also in the hotel and his room is quite near to mine. Later he joined us as we visited a project sponsored by World Vision.

Jorge of World Vision picked us up, together with his wife and two boys. We travelled in a large four-wheel-drive vehicle. We travelled out of the city for about 20 miles. We had a good view of the city. To get out of the city we had to drive in a straight line, ascending until we were almost level with the mountain rim and then descending on the other side. It is urbanised all the way. On the way I was suddenly informed there was to be a religious service and I would be the speaker. Unfortunately I hadn't even got my Bible or New Testament with me!

The place we visited was very poor. World Vision has supported the building of a social structure next to a work run by the Mennonite church. A woman of about 40 is pastor of the fellowship. She is a real Mexican, very dark and good looking. We had the service here, but first there was chorus singing. Quite a good number were seated in the open air section. There were large tarpaulin sheets overhead to keep out either the rain or the sun. I preached on the Feeding of the Five Thousand and the three principles which are shown by the Lord's words. There was a good response. Hans Filker and Raimo were pleased to be there with me.

Afterwards we walked around the area which was reminiscent in some respects to the slum area in Bombay though here it was much more up-market. However, the houses were very poor. It seems as if they are built by the people themselves. We could see some in the course of construction. They build a lower floor and live in that, then continue to build a second storey above it. We visited the home of a woman who is active in the fellowship. Her husband is evidently an alcoholic. He came in wearing a sombrero, very Mexican. The home consisted of one room with a curtain which divided it from a little shop they had, selling a few sweets, confectionery, fruit and vegetables. She also had a few items of clothing. To encourage her I decided to buy something I could take home. The articles were very cheap.

I was accompanied by a young man who lived next door to the shop. He told me he was a student who also works a little to support himself. He spoke reasonable English. It is interesting to see how many football pictures there are about. Wherever I have gone, people are playing football or tennis.

We had a meal here consisting of dark-coloured beans, rice and a mixture of something with shrimps and vegetables. We declined the drinks offered as it was local water and we were afraid it might make us ill, but we did have some oranges instead.

We returned to the hotel, where I was able to have a real rest. We were picked up at 6.30 p.m. and taken to a large restaurant where 10-12 of us sat down: the pastor and his wife from the church where I will be preaching tomorrow, Elizabeth and Arturo and some others. We had a good meal and there was much laughter and fellowship together. I praise God for all His goodness to me.

Sunday, 24th March
Mexico Presbyterian Church

In the morning I was met by Arturo and Elizabeth and taken to a large Presbyterian Church here in the city. I wasn't prepared for the kind of church I was going to. I had thought I was going to meet the pastor whom I had met yesterday evening. I was surprised to find that this was a "society" church with around 500 well-to-do people present. The pastor, a very tall, bearded, Spanish looking man, met me and in fact interpreted for me. The service was quite formal, the singing was good and a number of people took part. There was a typewritten programme, not timed, but down to detail. Everything ran like clockwork and as soon as one finished another began. I preached on John 6 - the three statements of Jesus, focusing on (a) overwhelming need, (b) overcoming faith, and (c) overflowing blessing. We had a good time there and it seemed to me there was a good response. At the service I was escorted to the outside gate where I could meet the people. A number spoke English and said they appreciated my message. The church was a large modern building in a kind of square shape with the seating arranged diagonally. There was good music and a choir. As we were leaving the sun was shining bright with the temperature in the 70s.

From there we went for a walk through the main square in the city. This is regarded as the largest square in the Western world, if not the whole world. There were thousands and thousands of people present; all kinds of things - organ grinders, street theatres, vendors of every kind, all sorts of musicians - a real festival air about the place. There were also a number of beggars - elderly, sick, Indians with tiny children etc. There were properly laid-out stalls but some vendors were also displaying their goods on the floor. It was an ideal area for open-air witness. I offered to lead a meeting next Saturday. On the one side of the square is an enormous cathedral. There are also many restaurants around and we went into one for our lunch (15 of us altogether). I was concerned because I knew I had to preach and the time was going so we had to move quickly. My next service was about 40 miles out of the city. The roads are excellent; most of the way there six lanes in each direction, with the metro (two railway lines) alongside. The traffic was fast-moving. Turning off, we drove along a dual-carriageway with three lanes either side. Even on these roads there are occasional traffic-slowing bumps.

Elizabeth, Arturo, Paco, his wife and two little boys also accompanied me. They are very bright and happy children. They quite took to me and in fact played a trick on me: they handed me an envelope out of which I took a letter. As soon as I opened it a spray of confetti or similar material shot out.

A Missionary Church

The evening service was held in a very large building which didn't look like a church. Above it was a huge sign saying "Jesus" with the cross. When we entered it was like a large school, impressively decked out with rows of flags across the ceiling and beside each flag the name of the relevant country. There were about 250 people present. There were curtains on both sides and I was told that, in the morning, these are removed as they have around 1,000 attending. It was very charismatic, with good singing, and some were dancing. They had a prayer time when everyone had to point to the flag above them and pray for that country – a real Operation World system. I was asked to preach.

The pastor had suggested I preach on Acts 1:8, so it was a real missionary meeting, involving my testimony and accounts of some of what is going on around the world. The ministry was well received and I met many people who were enthusiastic. I was asked if I would have dinner with the pastor but as it was getting late I suggested I just have coffee with them. That was about 8.30 p.m. The pastor lives across the car park at the rear and apparently there are four pastors who live in small houses at the back of the church. The cup of coffee turned out to be a little bit more than that and I ate quite a bit of Mexican food. Although it wasn't a full dinner it took some time and it was about 10 p.m. by the time I left for the 40-mile drive back to the city.

It was a good day. I was impressed by the pastor's son, a young man of 23 who has been with YWAM. He is going with a group down to one of the central Asian countries and also to Brazil for short-term outreach on the Amazon. They are also recruiting people to do outreach at the Olympic Games in Atlanta. It was altogether a very happy time.

Monday, 25th March
CMWA Board Meeting

The CMWA committee meetings have been held in a ground floor conference room in this hotel. People present: Charles Chambers (Chairman), Vooma Kennedy (Secretary), Steve/Delores Burger (IUGM, USA), Raimo Sinkonnen (Helsinki C.M.), Hans-Gorge Filker (Berlin City Mission). We had observers in Del Maxfield (Denver City Mission), Giff Claiborne (Los Angeles Mission), he also brought another Caribbean brother with him and there was also an elderly couple, Wayne and Dot Pritchard. This was a full day of discussions, much of which focussed on financial concerns.

Tuesday, 26th March

There was a different programme today and we in fact went out to tour the work of the Ninos de la Calle project, and also visited World Vision headquarters. Both of these I had done before so they were not too productive, except that at the children's work we met the Street Educators for a time of worship; they sang quite well and we also had a sermon from one of the pastors who preached on Romans 1:16. He spoke very strongly but I felt he was not really in touch with who we were.

More Street Children

We returned to the hotel for a break and lunch and went out again to a park area near the bus station. However, it was quite a small grassed area, where we met with half a dozen young people who were glue-sniffers. I would say they were similar to the folk who come along to our BCM Care Bus in the evenings. We were told there had been a police raid in the area and most of them had fled. There are reported to be about the two million street children in the city. This would represent ten per cent of the population, but I would think the proportion of street people is much smaller than this. The term "street children" seems misleading. Those I have seen are mainly 11 or older, typically around the age of 15 or 16 years. This was made clear later when a few of us visited the boys' home.

Here in the boys' home there are at present five residents who have been here for some weeks. One of them gave his story, which was very sad. He had been ill-treated by his step-mother, but also had a road accident which had left him disabled. There had been a lot of pressure upon him, as a result of which he had run away to the streets. He had been involved with drug addiction and had spent some time in a youth prison; eventually he found this work on the streets and had been brought into this home. He was a lovely lad with a bright smile who appreciated the love and warmth shown to him. I asked about his future and he was obviously dreaming about great things and one wonders just where he will go to next. We had a time of prayer for him.

One of the other boys was heavily disfigured, having been badly burned across his face and chest following an accident at home. Again, eventually this had led to him moving out on to the streets. It seems that most of these street children have families somewhere. They appear to run away because of problems at home or through neglect and poverty. They just find their way onto the streets. The weather conditions here allow them to sleep out and they either beg or do little jobs to eke out a living. One lad was cleaning car windows for a few coins. Others find a little business – something to sell on the streets. I bought a bottle of mineral water from one.

Later, on Tuesday evening we went to the "patio", which is in the centre of the children's work. There we met some poor young families with quite young children. We talked to one couple who have a child of around two years of age. Apparently the man is not the father of the children but this couple have teamed up and this is now their home - a rather sparse room with no privacy. They are here for the night. Again, this man has high hopes of eventually setting up in business somewhere. There are genuine needs among these people. Clearly they need feeding, clothing and counselling. I am impressed by the Street Educators (Elizabeth Camacho is one of them) and the way they reach out on the streets, get to know the young people and gradually get them into the centre. There was one young lad, about 16 years of age, who looked in a poor condition. He was in the shelter for the first time last night.

Wednesday, 27th March

Our committee meeting began at 8.30 a.m. with Raimo Sinkonnen taking devotions. The agenda began with Eastern Europe, with Hans Filker leading. Questions were raised regarding the work in Bulgaria and Russia. It was proposed that we should work more closely with the European Association of Urban Mission.

I was asked to give a report on the Indian missions and I simply described my contacts, the pastors' conference in Bombay last September, the pastors' conference and other events in Bangalore and finally my visit to Hyderabad. I mentioned the forthcoming visit when I will be addressing the Good Shepherd Seminar in the OM centre and how we were trying to find the funding for that.

Raimo Sinkonnen gave a report on the work of the Tallinn City Mission. We went on to discuss the forthcoming 1997 conference in Helsinki, concluding the session at 6.30 p.m. After dinner in a local restaurant there was discussion of the CMWA's future, followed by further discussion on the matter of Mexico City Mission. I believe there is a real need to define what a "city mission" is and what our aims and objectives are as to the future of the Mexico City Mission.

Friday, 29th March

The final meetings of the CMWA Conference took place in the morning. There was discussion regarding the children's work in Mexico. It was decided that they should become independent from World Vision. The CMWA will continue to give non-financial support. There is to be a close practical relationship between Mexico City and Los Angeles Mission.

In the afternoon I was called for by Arturo, who took me back to their home for the final days before my departure. At one point I went to see Elizabeth's mother. She is a very dear Christian who very much appreciated all that had been done for Elizabeth during her time in England.

Teotihuacan Pyramids

This was a wonderful day in which we visited the Teotihuacan pyramids 25 miles northeast of Mexico City. It was a glorious sunny day. There was some confusion over the arrangements. We were to meet up at a gas station with some folks from World Vision and others from CMWA. We eventually arrived at the pyramids having missed the folks at the gas station by about ten minutes. We later met up with some of them and travelled round to the Pyramid of the Moon. I was amazed that others in the party, from America, had just seen something of the Pyramid of the Sun and were bored by it. This is one of the wonders of the world and a visit not to be missed! The pyramids are man-made and enormous. They pre-date the Aztecs. There is a vast avenue called the "Way of the Dead". There were signs of human sacrifice on these pyramids. I was able to take a number of photographs. It was quite a climb but I found that by resting after every 10-12 steps it was possible to reach the top. It was sunny and very hot but very enjoyable.

I then went on to the Pyramid of the Sun, which is much higher. At the top there was a magnificent view of the valley. Strangely on this pyramid there were those who practice the worship of water. We found several families with bottles of water meditating around the top of the pyramid. These pyramids are arranged in line with the sun and moon and there is great interest in astrology. It is very sad to see such superstition although the Valley of Water is such a dry place. We visited various areas where the butterfly gods were worshipped. There are some amazing sculptures and carvings, some still with their original colours. Much has been restored. It is an enormous area, larger than the Great Pyramid in Egypt.

At the conclusion of our visit we went into the museum. One area was very spectacular: a glass floor beneath which was a huge model of the whole complex of the city and the pyramids.

On our return there were many people out in the surrounding streets, plying us with invitations to their restaurants. We had a good Mexican meal with Arturo and Elizabeth. The rest of the party had gone back into the city to have their meal. On our way back we called in at the home of friends of Arturo's. They lead marriage counselling on Saturday evenings, so this involved a wait. Then Elizabeth insisted I visited her home to meet her father. It was good to meet him but we were then very late getting home. I was due to preach the following morning.

Sunday, 31st March
Volcanoes

I was due to preach at the church that Elizabeth and Arturo attend. It is a small church and they rent the building. Around 30-40 people were present. We had some good singing, led by Arturo. The pastor is young. I spoke on John 21 and the message was well received. The pastor's wife interpreted for me. She is a very intelligent young woman. The people were very friendly. It was 2.30 p.m. by the time we left the church.

I was then taken to see a volcano. The scenery was magnificent and I was able to see the volcano in action. There was a marvellous valley with a series of mountains called the "Sleeping Woman". We climbed a hill on the other side of the valley which is evidently of special religious significance for the Roman Catholics. There is a church here.

My final day in Mexico

We then went for a drive to a real Mexican village where we the meal we had was a typical dish consisting of chicken, rice, chillies etc. At the conclusion of the visit we went back to the home of Alfredo and Sarah where the family was gathered. We talked for a while and I was introduced to their young people. Their daughter Sarah wants to go on an international tour, visiting a number of countries. She may come to England. It looks as though she will be funded by a charity.

We then visited Elizabeth's brother. Because of the pollution here they have a system in which the cars here are off the road one day a week. Because their car was off the road on Monday we borrowed a car which had recently been repaired following an accident. This was really Elizabeth's father's car but her brother uses it. When we arrived there we were told the story of his girlfriend's family, who were in great trouble. Their son had been very badly beaten up, robbed in his own home. At one time he had been on drugs and lived in a poor part of the city. It was interesting to come face to face with the realities and violence of these people on drugs. This young man had two very bloodshot eyes, cut lips and bruising all over. He was attacked on Friday when three youths broke into his home and attacked him. One had scissors. He was very agitated and talked the whole time. I prayed for him. We went into another room where I met his sister and her two young children; 9 months and 3 years. Apparently this attractive young woman had been deserted when she became a Christian. Her husband was a policeman and a Roman Catholic, but because of her stance as a Christian he left and divorced her. She is now living in this one room. Her mother was very distressed about the situation. I prayed and counselled her.

By the time we reached home it was 1.30 a.m. I had to be up at 5.15 a.m. to leave for my flight home. On the freeway to the airport we were involved in an accident. A huge dog was sitting in the middle of the road having been hit by another car. We slowed down and came to a stop but unfortunately another car behind drove into the back of us. This created many problems and our car was damaged. We had some difficulty in opening the boot where my luggage was stored. We prayed about it and eventually managed to release the catch. I realised Arturo had no insurance cover so when we arrived the airport I exchanged some travellers cheques and gave him what I could. Elizabeth's mother also turned up to see me off. She is very warm and grateful for the fellowship and contact. There were many tears on my departure. They feel that I am part of their family in Mexico. I must say this has been a wonderful visit. I have made many friends, communication has been good, and my ministry has been appreciated. And I am now on my way home.

15

More India Stories

August 1997 saw the third Triennial Conference of the City Mission World Association (CMWA). It was to be held in Helsinki Finland. Over 120 delegates from 21 countries would attend. Among them Gnana Pragasam was invited to represent the Bangalore City Mission.

Gnana Pragasam

The head office in Sydney, Australia offered to fund Gnana Pragasam's trip and sent him the money ahead of time, ensuring that he could book his flights and accommodation. However, when the CMWA members gathered it became clear that he was not going to show up. Unfortunately it was not uncommon for this sort of thing to happen. Receiving a relatively large sum of money can prove too much of a temptation for some men. Yet Gnana Pragasam was not such a man and we knew this. Something must have happened to prevent him from attending the conference.

It was some time later that I discovered that something had indeed happened, something awful. Gnana's eleven-year-old son had been knocked over and killed by a police car which was being driven the wrong way up a one-way street. The police officer was arrested and taken to court, tried and found guilty, where it was the custom for the victim's family to agree the judgment on the accused. For such a crime the officer would surely be sentenced to prison for a very long time.

However, when it came time for Gnana to pass judgment, he stood and boldly addressed the court, "Let him go free. He has suffered enough. He knows that he has killed my son and he has lost his job as a result. So let him go. I forgive him."

The judge and the rest of the people in the court had never heard anything like this. How could anyone forgive his child's killer and let him go free without punishment? For Gnana the answer was simple: because as a Christian he believed that this was what God has done for him through His own Son Jesus. The grace of God was manifest in the court that day.

What the Rickshaw Driver Heard

Pastor George insisted that we visited his work in the slums on the outskirts of Bangalore. He called for us on his small motorcycle, led us to the street and spent some time hailing rickshaw taxis. When one stopped, Dorothy, Janet and I squeezed into the one seat. George led the way on his motorbike, being distinguished among the hordes of other road users by his prematurely grey hair. He conversed with our driver when we stopped at traffic lights, and we guessed that he was witnessing to the driver in the local Indian language.

After a long drive we climbed up rickety stairs and along dark alleyways illuminated only by candlelight. The church meeting was held in a small room in a primitive tenement block. The welcome was as if we were royalty. The driver had left his rickshaw and stood listening at the open window of the crowded room as we shared the gospel, with George translating. There were other meetings that night in various places accompanied by the same rickshaw driver. Eventually we arrived at Pastor George's house for the customary meal. I made sure that the driver was also fed and watered!

It was a long way home and we returned at midnight. As we worked out how much we owed for this extended taxi ride the driver fell at our feet. Obviously he was very moved.

We paid him, and off he went. Next day we saw the pastor again. "What did you make of the taxi driver?" I asked. Then he told me that as he drove through the city and stopped at traffic lights he found the driver beside him again. "How can I become one of your people?" he enquired, "I have never seen such love, or felt such kindness. I want to be like that."

Pastor George took him home, led him to Christ and began to disciple him.

Henry Nerella

I cannot remember who introduced him to us but I was immediately impressed with this distinguished, handsome Indian pastor who came to us in Birmingham. Here was an intelligent man of God who was fully committed to serving his Lord.

I made two visits to meet Henry Nerella in his home country and both were memorable. The first involved an overnight train journey from Bangalore to Bellary, Karnataka. He came from Bellary especially to meet me and had booked a sleeper for our return. I was expecting to go straight to Henry's house to meet his wife Pansy and their four children, but on arrival at the station we went to an upstairs room and I was left to settle in. I think, perhaps, that Henry thought his house was not grand enough for me, which was a great pity. His own home was, in fact, above a former elephant house which served as their assembly meeting room. Although small this was the centre for his fanning out in evangelistic endeavours which should be recorded.

Bellary High School

Next morning he called for me on his motorcycle to visit a school of which I had no prior knowledge. It was quite early when we were invited to meet the headmistress in her office. This part of India was then not frequented by foreign visitors so she was delighted to have me there. We exchanged courteous greetings and then she escorted me into an adjoining room in which all the teaching staff were assembled and I was invited to address them. At times like these it is comforting to know that the Lord is near and reads our hearts as we cry to him for help. I suppose there were upwards of sixty teachers present and it was a privilege to encourage them in their work and speak to them on behalf of the greatest Teacher of men.

Then I was asked to perform another formal duty. They had constructed a new library and I was invited to open it. A school prefect brought me a splendid pair of scissors on a wooden dish embossed with a picture of Mahatma Gandhi. A golden sash was stretched across the doorway to the library and I was asked to cut it and declare that the new library was now open!

But that was not the end of this school visit for which I had not been prepared. After a pause for refreshments I was taken outside for the main event. On the wide open space, which would have been the sports field except in the heat there was no grass, the whole school was gathered and I was invited to address them. Fortunately I have had experience of addressing large school assemblies at home in England. The Indian situation was easier because the children were well disciplined and attentive. I am thankful that I have been blessed with a good imagination and a strong sense of humour which are necessary ingredients in holding the attention of the young.

The Beggars' Village

On one occasion Nerella's evangelistic team came across a "holy man" with flowing grey hair and whose elderly frame was covered in a long saffron robe. The team talked to him about the Lord Jesus Christ and the man was genuinely interested and took everything in, inviting them to go to his village. They duly went to the place and asked for an aged holy man, but this was met with consternation. They had no "holy man" there but one young man chuckled and took him to his house. As they entered the young man's home, they saw the grey wig and flowing robes of the "old" man, hanging behind the door.

The man has since turned to Christ, given up his deceit and earned an honest living by making objects for sale, and giving out Christian literature outside Hindu temples. Alongside other converted beggars they made small rattles, toy windmills and other toys for sale where they used to beg. I was so humbled visiting this man and his wife in their small home. She made a living from selling eggs, one at a time, which their own hen had laid. Many other beggars had come to Christ, and together they had built the "Beggars Village". He became their pastor.

The Lepers' Village

We also went on Henry's motorbike to the Lepers' village on as very hot day. The campus sported a very impressive set of buildings but had no medical provision. The reason for this was that the charitable effort of the Lions in England had given money to set up a centre but had not provided follow-up funds. The Leprosarium housed at least 100 patients. When they were called together, Henry translated into Telegu as I greeted and shared the gospel with them. Lepers are usually ostracised so they were pleased to have my visit and were warm in their welcome.

It was there that I witnessed a very moving spectacle: one blind leper was being led about by a tall gentleman with a rope. The leper depended entirely upon the help given to him by this man, who was a former policeman of some rank. On his conversion to Christ he had refused to continue to take bribes. This resulted in him being ostracised by his colleagues and in the loss of his job. He maintained his dignity in spite of his poverty and I have rarely seen such a humble servant spirit in a man.

Weep with those who weep

On another occasion I was moved to tears when Henry showed me another spot, this time in a churchyard near his home where his youngest daughter was buried. This much loved child would normally have been cremated if local Hindu custom had been followed but Henry and Pansy wanted a Christian burial for their child. They asked the local CSI (Church of South India) church if she could be interred in their burial ground but they refused as they were not part of their denomination. In desperation and love, Henry climbed over the churchyard wall at night and buried her with his own hands. People often say that life is cheap in the subcontinent but grief is felt as keenly in all parts of the world.

The Bellary Brethren Assembly

A week of meetings was arranged for me in the former Elephant House in the Fort at Bellary. People came from long distances; I remember one elderly lady had brought her bed-roll so she could settle in for the night and be early for the next morning meeting. Some could understand my English but others depended on Henry Nerella's translation. They were a mixed group, one man being the railway official responsible for the station where I was sleeping. Another elderly couple were, to my surprise, highly qualified medical consultants who had been working in the UK until their retirement back home in Bellary. The meetings were well attended and the fellowship good. It was very hot so we were glad of fans and the very high ceiling. At all the meetings food was served in Indian fashion, to be eaten seated on the ground without cutlery. Singing was chiefly in Telegu to the accompaniment of harmonium and drums.

Church planting near Bellary

We travelled by bus and train to an area which was being reclaimed under a government scheme from virtual desert to fertile farming land. Large canals had been cut and irrigation channels opened onto newly planted fields. Experienced farm workers were imported from the state of Andhra Pradesh to labour in this district of Karnataka. A new church was being built on the land of one of these Telegu-speaking farmers who were sympathetic to the gospel. I was invited to his lovely rustic home and was given a warm welcome. The new building was of course without electricity and therefore we used oil lamps for light and there were no fans. It was a hot night but a wonderful time of Christian fellowship in that remote rural village. Together we sang and I preached as Henry Nerella translated. We had brought food with us and after all the congregation had eaten we were provided with simple bedding and settled down to sleep on the ground.

I felt so privileged to observe at close hand such a work of God which was entirely Indian without foreign mission support.

Bombay Slum Boy

At the end of an Indian tour I often found myself in the Bombay home of Samuel Thasiah. Realising how tired I must be he usually suggested some small outing. On one occasion he asked if I would like to see the Gateway to India, an imposing structure built by the British and opened by King George V. As usual it was a hot sunny day as we watched the small boats in the harbour alongside and the motley crowd of visitors thronging the quayside and in the well-kept gardens beside the Gate. In the heat Samuel sensed I might be thirsty and asked if I would like a drink.

In India it is always prudent to be careful of contaminated water and other fluids. It is therefore wise to drink chai (tea, milk, sugar and water) as it has been boiled. There was nearby a small kiosk where chai was being sold in small paper cups so we bought one each.

We were drinking and Samuel was enthusiastically telling me of the history and grandeur of the Gate when I felt a tug at my trouser-leg. Looking down I saw a bedraggled, bare-footed urchin looking up. He opened his mouth and pointed to it and held out his hand. It was obvious he was asking for money to buy food. Had I not been warned about children begging in the tourist area I would have immediately given something to him. So often children are sent by adults who spend the money on drugs or alcohol and the child gets nothing. I therefore interrupted Samuel and asked him how I should respond.

The cup in his hand was still three-quarters full and he quietly presented it to the lad who received it with a smile. Not to be outdone by my Indian brother my English pride came to the fore. Being thirsty I had drunk most of my chai but I handed the over the paper cup to this poor boy who rewarded me too with a broad smile.

While Samuel Thasiah continued expounding on the glories of the Gate of India, and I was listening but my eye was on the beggar boy, not so much on his torn shorts, ragged shirt and dirty skin as on his behaviour. Carrying the two cups at arms-length he was pouring one into another and making sure that the contents were equal. When he was almost out of sight, from behind a low wall appeared an equally ragged little girl with matted hair but whose dirty face shone as she was presented with her share of the drink.

I could have cried. Such poverty! Such love! O that I could love like that!

16

OM Good Shepherd Ministries

The work of OM India started when at a conference in Europe George Verwer issued the challenge for a team to travel there overland. Ron Penny from England was one of those who volunteered. When asked where India was George replied, "Just keep travelling east, you can't miss it!"

This is not the place to tell the wonderful story of how the unprepared teams travelled long distances through unknown territory along poor roads to get to India. It was a dangerous step of faith. The did not know many people in the vast sub-continent, but they met brother Bakht Singh, the renowned evangelist and church-planter and a young Alfie Franks, who would become a life-long leader of the movement.

Stories of my early involvement with OM India have been recorded earlier in this book (Chapter 4) but in recent years I have returned annually to support what I believe is a most important aspect of its work, the Good Shepherd Ministries. It was pioneered by a team working in Bombay under the leadership of V.T. Jacob and later by Sam Paul. Operation Mobilisation was committed to reaching as many people as possible with the Christian gospel, mainly by means of literature. As the team moved into the poverty-stricken slums of Bombay they were moved to do what they could to give practical help for the poorest of the poor. It was a new departure for them and was met with scepticism by some. In India there were many social workers, though never enough, but they tended to be preoccupied with practical problems to the neglect of the spiritual needs.

This proposal was brought to my attention at the new OM centre, Logos Bhavan, near Hyderabad in 1993. I had been invited to do some ministry to several teams who were attending a kind of retreat in that beautiful campus. These conferences, which lasted a week, became known as Good Shepherd Seminars and became an annual event for workers and their families to take a break from the appalling conditions in which they lived in city slums.

Rev. Retimony was minister of a Methodist church in Bombay who visited me at my home in the UK. He invited me to preach to his congregation which met in two language groups following each other on Sunday mornings. I had a different interpreter for each well-attended service and was surprised to meet highly qualified professionals there.

The church had a substantial involvement in a desperately poor slum overlooking the river. They were running a much-needed school and medical clinic and it was good to see a church of this quality with such a concern for the poor.

It was in the Methodist church building that I met for Bible study with the OM Good Shepherd team led by Sam Joseph. They were privileged to possess a good ambulance vehicle bearing a red cross and flashing lights. I asked who were the medically trained staff and found there were none, not even a first-aider. As a result of this my wife Dorothy accompanied me to the Seminar at Hyderabad the following year. She had much experience training students in health education in the UK and was able to obtain various kinds of medical supplies for use in India. One item was a doll used for demonstrating artificial respiration. This item took a little explaining to the customs officials at the airports! Dorothy continued to go and teach in India over a number of years until her decreasing mobility prevented her.

Another need at the seminars was for someone to teach handicrafts with local materials which could provide some income for the poor. I knew of no one suitable until in

England I was preaching at a Christmas-toy service at Henley-in-Arden Baptist church. As I moved to conduct the service a deacon asked me to mention something of my experiences in India. I made a brief report and then simply said that if anyone who had artistic and handicraft skills and was willing to come with us to India would they please see me after the service. To my astonishment Mrs. Janet Chisholm came and said that God had spoken to her that day. She was the one who had made the Christmas decorations for the church and had lived in Bombay for several years when her husband was employed there. She came with his permission and financial support on several occasions. She became very dear to the Good Shepherd teams.

The teams appreciated meeting one another and sharing their experiences. They had much prayer, worship and Bible teaching, and various problems of slum dwellers were addressed and specialist speakers invited. Each year these seminars have been held in different locations, usually near one of the teams so that their own people could be involved. Of course it meant long-distance travelling for the other groups and the whole event was becoming expensive and at one time was threatened with closure. At that point I felt drawn to a step of faith by offering to obtain support for the seminars. For many years our home church has given annual gift day funds for this ministry and together with gifts from individuals we have always had sufficient money.

Near Hyderabad a Good Shepherd team worked in an area called the Pipe Village. There was a manufacturer of very large sewerage pipes and from time to time there was a faulty one which meant the pipe was rejected and rolled out into the field. Many poor homeless people made their habitation in them, blocking up one end with bricks, and building a doorway in the other. Of course there was no running water, sanitation or electricity, no medical care and no education for the children. The OM team was helping them in these areas in ways such as running medical camps, schools and giving advice on how they could improve their living standards. When the

OM International Leaders Meeting was held in Hyderabad it was wonderful to see children from the Pipe Village performing cultural dances on the stage during the India Night. They were dressed in bright costumes and sang beautifully to the hundreds of visitors from many lands.

Other Good Shepherd Seminars have been held in Lucknow, Utter Pradesh in a centre which used to belong to WEC missionaries but now is owned by OM. There is a Good Shepherd team based there and also in nearby Kanpur. Both these cities were significant in the time of the British Raj but there are great spiritual and physical needs there.

While at Lucknow we were visited by the director of OM India, Dr. Joseph D'Souza who is much involved in emancipation for India's Dalits (formerly called Untouchables, or lowest caste Hindus). There has recently been an amazing movement of God among these people who number about 250 million nationwide. Joseph arranged for me to address a crowd of an estimated 12,000 with translation into Hindi. It was a moving sight, reminiscent of an epic film with people coming from every quarter, mostly walking, some being carried, some on crutches. The main preacher was a local evangelist who was obviously being much used of God to judge by the response he was getting from the crowd.

It was not all work at Lucknow for Dorothy and me. The wife of one of the leaders asked us if we had ever visited the Taj Mahal. Though we had been to India many times over the years we had not seen it. We do not consider ourselves to be tourists and we are careful with our money. However our friends said that Agra, the site of the world's most beautiful building, was nearby and they would make arrangements for us to go. We were taken to Lucknow railway station and put on an all-night sleeper train! There were four bunks in our compartment, we occupied two. Dorothy said that it was the first time she had slept in a room with three men! We were met in Agra by a taxi and guide and spent the day exploring the fabulous Taj Mahal, and we have photos to prove it!

It was while we were at Lucknow that there was a severe earthquake in the state of Gujarat. It was decided that a team should travel there to help give relief. Among those who went was Shaji Amos, originally from Kerala in the south, but then leading a Good Shepherd team in Calcutta. This was a great challenge, for each state has its own culture and language and therefore there was much learning to be done. Shaji and his wife Beena moved there with their two little boys and stayed several years. They have now returned to Kolkata (Calcutta) and Shaji Amos is the founder director of the new Kolkata City Mission, doing an excellent work in some of the city's enormous slums.

The Good Shepherd Ministry team in Kolkata is now led by Mahadeb Mondal. We visited him soon after a horrific fire had destroyed more than 200 slum homes where he was working. The home of Border, a widow whom we visited on another occasion, lost her tiny slum home to the flames. She had rescued her prized possession, her Bible, and was thanking God for it. Mahadeb's wife Rita keeps their home as a base for OM people passing through. Things have changed so much in India since I first visited in 1978. Now in 2012 we keep in touch with such wonderful friends by Skype. Their teenage son makes excellent promotional DVDs of the OM Good Shepherd work in Kolkata.

The Good Shepherd team in Bombay (now called Mumbai) is now led by a woman called Bama K.R. Her work in one of the slums of that huge city of more than eighteen million people is of a high order. Having come from a Hindu background she organises church and school activities and arranges for 1,000 children to go on VBS (Vacation Bible School) in the summer. She takes a lead in organising the Good Shepherd Seminars wherever they are held.

There are similar works in Bangalore, Bhopal, Pune, Orissa, and several other cities in India. My prayer is that more will be done and more workers recruited. All the regular members of OM Good Shepherd Ministries are Indian nationals with a deep commitment to Christ and a genuine love for the poor, for whom they make great sacrifices.

The OM work among the Dalit people has grown on a huge scale to form the Good Shepherd Community Church, an association of churches across India which has required the training of thousands of pastors. It is an example of God at work on His own lines, the result of many steps of faith.

17

A Task Unfinished

When Bishop Frank Houghton of the China Inland Mission wrote his famous hymn, "Facing a task unfinished", before the Second World War, he had no idea of the imminent apparent destruction of the church in China or of its strong revival today. The task of taking the good news of Jesus Christ to a needy world is still unfinished, but it is progressing. Opposition and even persecution have continued and increased but there has never been a time when there were more followers of Christ or a greater desire to share his gospel.

The preceding chapters present a factual account of an ordinary man's experience of God at work in our generation. They may raise certain questions, such as, Is He still the same? Can God be trusted? Can He do it for me? My answer is, Yes! Yes! Yes! *How can He do it for me?* This is a question that requires an answer.

First, as the Bible puts it, "Anyone who comes to him must believe that he exists and that he rewards those who earnestly seek him" (Hebrews 11:6). If we cry, "Help my unbelief!" we are on the way.

Secondly, we need to hear his call. Throughout the Bible there are examples of people in unlikely places hearing the call of God: Abraham, Moses, Hannah, Samuel, Mary, Peter and Paul to name but a few. Jesus said that he calls his sheep by name and they follow him (John 10:2-4).

Thirdly, we need to cultivate our dependence upon God, which we call prayer. He says, "Ask, and it will be given you;

seek and you will find; knock and the door will be opened to you." Then he underlines his promise with, "Everyone who asks receives; he who seeks finds; and to him who knocks, the door will be opened" (Matthew 7:7-8).

Finally, we need to do something: what the Bible calls the obedience of faith. It may be to tell someone that we have trusted Christ, or write a letter of application, or step out in faith in some other practical way. He will not fail to keep his promises.

One of the promises of God that have kept me over the years is, "He is able to keep you from falling" (Jude 24). Many times I have felt that I was falling, and if left to myself I would have fallen, but he has held me up. I have many cracks and chips and bruises, but what soldier or workman or athlete doesn't? The important thing is to get up again and run the race.

It has been a privilege for me to meet so many wonderful people of different races and languages in all five continents and observe the work of God of many kinds. What little good I may have done is entirely by his grace. Obviously it has been very costly with air travel and accommodation but I can testify that I have lacked nothing. It has been a principle for my wife and me not to be in debt and to make no appeals for our own support. Though God has kept us dependent on him we have not lacked money either for ourselves or for the education of our four children. He does not fail. Our practical experience is that he "is able to do immeasurably more than all we ask or imagine ... To him be all the glory!" (Ephesians 3:20).